T0318724

Technology, Change and the Academic Library

Technology, Change and the Academic Library

Case Studies, Trends and Reflections

Edited by

Jeremy Atkinson
Jeremy Atkinson Consultancy, Cardiff, Wales, United Kingdom

Chandos Publishing is an imprint of Elsevier
50 Hampshire Street, 5th Floor, Cambridge, MA 02139, United States
The Boulevard, Langford Lane, Kidlington, OX5 1GB, United Kingdom

Notices
Knowledge and best practice in this field are constantly changing. As new research and experience broaden our understanding, changes in research methods, professional practices, or medical treatment may become necessary.

Practitioners and researchers must always rely on their own experience and knowledge in evaluating and using any information, methods, compounds, or experiments described herein. In using such information or methods they should be mindful of their own safety and the safety of others, including parties for whom they have a professional responsibility.

To the fullest extent of the law, neither the Publisher nor the authors, contributors, or editors, assume any liability for any injury and/or damage to persons or property as a matter of products liability, negligence or otherwise, or from any use or operation of any methods, products, instructions, or ideas contained in the material herein.

British Library Cataloguing-in-Publication Data
A catalogue record for this book is available from the British Library.

Library of Congress Cataloging-in-Publication Data
A catalog record for this book is available from the Library of Congress.

ISBN 978-0-12-822807-4 (print)

ISBN 978-0-12-823228-6 (online)

For information on all Chandos Publishing publications
visit our website at https://www.elsevier.com/books-and-journals

Publisher: Glyn Jones
Editorial Project Manager: Andrae Akeh
Production Project Manager: Surya Narayanan Jayachandran
Cover Designer: Alan Studholme

Typeset by MPS Limited, Chennai, India

Working together
to grow libraries in
developing countries

www.elsevier.com • www.bookaid.org

Dedication

To Chris and Verity

Contents

Section III   Case Studies   43

Section IV   Reflections   **183**

List of contributors

Karen Abel University Library, University of Leeds, Leeds, United Kingdom

Jeremy Atkinson Jeremy Atkinson Consultancy, Cardiff, Wales, United Kingdom

Amanda Bellenger University Library, Curtin University, Perth, WA, Australia

David Bennett University Library, University of Portsmouth, Portsmouth, United Kingdom

Kylie Black University Library, University of Western Australia, Perth, WA, Australia

Sarah Cesare University Library, University of Western Australia, Perth, WA, Australia

Tracey Clarke Tracey Clarke Consulting, Sheffield, United Kingdom

Elly Cope University Library, University of Leeds, Leeds, United Kingdom

Gionni di Gravio University Library, University of Newcastle Australia, Newcastle, NSW, Australia

Nel Duffield Information Technology and Digital Services, University of Adelaide, Adelaide, SA, Australia

Susan Halfpenny Information Services, University of York, York, United Kingdom

Ann Hardy University Library, University of Newcastle Australia, Newcastle, NSW, Australia

Mark Hughes Library Services, Cardiff Metropolitan University, Cardiff, Wales, United Kingdom

Neil Jacobs UK Research and Innovation, Swindon, United Kingdom; Formerly Jisc, Bristol, United Kingdom

Stephanie Jesper Information Services, University of York, York, United Kingdom

Alison Little University Library, University of Sheffield, Sheffield, United Kingdom

Ciara McCaffrey Glucksman Library, University of Limerick, Limerick, Ireland

Katie Mills University Library, University of Western Australia, Perth, WA, Australia

Alison Morton University Library, University of Sheffield, Sheffield, United Kingdom

William J. Nixon University of Glasgow Library, Glasgow, Scotland, United Kingdom

Mary O'Connor Formerly University Library, University of Adelaide, Adelaide, SA, Australia

Ferg Roper South Metropolitan TAFE, Perth, WA, Australia; Formerly Capability Development, University of Western Australia, Perth, WA, Australia

Jaime Royals University Library, University of Adelaide, Adelaide, SA, Australia

Jane Saunders University Library, University of Leeds, Leeds, United Kingdom

Linda Sheedy University Library, Curtin University, Perth, WA, Australia

Lynn Sykes Formerly University Library, University of Sheffield, Sheffield, United Kingdom

Wendy Walker University of Glasgow Library, Glasgow, Scotland, United Kingdom

David Wells University Library, Curtin University, Perth, WA, Australia

Andrew Williams University Library, University of Adelaide, Adelaide, SA, Australia

Colin Work University Library, University of Portsmouth, Portsmouth, United Kingdom

About the editor

Jeremy Atkinson has a wide-ranging experience and expertise in the leadership, management and development of academic library services. Since 2012, he has been a Library and Information Services Consultant working with a number of high-profile clients, including Jisc, SCONUL and individual UK universities. Before that, he had overall responsibility for the strategic and operational management of library and information services at the University of Glamorgan (now University of South Wales) from 1991 to 2012. Previously, he held library posts at the University of Northumbria, Cardiff University and Manchester Metropolitan University.

Jeremy has had a long-standing and active involvement in a large number of UK strategic committees and groups, notably those of Jisc, SCONUL (including 3 years as a trustee and member of SCONUL Executive Board) and Wales Higher Education Libraries Forum (WHELF). His work with WHELF included a key leadership role in the development of Wales Higher Education Electronic Library (WHEEL), and his Jisc work focused on electronic resources, digitisation, collections strategy and infrastructure. Recent consultancy activity has included work on open access, repositories and copyright.

Jeremy has produced a wide range of publications and conference papers on topics including change management, quality assurance, electronic resources and library collaboration. He is the editor of *Collaboration and the academic library: Internal and external, local and regional, national and international*, published by Chandos in 2018, and *Quality and the academic library: Reviewing, assessing and enhancing service provision*, published by Chandos in 2016.

Acknowledgements

Thank you to everyone who has made this book possible: to Ann Rossiter of SCONUL in the United Kingdom and Diane Costello of CAUL in Australia for their help in identifying potential contributors; to all the authors of the case studies and chapters for agreeing to be involved and for producing relevant and interesting contributions; to Glyn Jones, Andrae Akeh and Surya Narayanan Jayachandran of Chandos Publishing and Elsevier for their support at all stages of the project; and to my family and friends for their support, patience and suggestions during the research, writing and editing processes.

Jeremy Atkinson

Section I

Introduction

Introduction

1

Jeremy Atkinson
Jeremy Atkinson Consultancy, Cardiff, Wales, United Kingdom

Considerable change has affected universities and academic libraries in recent years, and the pace of change is only likely to accelerate. The significant changes affecting academic libraries include the following:

- Increasing client expectations, with the consequent need to maintain and enhance the student experience.
- Disintermediation and the invisibility of library support in the digital age.
- Current and future generations of students and researchers considering themselves self-sufficient in information skills.
- The decline in the importance of the library as a physical entity.
- Changing user needs and working styles.
- The availability of alternative sources of information for learners and researchers, with other providers in the digital environment and the library no longer being the principal information provider.
- The changing nature of universities, with new ways of working, changes in pedagogy and increased online delivery.
- Greater remote working with a requirement for 24/7 access on a range of personal devices.
- Library users shifting from being consumers to creators of content.
- Changes in scholarly publication (e.g. open access) and the research environment.
- Rapidly changing technologies and personalisation approaches. Use of some technologies (e.g. social media, mobile technologies) particularly favoured by younger students.
- Requirement for greater integration and interoperability of systems.
- Financial uncertainties and institutional cutbacks.
- Increasing emphasis on efficiency gains, value for money, accountability, impact, and evaluation and monitoring of performance and effectiveness. Importance of student retention.

At the time of writing, the coronavirus pandemic was causing considerable concern and major changes to the ways in which society operates. The consequences of the pandemic are likely to be far reaching for higher education, not just financially, but also in terms of the impact on student recruitment, ways of working and studying, the provision of support, and, potentially, the increasing importance of technological solutions.

Academic libraries have shown great ingenuity in taking up and implementing a range of technologies to help deal with or alleviate these trends, to meet the

Technology, Change and the Academic Library. DOI: https://doi.org/10.1016/B978-0-12-822807-4.00001-4

needs of their users and to support the aims and objectives of their universities. The adoption of different technologies in academic libraries has expanded considerably. Early automation work focused on areas such as library management systems, but in 2020 the use of technology applications is extensive. There is large-scale use of different systems, devices and software such as self-service technologies, repositories, mobile devices and social media. Academic libraries have moved from being collections-based to more service-based, with a wider range of services to users including research data management, bibliometrics, open access presses, virtual reference and digital literacy. Libraries have moved focus from physical to online collections, with provision of access to an increasing range of electronic resources. Moreover, areas such as artificial intelligence, the internet of things and wearable technologies present opportunities and challenges for the future.

The success of academic libraries will increasingly be contingent on their ability to thrive in a technology rich environment. This book aims not just to concentrate on the technologies themselves, but to consider fully the change management issues relating to their implementation and use. Coverage will include consideration of leadership and management, planning and implementation processes, staffing and organisational issues, financial aspects, culture, skills and values, and the impact on services, staff, users and the organisation as a whole.

The literature relating to technology, change and academic libraries is fairly substantial and complex and can be difficult for the nonexpert librarian or librarianship student to gain access to and understand. I have tried to deal with this by taking a similar approach to the one I used in previous volumes on quality and academic libraries (Atkinson, 2016) and collaboration and academic libraries (Atkinson, 2018). A wide-ranging introduction and overview of the area is provided, followed by a series of case studies giving a practical approach and up to date and reflective content for the more experienced information professional. Hopefully, the book will present varied perspectives, information on the 'who', 'why', 'what' and 'how' of technology and change in academic libraries, and the skills required.

The book also seeks to offer a relevant approach for a wide readership by the following:

- Providing *accessible* content within the overview, and including identification of the more readable articles in the references and further reading sections.
- Providing *signposts* to the key themes and trends, key developments and key resources.
- Covering the *different aspects* of technology and change in academic libraries. There is a general consideration of the application of change management principles in academic libraries, and the wide-ranging case studies look at the adoption of different technologies, the impact and significance of the changes made and the change processes used.
- Providing information on the *context and changing environment* in which academic libraries are operating. Where appropriate, the contributors consider the political, economic and social aspects of the technological developments in academic libraries, the changing nature and requirements of students and other users, the changes in teaching, learning,

research and scholarly communication, and the changes in roles, responsibilities and organisational structures of libraries and librarians.

- Taking a *UK focus* but including *international perspectives*. Although the editor and
a number of the contributors are from the United Kingdom, the book also includes a
contribution from Ireland and a number of contributions from Australia. The coverage of the literature in the overview and further reading sections is international in
scope.

I thought it would be helpful if I asked the contributors to adopt an approach of
critical reflection, where appropriate. This method was also used in the previous
books, *Quality and the Academic Library* (Atkinson, 2016) and *Collaboration and
the Academic Library* (Atkinson, 2018). Much of the literature relating to technology, change and academic libraries very usefully describes and analyses developments in the field. Although this approach is also taken here, in addition, I asked
contributors to reflect on their technology developments and projects as well as the
implications, impact and significance of the work carried out. I hope this will help
readers to gain a deeper understanding of technology and change involving academic libraries and of the benefits and constraints of different approaches and methods, to reflect on their own previous technology and change projects, and to plan
future initiatives.

The ideas of reflective practice and critical reflection have been used increasingly in recent years in a number of professional fields, including health and care
sciences. The development and understanding of specialised knowledge are essential for professional practice, and using approaches of self-consciousness (reflection) and continual self-critique (critical reflection) have been found to be useful
to the development of continuing competence (Williams, 2001). In contrast,
reflection has had less attention in the management and leadership literature with
managers often placing more emphasis on action and outcomes (Gray, 2007).
With some exceptions, there has also been little use in librarianship and information science (Greenall & Sen, 2016; Sen, 2010). The pace of change in organisations and the day-to-day demands of the workplace often leave little time for
reflection.

The aims of critical reflection are for practitioners to understand the nature and
meaning of practice; correct and improve the practice through self-reflection and
criticism; generate models of good practice and theories of application through
reflection and critique of actual occurrences. Critical reflection has three phases: a
descriptive phase, with descriptions of practice or events; a reflective phase, with
reflective analysis of events or situations; and a critical phase, with a critique of
practice (Kim, 1999).

I used this approach and, in particular, Borton's Developmental Model (1970)
of 'What? So What? Now What?' to develop a simple critical reflection framework for the contributors to this book to help them in the writing of the chapters
and case studies. This framework is given in the following table. Additional references on critical reflection are given in the "Further reading" section at the end of
the book.

Critical reflection element	Questions
What? Description	• What were the activities and services that were being looked at as part of the innovation and development? • What were the aims and objectives, rationale and context for the work? • How was the work planned, funded and carried out? • What methods were used? • What were the outcomes of the work? • Who carried the work out? • Who else was involved? • What was my own role in the work? • What did I do?
So what? Analysis	• Was the planning and implementation work for the innovation and development effective? • Have you carried out any evaluation of the work? • What worked well? • What worked less well? • What lessons were learned? • What were the challenges, barriers and risks in carrying out the work? • What were the key issues relating to leadership and management and the attributes, skills and behaviours of the participants involved in the work? • Were there any important issues relating to values or ethics during the work? • Were the methods used for the development or innovation adapted during the work as a result of experience gained? • On reflection, did the methods used work as originally intended? • How would I do the work differently if I was to do it again? • What different methods/approaches would I use? • What would be your main conclusions and recommendations arising from the work on the development?
Now what? Synthesis	• What were the benefits of the work? • What changes have been made as a result of carrying out the innovation and development work? • Of the changes made what has worked well and what has worked less well? • What has been the impact and significance of the changes made? • What has been the impact of the work on library services, systems, collections or spaces? • What has been the impact of the work on university teaching, learning and research and on the university as a whole?

(*Continued*)

Critical reflection element	Questions
(Continued)	
	• What has been the impact of the work on library staff and users, roles and responsibilities, organisational structures and skills, capabilities and behaviours? • What potential is there for follow on work?

References

Atkinson, J. (Ed.), (2016). *Quality and the academic library: Reviewing, assessing and enhancing service provision.* Oxford: Chandos Publishing.

Atkinson, J. (Ed.), (2018). *Collaboration and the academic library: Internal and external, local and regional, national and international.* Oxford: Chandos Publishing.

Borton, T. (1970). *Reach, touch and teach: Student concerns and process education.* New York: McGraw-Hill.

Gray, D. E. (2007). Facilitating management learning: Developing critical reflection through reflective tools. *Management Learning, 38*(5), 495−517. Available from https://doi.org/10.1177/1350507607083204.

Greenall, J., & Sen, B. A. (2016). Reflective practice in the library and information sector. *Journal of Librarianship and Information Science, 48*(2), 137−150. Available from https://doi.org/10.1177/0961000614551450.

Kim, H. S. (1999). Critical reflective inquiry for knowledge development in nursing practice. *Journal of Advanced Nursing, 29*(5), 1205−1212. Available from https://doi.org/10.1046/j.1365-2648.1999.01005.x.

Sen, B. A. (2010). Reflective writing: A management skill. *Library Management, 31*(1/2), 79−93. Available from https://doi.org/10.1177/0961000614551450.

Williams, B. (2001). Developing critical reflection for professional practice through problem-based learning. *Journal of Advanced Nursing, 34*(1), 27−34. Available from https://doi.org/10.1046/j.1365-2648.2001.3411737.x.

Section II

Technology and Change Management in Higher Education and Academic Libraries

Technology and change management in academic libraries: An overview and literature review

2

Jeremy Atkinson
Jeremy Atkinson Consultancy, Cardiff, Wales, United Kingdom

2.1 Introduction

The chapter provides an overview and extensive literature review of technology and change management in academic libraries. There is consideration of technology developments that are relevant to academic libraries, trends, use of specific technologies, change management in academic libraries, and developments in related sectors.

The total literature of the area is substantial and it is only feasible to be very selective within an overview of this kind. In selecting articles, books and other sources for the literature review, I have opted for items that, in general, are recent, readable and accessible and that help to illustrate the key themes clearly and in an interesting way. Some additional resources are given in the Further Reading section at the end of this book. Other material can be located via librarianship journals and abstracting and indexing services.

Many articles and books rightly emphasise that in technological developments and innovations in academic libraries it is important not to let the technology dictate. Technology should be viewed as the enabling agent, not the driver. In reviewing the literature, it became clear to me that there were a number of 'softer' issues and themes that were key when considering technology developments and change management in academic libraries. These are listed below and are expanded on in many of the case studies that follow. They also form the basis of a more detailed consideration and reflection in Chapter 18.

- Strategic planning, and relationship to strategies, policies and procedures
- Leadership and management
- Project management, change management, governance and communication
- Finance and staffing
- Advocacy, consultation and engagement
- Institutional culture and cultural change
- Values
- Changes in roles and responsibilities
- Partnerships and collaboration

Technology, Change and the Academic Library. DOI: https://doi.org/10.1016/B978-0-12-822807-4.00002-6

- Impact on staff, services and users, on workflows and processes, and on university teaching, learning and research
- Skills, attitudes and behaviours of library staff
- Skills, attitudes and behaviours of users
- Ethical and legal issues, including privacy, confidentiality and security
- Technical infrastructure and support
- Promotion and marketing
- Evaluation, monitoring and review

2.2   Technology in academic libraries

A number of books published in recent years have sought to identify current and future technology developments that are likely to be relevant to libraries. They also describe the ways in which the different technologies have been adopted and adapted by library services in order to address user needs and discuss their impact on library staff, services and users. Examples are the books by Joiner (2018), King (2018), and Koerber and Sauers (2015). Other examples are given in the Further Reading chapter. Moss, Endicott-Popovsky, and Dupuis (2015) consider the ways in which available technologies have, in particular, transformed the creation, capture, preservation and discovery of content, as well as the potential of the digital environment to transform research and scholarship. In a similar vein, Dempsey (2016) looks at the changing nature of academic library collections and services in a networked environment. He identifies two major trends: the increasing role of the library in managing the research and other outputs of the university; and the facilitation of access to a broader range of local, external and collaborative resources organised around user needs.

Values are also an important issue in the context of emerging technologies. Technologies come embedded with their own set of values and assumptions, with the consequence that the professional values of libraries may be in conflict with the values embedded in the technology (Fernandez & Tilton, 2018). Libraries can also potentially play a partnership role in the commercialisation strategies for innovations and inventions arising from university research (Elliott, Dewland, Martin, Kramer, & Jackson, 2017). In Chapter 10, there is consideration of collaboration of this kind between the Library and computational biologists at the University of Western Australia.

2.3   Change management in academic libraries

Jantz (2016, 2017) emphasises that academic libraries need to change and adapt to a rapidly changing environment. He argues that the culture in many academic libraries is deep seated and can tend to preserve the status quo, making it difficult to implement major new innovations that require flexibility and creativity. He advocates the use of management innovation that departs from traditional management principles and practices and can become the primary enabler of transformation in academic libraries. Mossop (2013) also looks at transformational change in academic libraries to achieve deep level cultural change. In other relevant material, Almquist and Almquist (2017) look at the art of intrapreneurial innovation, stressing the importance of creativity, communication and collaboration, Bieraugel (2015) considers the use of the lean start-up method for managing library innovation, Kelly (2010) describes the use of appreciative enquiry as an approach to change management, and Duren (2016) highlights the importance of the communication process in change management. Chapter 3 looks at how change management theories and approaches can be applied in an academic library context.

2.4 Technology and change management in academic libraries

The division of content between these first three sections is not precise, but a number of resources look at both technology and change management in academic libraries. In their volume on trends, discovery and people in the digital age, Baker and Evans (2013) explore the impact of developing technologies on the information world, including the future of librarianship. They reflect that there has been a significant move away from the librarian as intermediary between the content and user towards roles as 'content aggregators, access managers and educators in digital literacy'. They stress the importance of innovative leadership and appropriate changes to organisational structures. Booth (2009) highlights the importance of identifying student behaviours relating to emerging and social technologies and the implications for academic libraries. In the move to digital resources, Choy (2011) emphasises the importance of the library-user relationship to ensure that users continue to use and value libraries. Coghill and Russell (2016) look at the development of librarian competencies for the digital age and a series of books edited by Eden (2015a, 2015b) provide useful case studies of technology and change projects in academic libraries.

2.5 Related areas

It is also interesting to explore some of the same issues relating to technology and change in other sectors. Bautista (2013) looks at the use of technology in museums and proposes that technology should be adopted and adapted by museums based on their particular missions, communities, cultures and places. The book includes five case studies of the most technologically advanced art museums in the United States and each case study helpfully ends with a lessons learned section. Parry (2009) argues that the influence of digital technology in museums and the cultural heritage sector has been pervasive and profound. There are parallels with academic libraries, with museums now reliant on technology to manage collections, which contain digital as well as material objects, and with their activity online as important as their physical presence on site. Chapters include consideration of empowering the remote user, accessibility, digitisation and preservation, and the usability of websites. A chapter on the changing role of information professionals in museums in the digital age looks at ways in which museums have changed their priorities, staffing, organisational structures, systems and procedures.

Cuban (2018) considers the uses and effects of digital technologies in classrooms and schools, exploring if and how technology has altered classroom and teaching practices and, in consequence, whether there has been a positive impact on student learning.

2.6 Trends

A number of reports (ACRL Research Planning and Review Committee, 2019; EDUCAUSE, 2020) and recent articles (Cox, Pinfield, & Rutter, 2019a; Gwyer, 2015) help to provide information on the trends impacting on academic libraries. Their coverage is wider than technological trends, but the resources present important guidance on developments in technology. Additional resources are listed in the Further Reading section.

2.7 Specific technologies

There are many different technologies that have been applied successfully in academic libraries, with other technologies having the potential to be utilised. The sections that follow consider some of the more important applications.

2.7.1 Library systems and library services platforms

Some of the most common large scale change management projects for academic libraries relate to the procurement and implementation of new library management systems and online services. Beard and Land (2012) emphasise the importance in these projects of remaining focused on the user experience and maintaining close partnerships of the library with IT services, vendors and the academic community. Effective governance, communication, and change and project management are key to success. The changing information searching behaviour of users, particularly digital natives, has required libraries and library vendors to provide simple search interfaces to discovery systems, in line with services such as Google (Wells, 2016). The cost and complexity of library system replacement has encouraged some groups of academic libraries to consider developing and implementing shared systems as in the WHELF project in Wales for a shared library management system (Owen, 2016). The impacts of this project on one of the participants, Cardiff Metropolitan University, are considered in Chapter 11. The use of cloud computing can also have financial benefits and reduce local storage capacity concerns, although implications such as information security, ownership and control of data, and privacy need to be considered (Mavodza, 2013). Use of systems such as EDI (electronic data interchange) (Kelsey, 2015) and customer relationship management systems (Fouad & Al-Goblan, 2017) by academic libraries can also have benefits in terms of cost saving, streamlined workflows and improved customer satisfaction. Chapter 5 looks at the implementation of the Leganto reading list software within the library management system at Curtin University.

2.7.2   Research support

Advances in technology, changes in higher education, research and scholarly communication, and financial constraints have all had a significant impact on the nature of support required for university research activities (Kennan, Corrall, & Afzal, 2014). These are at all points in the research lifecycle, and not just those traditionally supported by academic librarians, and include research data management, bibliometrics, e-research (Johnson, Butler, & Johnston, 2012), the creation of online research profiles (Ward, Bejarano, & Dudas, 2015), and grant writing. There are opportunities for librarians to expand their role, but there are also gaps and constraints to overcome in terms of staff skills, knowledge, confidence, capability and capacity (Brewerton, 2012). Programmes to reskill librarians in areas such as open access and research data management may be required, alongside a greater emphasis on partnership and collaboration with other areas of the university, including research offices, and the creation of particular functional roles in library staffing structures (Sewell & Kingsley, 2017). Specific areas of research support are also explored in the sections immediately below.

2.7.3   Open access, scholarly communication and repositories

From an academic library perspective, open access has helped to provide an alternative to the unsustainable pricing of journals, with library budgets dominated by a small number of multinational publishers, as well as supporting the value of openness in the distribution of research (Steele, 2014). Initial progress with institutional repositories was slow with researchers often having a lack of awareness of repositories and related institutional policies (Creaser, 2010) and with varying levels of interest, participation and compliance, including some suspicion of the status of open access journals. In recent years open access has become more of 'a scholarly norm' (Willinsky, 2018), with open access and scholarship more embedded in the research environment, culture and activity, particularly in the UK, with funding bodies implementing mandates and policies relating to open access and research assessment, and academic libraries playing an important central role. Chapter 17 provides details of Jisc's role in these developments in the UK, including its close working relationships with academic libraries. Other key issues include the development of skills and competencies in librarians and 'scholarly publishing literacy' in researchers (Zhao, 2014), the additional costs of article processing charges, and the need for repositories to be interoperable with other university systems, including current research information systems.

2.7.4 Bibliometrics

Many academic libraries have sought to redefine and widen their role by providing research impact services using bibliometrics, which can support the promotion of research, grants and institutional comparisons (Drummond & Wartho, 2009). This can help to increase the visibility and status of libraries, but can also affect how libraries are perceived in adopting a monitoring function in addition to a service-orientated role (Astrom & Hansson, 2013). There can be competency issues, with gaps in knowledge, skills and confidence being significant constraints (Corrall, Kennan, & Afzal, 2013). These can be addressed through workshops and other staff development activities, with opportunities to share skills and identify gaps and future support requirements (Powell & Elder, 2019).

2.7.5 Open access university presses

As traditional university presses have struggled to maintain the publication of scholarly monographs, new opportunities have arisen for a more diverse publishing ecology with the development of open access publishing through collaboration between the presses and academic libraries and the combination of digital repositories and scholarly publishing (Adema & Stone, 2017). There can be issues of obtaining faculty buy-in and the perceived quality of the outputs from this non-traditional publishing model (Sandy & Mattern, 2018). There can also be value in academic libraries working together to establish publishing cooperatives (Walters, 2012) and in Chapter 9 there is a description of the development of the White Rose University Press created by the universities of Leeds, Sheffield and York.

2.7.6 Research data management

In the last few years, academic libraries, particularly in large research intensive universities, have sought to extend their role in supporting researchers into the area of research data management, often in conjunction with other departments, such as IT services and research offices (Morgan, Duffield, & Hall, 2017). Research funders have required institutions to demonstrate how they will preserve and share research data and there are key issues in the development of local policies, training, advocacy, ethics and technical infrastructure. Cox, Pinfield, and Smith (2016) highlight the complexity of research data management, with issues often viewed and defined differently by different stakeholders. Librarians need to be able to demonstrate that they have the appropriate expertise and skills to operate efficiently in this area of activity. Chapter 15 describes a research data management project at the University of Adelaide.

2.7.7 Web services

The importance of academic library websites as gateways to library services and resources has increased in line with the increases in digital resources and usage of the internet by students and staff (Mierzecka & Suminas, 2018). Supporting resources such as subject guides are more easily updated, repackaged and made accessible via the web (McMullin & Hutton, 2010). Issues to consider include the staffing requirements for the web team (Dethloff & German, 2013), the constraints imposed by institutional procedures and processes (Manuel, Dearnley, & Walton, 2010) and evaluation (Al-Qallaf & Ridha, 2019).

2.7.8 Digital resources, including e-books

Over recent years, there has been a major transition from print to electronic formats for academic journals and a consequent significant impact on academic libraries, with a huge rise in the availability and take-up of e-journals by academic staff, researchers and students (Williams, Nicholas, & Rowlands, 2010). There have been considerable benefits in terms of convenience and remote access, although there have been issues around availability of back files and publisher 'bundles' or 'big deals' have had both advantages and disadvantages for academic libraries and their users (Strieb & Blixrud, 2014). The transition to electronic formats from print has been much slower for academic books. Although there are advantages such as convenience and cost for e-books, there is evidence that many students still prefer print texts for reasons such as accessibility, eyestrain, tactile features and the ability to highlight and take notes (Johnston & Salaz, 2019). A number of e-book studies (Blummer & Kenton, 2020) have highlighted issues relating to information seeking behaviour, technology acceptance, and user attitudes and preferences, and concerns about ease of use, licensing and access restrictions, and competing formats. There are also implications for academic libraries in terms of workflows and the need for promotional activities. Chapter 16 details the steps taken by Leeds University Library to improve the curation of its e-books and access to these resources for users. There are also opportunities for academic libraries to work collaboratively in the procurement of e-resources as in the SHEDL (Scottish Higher Education Digital Library) initiative (Stevenson, Ashworth, & Evans, 2018) and Chapter 12 describes recent SHEDL collaborative procurement activity in the area of e-books.

Digital technology, particularly digitisation, has had a great impact on special collections in university libraries, enabling much wider access to rare and unique titles. To ensure digitisation meets user needs, institutions have made consultation and user participation central to digitisation initiatives and selection processes (Mills, 2015). Academic libraries have also supported the creation, revision and adoption of OER (open educational resources), which has encouraged pedagogical innovation in the classroom and often saved students money (Gumb, 2019). Academic libraries may need to acquire and integrate research datasets as part of their library collections, in support of university research. This will involve issues around acquisition procedures, licensing, discovery, access and technical support

(Foster, Rinehart, & Springs, 2019). In addition, requirements from research funders have placed an increasing pressure on institutions to store their own raw research data in a secure way. This has provided opportunities for academic libraries, working in partnership with researchers and IT services, to undertake roles in data curation and data analysis (Maxwell, Norton, & Wu, 2018). New competencies, including technical skills, will be required of librarians helping to manage research data (Semeler, Pinto, & Rozados, 2019).

2.7.9 Library spaces

Developments such as digitisation, the proliferation of electronic resources and remote access could be seen as making the 'library as place' increasingly irrelevant. However, academic libraries have responded energetically and proactively to a number of trends and developments (Seal, 2015) to become more user- and service-based rather than collection-based through the provision of innovative learning spaces. The trends include:

- Students preferring flexible, comfortable places to work singly or collaboratively in groups
- Need for assistance to navigate a large and complex array of online resources
- Need for access to a range of technologies
- Increasing focus on knowledge creation and new forms of learning and pedagogy
- Requirement for the integration of service provision

Different space models such as Information Commons and Learning Commons, involving academic libraries, have become increasingly common. Turner, Welch, and Reynolds (2013) comment that Information Commons initiatives generally bring together library space and IT services in a largely library-centric model. Learning Commons developments have a wider remit focusing on the support and facilitation of learning and involve other academic and student support services. Information and Learning Commons developments have a focus on undergraduate students; initiatives such as Research Commons or Scholars' Commons (Dallis, 2016) aim to provide facilities and services for faculty and graduate research. All the models require new approaches to leadership and management within a collaborative arrangement.

Academic libraries can also have a role with other stakeholders in defining a university strategy for informal learning spaces. Harrop and Turpin (2013) describe a study exploring learners' behaviours, attitudes and preferences towards informal learning spaces and present a number of learning space preference attributes which can be used to evaluate existing spaces and inform development.

Some academic libraries have followed the lead of public libraries in developing and hosting makerspaces. Makerspaces are physical locations where people can gather to share resources and knowledge, work on projects, network and build (Wong & Partridge, 2016). In some universities, pop-up makerspaces have been set up as an exploratory stage to gauge interest before implementing a permanent space. Technical facilities in makerspaces typically include 3D printing (Pryor, 2014) and laser cutting.

Makerspaces can provide academic libraries with a role in supporting new approaches to learning and knowledge creation, often in cross-disciplinary initiatives, with opportunities to teach information, digital and critical literacies (Curry, 2017).

2.7.10 Virtual reference services

Academic libraries are making increased use of virtual reference services to allow users to submit questions and receive answers via methods such as email, messaging and chat. Staffing and workflow efficiencies have resulted, but this has often involved significant changes to traditional practices and has challenged long held beliefs about the delivery of library reference services. This has required library staff to be supported and be trained to develop new skills and adapt to new practices (Hockey, 2016). There are also examples of groups of academic libraries, such as Northern Collaboration[1] in northern England, providing out-of-hours virtual enquiry services (Jolly & White, 2016), which can provide value for money, but which require effective communication within and between institutions. Statistics collected about virtual reference usage can give information about high and low users, which can help to provide insights to assist with marketing (Nolen et al, 2012). Chapter 6 looks at virtual help and advisory services at the University of Sheffield.

2.7.11 Digitisation

Digitisation offers potentially significant benefits for university libraries holding unique and important library materials, particularly in special collections. Large scale digitisation projects can help to preserve and protect original material, whilst also increasing its availability for research and teaching both within the institution and more widely. However, mass digitisation projects present major resource issues, both in staff time and cost. Prioritisation frameworks, identifying user priorities for digitisation, can be helpful (Birrell et al., 2011), but external funding is often required to make rapid progress, as in the partnership with Google at Complutense University Library in Madrid (Magan, Palafox, Tardon, & Sanz, 2011) or with the UK-wide Jisc digitisation programme[2] between 2003 and 2013 (Sykes, 2008). Chapter 13 considers a project to engage students with university archival collections and digitisation processes at the University of Newcastle (Australia).

2.7.12 Social media technologies in learning, research, communication and marketing

Many academic librarians now use social media for the communication and promotion of services, in instruction and training, and for professional communication and development within and outside their organisation. Librarians have traditionally sought to communicate with their users in the places they visit or via the tools they use and social media platforms are spaces students, in particular, currently occupy

(Joe, 2015). Chatten and Roughley (2016) report on the ways in which social media can enhance audience engagement and create a community of users, and they emphasise the value of a team approach to ensure diversity and breadth of output. Services such as Facebook and Twitter are increasingly used by academic libraries, but there is a need to explore and consult about students' preferred social media tools and the kind of information they would like to receive about academic library services (Polger & Sich, 2019). Some libraries have reported on their role in supporting some groups of users, such as researchers, in social media use (Persson & Svenningsson, 2016). Other points referred to include privacy, legal and ethical issues, the need to produce social media policies, and the hesitancy of some library staff to get involved in social media work. In addition, Jones and Harvey (2019) report on some libraries struggling to get students to engage with their social media initiatives, with students perhaps preferring to separate out social and study activities.

2.7.13   Identity and access management

Access and identity management have become important issues for academic libraries as electronic resources increase and librarians want to implement policies about who can access resources and under what conditions. Garibyan, McLeish, and Paschoud (2013) explain the underlying principles, the available technologies and how they work, including federated access management technologies such as Shibboleth. Streamlining the user experience of accessing electronic resources for staff, researchers and students needs to be balanced against user privacy with institutions protecting users' personal data with GDPR and information security measures (Reid, 2019).

2.7.14   Learning analytics

Academic libraries have a long history of collecting data to inform decision making, improve the student experience and develop new services. Examples include gate counts, use of collections both printed and electronic, and reference or customer service interactions. The data have typically been siloed to the library, non-identifiable to individual users, and private and confidential (Oliphant & Brundin, 2019). More recently, academic libraries have begun to participate in learning analytics, which involves gathering data about students and using the information to improve learning and institutional outcomes. Many library professionals have expressed concern about the ethics of this kind of activity, particularly around issues of privacy, confidentiality and intellectual freedom (Jones, 2019). Oakleaf (2018) also refers to librarians' concerns about individual level data, but advocates the integration of libraries into institutional learning analytics to gain insights into library value in an institutional context, particularly around student attainment and retention. There are also issues around the development of data fluency in librarians involved in this activity (Kirkwood, 2016).

2.7.15   MOOCs

Massive Open Online Courses (MOOCs) have recently emerged in higher education and offer free participation, are delivered entirely online and are massively scalable, being designed for thousands of users. Some developments have seen little involvement of librarians, but potential academic librarian participation is in traditional areas such as instruction, reference and collection development, as well as in copyright clearance and content licensing (Barnes, 2013; Gore, 2014; Mune, 2015). University libraries are also beginning to consider developing their own courses in this area and Chapter 4 describes the development of MOOCs on digital citizenship and digital wellbeing at the University of York.

2.7.16   Online learning

In recent years, online learning, including e-learning and blended learning, has changed pedagogical approaches in universities. Academic libraries need to adapt their services or develop new service models, create staff development opportunities, and, in some cases, adjust organisational structures to support online and blended learning (Keisling, 2018). Libraries are increasingly involved in the creation of learning objects that can either be linked to or embedded within learning management systems (Mestre, 2010) enabling access to library resources or activities such as information literacy instruction (Courtney & Wilhoite-Mathews, 2015). More recent developments involve support within virtual reality learning environments (Hahn, 2018). Chapter 7 describes the adoption of adaptive learning technologies to redesign and enhance an online communication and research skills unit at the University of Western Australia.

2.7.17   Digital scholarship and digital humanities

Multidisciplinary collaboration, involving librarians, archivists and IT developers working with academic staff, has seen the creation of new knowledge and resources in digital scholarship and digital humanities initiatives (Burns, 2016). This has involved the development of new roles and responsibilities for librarians. Zhang, Liu, and Mathews (2015) define the present and potential future role of the librarian as creator and contributor, curator, messenger and liaison, educator, mediator and interpreter, host, partner, innovator, 'hybrid scholar', advocate and consultant. Changes of this nature are challenging, and significant training and the revamping of organisational structures may be necessary to realise deeper collaboration. Cox (2016) comments that as the library seeks to move to being more of a partner than a service provider, the library's actual and potential collaborations will need to be communicated to a diverse range of university stakeholders in order to create and embed revised perceptions of the librarian's role. The activities involved in digital scholarship work (e.g. digitisation, housing research data, digital publishing, the development of software) are wide ranging and staff resource intensive, and work will need to be carried out to ensure that the library's involvement is scalable and sustainable (Vinopal & McCormick, 2013).

2.7.18   Disability technology and accessibility of services and resources

In many countries academic library provision for disabled students has become an increasingly important issue following legislative changes. Librarians often work closely with colleagues in IT services and student services to provide assistive technology, such as software and hardware, to enable disabled students gain access to information and study. In implementing technological developments, academic libraries need to ensure that disabled users are appropriately catered for. Examples cited in the literature include access to electronic resources (Majinge & Mutula, 2018), library websites (Cassner, Maxey-Harris, & Anaya, 2011) and repositories and learning management systems (Skourlas et al, 2016).

2.7.19   Digital literacy

Academic libraries have a long established role in information literacy training. More recently universities have begun to develop digital literacy provision, which has a wider scope including: data and media literacies; digital learning; digital creation, innovation and scholarship; and digital citizenship (Walton, 2016). Librarians have a role to play in digital literacy, although they need to expand their skills and competencies beyond traditional information resources to reflect changing faculty and student needs. This includes the use of data resources (MacMillan, 2015). Digital literacy is an area of activity that no one department can provide on its own, and effective delivery requires the development of effective partnerships and collaboration and, in many cases, a university-wide approach within an agreed strategic framework (Hallam, Thomas, & Beach, 2018).

2.7.20   Focus on the user

In order to respond to the increased expectations of users, particularly students, there has been a recent trend away from a totally centralised and generic library provision to offer more personalised services and support. In their influential book, Priestner and Tilley (2012) propose a 'boutique' approach, including responding and adapting to changes in technology to provide personalised digital resources and support within a virtual environment. In some ways this follows the approach of large commercial providers such as Netflix and Amazon in the delivery of personalised services and in the utilisation of user data. This user-centric perspective is also reflected in the increased take up of user experience (UX) techniques by academic libraries (Walton, 2015). UX helps service providers understand and improve the experience users have through the application of ethnographic techniques. The use of patron-driven acquisition (PDA), sometimes known as user- or demand driven acquisition (UDA or DDA), also provides a strong user focus for collection development, particularly for e-books, with the acquisition of resources related to high user demand (Carrico, Leonard, & Gallagher, 2016).

2.7.21 Mobile technologies and devices

The increasingly high percentage of mobile device ownership — laptops, tablets and smartphones — among university students has required academic libraries to provide BYOD (Bring Your Own Device) study facilities and have good wireless provision throughout library buildings. Mobile technology developments have allowed academic libraries to expand their reach to students and faculty beyond the library's walls through the provision of information and services to mobile devices, but are also likely to have an impact on provision that has been developed in recent years. These include the large scale provision of fixed PCs, laptop loan services (Gu, 2011) and e-reader loan services (Savova & Garsia, 2012). Academic librarians have utilised mobile devices and apps for activities such as information literacy (Basile & Matis, 2018) and tablets for roving support to students at their point of need outside the library (Sharman, 2014). There are some challenges for librarians to address in the diversity of needs and preferences among users and which technologies to adopt in a rapidly changing landscape, as well as the cost implications (Barnhart & Pierce, 2011). There are also staffing issues relating to the preparedness of library staff to deliver services through mobile technologies in terms of skills, knowledge and competencies (Saravani & Haddow, 2011). Chapter 8 describes the development of a mobile-friendly web-based book finding tool at the University of Portsmouth.

2.7.22 Robotics, including automated storage and retrieval

Adoption of robotics in academic libraries is in its infancy (Guth & Vander Meer, 2017), although one area where there has been significant progress is in the development of automated storage and retrieval systems (ASRS) for the storage of lesser used books. The first system was installed at California State University (Heinrich & Willis, 2014). Chapter 14 describes the implementation of an ASRS system at the University of Limerick.

2.7.23 Artificial intelligence

In the future, the development and application of artificial intelligence could have a dramatic impact on academic libraries. This could be in areas such as search and resource discovery, scholarly publishing and learning. Challenges could include libraries being sidelined in developments, ethical concerns, issues of data quality and threats to jobs (Cox, Pinfield, & Rutter, 2019b). More positively, artificial intelligence could have a role in data acquisition and curation, supporting user navigation and data literacy, and communication with users. Conversational artificial intelligence, including the use of chatbots, has the potential to create personalised experiences for library users. At the University of Technology Sydney a prototype chatbot has been developed to enhance the academic library experience of students. McKie and Narayan (2019) emphasise the need for librarians to work closely with technology developers in initiatives such as these.

2.7.24 Internet of things

In general, the term 'Internet of things' encompasses everything connected to the internet, but is particularly used to define objects that 'talk' to each other. Examples are RFID (radio frequency identification) and QR (quick response) codes. By combining these connected devices with automated systems, it is possible to collect information or data, analyse them and then create an appropriate action. In academic libraries particular use has been made of RFID in collection management and self service provision (Chelliah, Sood, & Scholfield, 2015). Implementation of RFID needs to take account of ethical and privacy issues (Ferguson, Thornley, & Gibb, 2015). QR codes have also been used by academic libraries in the promotion of services (Elmore & Stephens, 2012). There is potential for future applications in academic libraries with smartphones and wearables (Ajmi & Robak, 2017).

Endnotes

1. Northern Collaboration: https://northerncollaboration.org.uk
2. Jisc digitisation programme: https://www.webarchive.org.uk/wayback/archive/20140614072425/http://www.jisc.ac.uk/whatwedo/programmes/digitisation.aspx

References

ACRL Research Planning and Review Committee. (2019). *Environmental scan 2019*. Chicago, IL: Association of College and Research Libraries Retrieved from. Available from http://www.ala.org/acrl/sites/ala.org.acrl/files/content/publications/whitepapers/EnvironmentalScan2019.pdf.

Adema, J., & Stone, G. (2017). The surge in new university presses and academic-led publishing: An overview of a changing publishing ecology in the UK. *LIBER Quarterly*, 27 (1), 97−126. Available from https://doi.org/10.18352/lq.10210.

Ajmi, A., & Robak, M. J. (2017). Wearable technologies in academic libraries: Fact, fiction and the future. In R. Canuel, & C. Crichton (Eds.), *Mobile technology and academic libraries: Innovative services for research and learning* (pp. 249−263). Chicago, IL: ACRL.

Almquist, A. J., & Almquist, S. G. (2017). *Intrapreneurship handbook for librarians: How to be a change agent in your library*. Santa Barbara, CA: Libraries Unlimited.

Al-Qallaf, C. L., & Ridha, A. (2019). A comprehensive analysis of academic library websites: Design, navigation, content, services, and web 2.0 tools. *International Information & Library Review*, 51(2), 93−106. Available from https://doi.org/10.1080/10572317.2018.1467166.

Astrom, F., & Hansson, J. (2013). How implementation of bibliometric practice affects the role of academic libraries. *Journal of Librarianship and Information Science*, 45(4), 316−322. Available from https://doi.org/10.1177/0961000612456867.

Baker, D., & Evans, W. (Eds.), (2013). *Trends, discovery and people in the digital age.* Oxford: Chandos Publishing.

Barnes, C. (2013). MOOCs: The challenges for academic librarians. *Australian Academic & Research Libraries*, *44*(3), 163−175. Available from https://doi.org/10.1080/00048623. 2013.821048.

Barnhart, F. D., & Pierce, J. E. (2011). Becoming mobile: Reference in the ubiquitous library. *Journal of Library Administration*, *51*(3), 279−290. Available from https://doi. org/10.1080/01930826.2011.556942.

Basile, A., & Matis, S. (2018). Is there an app for that?: A review of mobile apps for information literacy classes. *College & Research Libraries News*, *79*(10), 546−550, Retrieved from. Available from https://crln.acrl.org/index.php/crlnews/article/view/17433/19224.

Bautista, S. S. (2013). *Museums in the digital age: Changing meanings of place, community and culture.* Lanham, MD: AltaMira Press / Rowman & Littlefield.

Beard, L., & Land, A. (2012). Staying relevant in the Google age: Implementing vertical search at the University of Manchester; A technological and cultural perspective. *LIBER Quarterly*, *21*(2), 238−248. Available from https://doi.org/10.18352/lq.8022.

Bieraugel, M. (2015). Managing library innovation using the lean startup method. *Library Management*, *36*(4/5), 351−361. Available from https://doi.org/10.1108/LM-10-2014-0131.

Birrell, D., Dobreva, M., Dunsire, G., Griffiths, J. R., Hartley, R. J., & Menzies, K. (2011). The DiSCmap project: Digitisation of special collections: Mapping, assessment, prioritisation. *New Library World*, *112*(1/2), 19−44. Available from https://doi.org/10.1108/03074801111100436.

Blummer, B., & Kenton, J. M. (2020). A systematic review of e-books in academic libraries: Access, advantages, and usage. *New Review of Academic Librarianship*, *26*(1), 79−109. Available from https://doi.org/10.1080/13614533.2018.1524390.

Booth, C. (2009). *Informing innovation: Tracking student interest in emerging library technologies at Ohio University.* Chicago, IL: ACRL.

Brewerton, A. (2012). Re-skilling for research: Investigating the needs of researchers and how library staff can best support them. *New Review of Academic Librarianship*, *18*(1), 96−110. Available from https://doi.org/10.1080/13614533.2012.665718.

Burns, J. A. (2016). Role of the information professional in the development and promotion of digital humanities content for research, teaching, and learning in the modern academic library: An Irish case study. *New Review of Academic Librarianship*, *22*(2-3), 238−248. Available from https://doi.org/10.1080/13614533.2016.1191520.

Carrico, S., Leonard, M., & Gallagher, E. (2016). *Implementing and assessing use-driven acquisitions: A practical guide for librarians.* Lanham, MD: Rowman & Littlefield.

Cassner, M., Maxey-Harris, C., & Anaya, T. (2011). Differently able: A review of academic library websites for people with disabilities. *Behavioral & Social Sciences Librarian*, *30* (1), 33−51. Available from https://doi.org/10.1080/01639269.2011.548722.

Chatten, Z., & Roughley, S. (2016). Developing social media to engage and connect at the University of Liverpool Library. *New Review of Academic Librarianship*, *22*(2-3), 249−256. Available from https://doi.org/10.1080/13614533.2016.1152985.

Chelliah, J., Sood, S., & Scholfield, S. (2015). Realising the strategic value of RFID in academic libraries: A case study of the University of Technology Sydney. *Australian Library Journal*, *64*(2), 113−127. Available from https://doi.org/10.1080/00049670.2015.1013005.

Choy, F. C. (2011). From library stacks to library-in-a-pocket: Will users be around? *Library Management*, *32*(1/2), 62−72. Available from https://doi.org/10.1108/01435121111102584.

Coghill, J. G., & Russell, R. G. (Eds.), (2016). *Developing librarian competencies for the digital age*. Lanham, MD: Rowman & Littlefield.

Corrall, S., Kennan, M. A., & Afzal, W. (2013). Bibliometrics and research data management services: Emerging trends in library support for research. *Library Trends*, *61*(3), 636−674. Available from https://doi.org/10.1353/lib.2013.0005.

Courtney, M., & Wilhoite-Mathews, S. (2015). From distance education to online learning: Practical approaches to information literacy instruction and collaborative learning in online environments. *Journal of Library Administration*, *55*(4), 261−277. Available from https://doi.org/10.1080/01930826.2015.1038924.

Cox, A. M., Pinfield, S., & Rutter, S. (2019a). Academic libraries' stance towards the future. *Portal: Libraries and the Academy*, *19*(3), 485−509. Available from https://doi.org/10.1353/pla.2019.0028.

Cox, A. M., Pinfield, S., & Rutter, S. (2019b). The intelligent library: Thought leaders' views on the likely impact of artificial intelligence on academic libraries. *Library Hi Tech*, *37* (3), 418−435. Available from https://doi.org/10.1108/LHT-08-2018-0105.

Cox, A. M., Pinfield, S., & Smith, J. (2016). Moving a brick building: UK libraries coping with research data management as a 'wicked' problem. *Journal of Librarianship and Information Science*, *48*(1), 3−17. Available from https://doi.org/10.1177/0961000614533717.

Cox, J. (2016). Communicating new library roles to enable digital scholarship: A review article. *New Review of Academic Librarianship*, *22*(2-3), 132−147. Available from https://doi.org/10.1080/13614533.2016.1181665.

Creaser, C. (2010). Open access to research outputs − institutional policies and researchers' views: Results from two complementary surveys. *New Review of Academic Librarianship*, *16*(1), 4−25. Available from https://doi.org/10.1080/13614530903162854.

Cuban, L. (2018). *The flight of the butterfly or the path of the bullet?: Using technology to transform teaching and learning*. Cambridge, MA: Harvard Educational Publishing Group.

Curry, R. (2017). Makerspaces: A beneficial new service for academic libraries? *Library Review*, *66*(4/5), 201−212. Available from https://doi.org/10.1108/LR-09-2016-0081.

Dallis, D. (2016). Scholars and learners: A case study of new library spaces at Indiana University. *New Library World*, *117*(1/2), 35−48. Available from https://doi.org/10.1108/NLW-04-2015-0023.

Dempsey, L. (2016). Library collections in the life of the user: Two directions. *LIBER Quarterly*, *26*(4), 338−359. Available from https://doi.org/10.18352/lq.10170.

Dethloff, N., & German, E. M. (2013). Successes and struggles with building web teams: A usability committee case study. *New Library World*, *114*(5/6), 242−250. Available from https://doi.org/10.1108/03074801311326867.

Drummond, R., & Wartho, R. (2009). RIMS: The Research Impact Measurement Service at the University of New South Wales. *Australian Academic & Research Libraries*, *40*(2), 76−87. Available from https://doi.org/10.1080/00048623.2009.10721387.

Duren, P. (2016). Change communication can be so simple!: The empathic change communication style. *Library Management*, *37*(8/9), 398−409. Available from https://doi.org/10.1108/LM-01-2016-0006.

Eden, B. L. (Ed.), (2015a). Creating research infrastructures in the 21st-century academic library: Conceiving, funding, and building new facilities and staff. Lanham, MD: Rowman & Littlefield.

Eden, B. L. (Ed.), (2015b). Enhancing teaching and learning in the 21st-century academic library: Successful innovations that make a difference. Lanham, MD: Rowman & Littlefield.

EDUCAUSE. (2020). *2020 EDUCAUSE horizon report: Teaching and learning edition*. Louisville, CO: EDUCAUSE Retrieved from. Available from https://library.educause.edu/-/media/files/library/2020/3/2020_horizon_report_pdf.pdf?la = en&hash = 08A92 C17998E8113BCB15DCA7BA1F467F303BA80.

Elliott, C., Dewland, J., Martin, J. R., Kramer, S., & Jackson, J. J. (2017). Collaborate and innovate: The impact of academic librarians on the commercialization of university technology. *Journal of Library Administration*, *57*(1), 36−48. Available from https://doi.org/10.1080/01930826.2016.1215674.

Elmore, L., & Stephens, D. (2012). The application of QR codes in UK academic libraries. *New Review of Academic Librarianship*, *18*(1), 26−42. Available from https://doi.org/10.1080/13614533.2012.654679.

Ferguson, S., Thornley, C., & Gibb, F. (2015). How do libraries manage the ethical and privacy issues of RFID implementation? A qualitative investigation into the decision-making processes of ten libraries. *Journal of librarianship and information science*, *47*(2), 117−130. Available from https://doi.org/10.1177/0961000613518572.

Fernandez, P. D., & Tilton, K. (Eds.), (2018). *Applying library values to emerging technology: Decision-making in the age of open access, maker spaces, and the ever changing library*. Chicago, IL: ACRL.

Foster, A. K., Rinehart, A. K., & Springs, G. R. (2019). Piloting the purchase of research data sets as collections: Navigating the unknowns. *Portal: Libraries and the Academy*, *19*(2), 315−328. Available from https://doi.org/10.1353/pla.2019.0018.

Fouad, N., & Al-Goblan, N. (2017). Using customer relationship management systems at university libraries: A comparative study between Saudi Arabia and Egypt. *IFLA Journal*, *43*(2), 158−170. Available from https://doi.org/10.1177/0340035216685103.

Garibyan, M., McLeish, S., & Paschoud, J. (2013). *Access and identity management for libraries: Controlling access to online information*. London: Facet Publishing.

Gore, H. (2014). Massive open online courses (MOOCs) and their impact on academic library services: Exploring the issues and challenges. *New Review of Academic Librarianship*, *20*(1), 4−28. Available from https://doi.org/10.1080/13614533.2013.851609.

Gu, F. (2011). The campus-wide laptop loan service and the library's role. *Library Management*, *32*(1/2), 6−21. Available from https://doi.org/10.1108/01435121111102548.

Gumb, L. (2019). An open impediment: Navigating copyright and OER publishing in the academic library. *College & Research Libraries News*, *80*(4), 202−204. Available from https://doi.org/10.5860/crln.80.4.202, 215.

Guth, L., & Vander Meer, P. (2017). Telepresence robotics in academic library: A study of exposure and adaption among patrons and employees. *Library Hi Tech*, *35*(3), 408−420. Available from https://doi.org/10.1108/LHT-03-2017-0059.

Gwyer, R. (2015). Identifying and exploring future trends impacting on academic libraries: A mixed methodology using journal content analysis, focus groups, and trend reports. *New Review of Academic Librarianship*, *21*(3), 269−285. Available from https://doi.org/10.1080/13614533.2015.1026452.

Hahn, J. F. (2018). Virtual reality learning environments: Development of multi-user reference support experiences. *Information and Learning Sciences*, *119*(11), 652−661. Available from https://doi.org/10.1108/ILS-07-2018-0069.

Hallam, G., Thomas, A., & Beach, B. (2018). Creating a connected future through information and digital literacy: Strategic directions at the University of Queensland Library. *Journal of the Australian Library and Information Association*, *67*(1), 42−54. Available from https://doi.org/10.1080/24750158.2018.1426365.

Harrop, D., & Turpin, B. (2013). A study exploring learners' informal learning space behaviors, attitudes and preferences. *New Review of Academic Librarianship*, *19*(1), 58–77. Available from https://doi.org/10.1080/13614533.2013.740961.

Heinrich, H., & Willis, E. (2014). Automated storage and retrieval system: A time-tested innovation. *Library Management*, *35*(6/7), 444–453. Available from https://doi.org/10.1108/LM-09-2013-0086.

Hockey, J. M. (2016). Transforming library enquiry services: Anywhere, anytime and any device. *Library Management*, *37*(3), 125–135. Available from https://doi.org/10.1108/LM-04-2016-0021.

Jantz, R. C. (2016). *Managing creativity: The innovative research library*. Chicago, IL: ALA Editions.

Jantz, R. C. (2017). Creating the innovative library culture: Escaping the iron cage through management innovation. *New Review of Academic Librarianship*, *23*(4), 323–328. Available from https://doi.org/10.1080/13614533.2017.1388055.

Joe, J. W. (2015). Assessment of social media in the library: Guidelines for administrators. *Journal of Library Administration*, *55*(8), 667–680. Available from https://doi.org/10.1080/01930826.2015.1085251.

Johnson, L. M., Butler, J. T., & Johnston, L. R. (2012). Developing e-science and research services and support at the University of Minnesota health sciences libraries. *Journal of Library Administration*, *52*(8), 754–769. Available from https://doi.org/10.1080/01930826.2012.751291.

Johnston, N., & Salaz, A. M. (2019). Exploring the reasons why university students prefer print over digital texts: An Australian perspective. *Journal of the Australian Library and Information Association*, *68*(2), 126–145. Available from https://doi.org/10.1080/24750158.2019.1587858.

Joiner, I. (2018). *Emerging library technologies: It's not just for geeks*. Oxford: Chandos Publishing.

Jolly, L., & White, S. (2016). Communication, collaboration, and enhancing the learning experience: Developing a collaborative virtual enquiry service in university libraries in the north of England. *New Review of Academic Librarianship*, *22*(2-3), 176–191. Available from https://doi.org/10.1080/13614533.2016.1156002.

Jones, K. M. L. (2019). 'Just because you can doesn't mean you should': Practitioner perceptions of learning analytics ethics. *Portal: Libraries and the Academy*, *19*(3), 407–428. Available from https://doi.org/10.1353/pla.2019.0025.

Jones, M. J., & Harvey, M. (2019). Library 2.0: The effectiveness of social media as a marketing tool for libraries in educational institutions. *Journal of librarianship and information science*, *51*(1), 3–19. Available from https://doi.org/10.1177/0961000616668959.

Keisling, B. (2018). Blended learning: Scaling library services and instruction to support changing educational landscapes. *Library Management*, *39*(3/4), 207–215. Available from https://doi.org/10.1108/LM-08-2017-0080.

Kelly, T. (2010). A positive approach to change: The role of appreciative enquiry in library and information organisations. *Australian Academic & Research Libraries*, *41*(3), 163–177. Available from https://doi.org/10.1080/00048623.2010.10721461.

Kelsey, P. (2015). Implementing EDI X12 book acquisitions at a medium-sized university library. *New Library World*, *116*(7/8), 383–396. Available from https://doi.org/10.1108/NLW-11-2014-0130.

Kennan, M. A., Corrall, S., & Afzal, W. (2014). 'Making space' in practice and education: Research support services in academic libraries. *Library Management*, *35*(8/9), 666–683. Available from https://doi.org/10.1108/LM-03-2014-0037.

King, D. L. (2018). *How to stay on top of emerging technology trends for libraries.* Chicago, IL: ALA TechSource.

Kirkwood, R. J. (2016). Collection development or data-driven content curation?: An exploratory project in Manchester. *Library Management, 37*(4/5), 275−284. Available from https://doi.org/10.1108/LM-05-2016-0044.

Koerber, J., & Sauers, M. (2015). *Emerging technologies: A primer for librarians.* Lanham, MD: Rowman & Littlefield.

MacMillan, D. (2015). Developing data literacy competencies to enhance faculty collaborations. *LIBER Quarterly, 24*(3), 140−160. Available from https://doi.org/10.18352/lq.9868.

Magan, J. A., Palafox, M., Tardon, E., & Sanz, A. (2011). Mass digitization at the Complutense University Library: Access to and preservation of its cultural heritage. *LIBER Quarterly, 21*(1), 48−68. Available from https://doi.org/10.18352/lq.8007.

Majinge, R. M., & Mutula, S. M. (2018). Access to electronic and print information resources by people with visual impairments in university libraries: A review of related literature. *Library Management, 39*(6/7), 462−473. Available from https://doi.org/10.1108/LM-04-2017-0038.

Manuel, S., Dearnley, J., & Walton, G. (2010). Strategic development of UK academic library websites: A survey of East Midlands university libraries. *Journal of Librarianship and Information Science, 42*(2), 147−155. Available from https://doi.org/10.1177/0961000610361424.

Mavodza, J. (2013). The impact of cloud computing on the future of academic library practices and services. *New Library World, 114*(3/4), 132−141. Available from https://doi.org/10.1108/03074801311304041.

Maxwell, D., Norton, H., & Wu, J. (2018). The data science opportunity: Crafting a holistic strategy. *Journal of Library Administration, 58*(2), 111−127. Available from https://doi.org/10.1080/01930826.2017.1412704.

McKie, I. A. S., & Narayan, B. (2019). Enhancing the academic library experience with chatbots: An exploration of research and implications for practice. *Journal of the Australian Library and Information Association, 68*(3), 268−277. Available from https://doi.org/10.1080/24750158.2019.1611694.

McMullin, R., & Hutton, J. (2010). Web subject guides: Virtual connections across the university community. *Journal of Library Administration, 50*(7-8), 789−797. Available from https://doi.org/10.1080/01930826.2010.488972.

Mestre, L. S. (2010). Matching up learning styles with learning objects: What's effective? *Journal of Library Administration, 50*(7-8), 808−829. Available from https://doi.org/10.1080/01930826.2010.488975.

Mierzecka, A., & Suminas, A. (2018). Academic library website functions in the context of users' information needs. *Journal of Librarianship and Information Science, 50*(2), 157−167. Available from https://doi.org/10.1177/0961000616664401.

Mills, A. (2015). User impact on selection, digitization, and the development of digital special collections. *New Review of Academic Librarianship, 21*(2), 160−169. Available from https://doi.org/10.1080/13614533.2015.1042117.

Morgan, A., Duffield, N., & Hall, L. W. (2017). Research data management support: Sharing our experiences. *Journal of the Australian Library and Information Association, 66*(3), 299−305. Available from https://doi.org/10.1080/24750158.2017.1371911.

Moss, M., Endicott-Popovsky, B., & Dupuis, M. J. (Eds.), (2015). *Is digital different?: How information creation, capture, preservation and discovery are being transformed.* London: Facet Publishing.

Mossop, S. (2013). *Achieving transformational change in academic libraries*. Oxford: Chandos Publishing.

Mune, C. (2015). Massive open online librarianship: Emerging practices in response to MOOCs. *Journal of Library & Information Services in Distance Learning*, 9(1-2), 89−100. Available from https://doi.org/10.1080/1533290X.2014.946350.

Nolen, D. S., Powers, A. C., Zhang, L., Xu, Y., Cannady, R. E., & Li, J. (2012). Moving beyond assumptions: The use of virtual reference data in an academic library. *Portal: Libraries and the Academy*, 12(1), 23−40. Available from https://doi.org/10.1353/pla.2012.0006.

Oakleaf, M. (2018). The problems and promise of learning analytics for increasing and demonstrating library value and impact. *Information and Learning Sciences*, 119(1/2), 16−24. Available from https://doi.org/10.1108/ILS-08-2017-0080.

Oliphant, T., & Brundin, M. R. (2019). Conflicting values: An exploration of the tensions between learning analytics and academic librarianship. *Library Trends*, 68(1), 5−23. Available from https://doi.org/10.1353/lib.2019.0028.

Owen, G. W. (2016). Delivering a shared library management system for users. *Library Management*, 37(6/7), 385−395. Available from https://doi.org/10.1108/LM-04-2016-0032.

Parry, R. (Ed.), (2009). *Museums in a digital age*. London: Routledge.

Persson, S., & Svenningsson, M. (2016). Librarians as advocates of social media for researchers: A social media project initiated by Linkoping University Library, Sweden. *New Review of Academic Librarianship*, 22(2-3), 304−314. Available from https://doi.org/10.1080/13614533.2016.1184693.

Polger, M. A., & Sich, D. (2019). Are they even following us? *Library Management*, 40(8/9), 503−517. Available from https://doi.org/10.1108/LM-06-2019-0031.

Powell, K. R., & Elder, J. J. (2019). A bibliometric services workshop for subject librarians. *Library Management*, 40(5), 305−312. Available from https://doi.org/10.1108/LM-03-2018-0014.

Priestner, A., & Tilley, E. (Eds.), (2012). *Personalising library services in higher education: The boutique approach*. Farnham: Ashgate.

Pryor, S. (2014). Implementing a 3D printing service in an academic library. *Journal of Library Administration*, 54(1), 1−10. Available from https://doi.org/10.1080/01930826.2014.893110.

Reid, P. (2019). Usability and privacy in academic libraries: Regaining a foothold through identity management. *Insights*, 32(1), 3. Available from https://doi.org/10.1629/uksg.487.

Sandy, H. M., & Mattern, J. B. (2018). Academic library-based publishing: A state of the evolving art. *Library Trends*, 67(2), 337−357. Available from https://doi.org/10.1353/lib.2018.0040.

Saravani, S.-J., & Haddow, G. (2011). The mobile library and staff preparedness: Exploring staff competencies using the unified theory of acceptance and use of technology model. *Australian Academic & Research Libraries*, 42(3), 179−190. Available from https://doi.org/10.1080/00048623.2011.10722231.

Savova, M., & Garsia, M. (2012). McGill Library makes e-books portable: E-reader loan service in a Canadian academic library. *Portal: Libraries and the Academy*, 12(2), 205−222. Available from https://doi.org/10.1353/pla.2012.0019.

Seal, R. A. (2015). Library spaces in the 21st century: Meeting the challenges of user needs for information, technology and expertise. *Library Management*, 36(8/9), 558−569. Available from https://doi.org/10.1108/LM-11-2014-0136.

Semeler, A. R., Pinto, A. L., & Rozados, H. B. F. (2019). Data science in data librarianship: Core competencies of a data librarian. *Journal of Librarianship and Information Science*, 51(3), 771−780. Available from https://doi.org/10.1177/0961000617742465.

Sewell, C., & Kingsley, D. (2017). Developing the 21st century academic librarian: The Research Support Ambassador Programme. *New Review of Academic Librarianship, 23* (2-3), 148−158. Available from https://doi.org/10.1080/13614533.2017.1323766.

Sharman, A. (2014). Roving librarian: The suitability of tablets in providing personalized help outside of the traditional library. *New Review of Academic Librarianship, 20*(2), 185−203. Available from https://doi.org/10.1080/13614533.2014.914959.

Skourlas, C., Tsolakidis, A., Belsis, P., Vassis, D., Kampouraki, A., Kakoulidis, P., & Giannakopoulos, G. A. (2016). Integration of institutional repositories and e-learning platforms for supporting disabled students in the higher education context. *Library Review, 65*(3), 136−159. Available from https://doi.org/10.1108/LR-08-2015-0088.

Steele, C. (2014). Scholarly communication, scholarly publishing and university libraries: Plus ca change? *Australian Academic & Research Libraries, 45*(4), 241−261. Available from https://doi.org/10.1080/00048623.2014.950042.

Stevenson, A., Ashworth, S., & Evans, J. (2018). The Scottish Higher Education Digital Library (SHEDL): Successes, challenges and the future. In J. Atkinson (Ed.), Collaboration and the academic library: Internal and external, local and regional, national and international ((pp. 195−204). Oxford: Chandos Publishing. Available from https://doi.org/10.1016/B978-0-08-102084-5.00018-3.

Strieb, K. L., & Blixrud, J. C. (2014). Unwrapping the bundle: An examination of research libraries and the 'big deal'. *Portal: Libraries and the Academy, 14*(4), 587−615. Available from https://doi.org/10.1353/pla.2014.0027.

Sykes, J. (2008). *Large-scale digitisation: The £22 million JISC programme and the role of libraries*. Presentation for the UKSG Annual Conference, 7−9 April 2008. Retrieved from: http://eprints.lse.ac.uk/25277/1/LargeScaledigitisationJISC%28LSEROversion%29.pdf

Turner, A., Welch, B., & Reynolds, S. (2013). Learning spaces in academic libraries: A review of the existing trends. *Australian Academic & Research Libraries, 44*(4), 226−234. Available from https://doi.org/10.1080/00048623.2013.857383.

Vinopal, J., & McCormick, M. (2013). Supporting digital scholarship in research libraries: Scalability and sustainability. *Journal of Library Administration, 53*(1), 27−42. Available from https://doi.org/10.1080/01930826.2013.756689.

Walters, T. (2012). The future role of publishing services in university libraries. *Portal: Libraries and the Academy, 12*(4), 425−454. Available from https://doi.org/10.1353/pla.2012.0041.

Walton, G. (2015). What user experience means for academic libraries. *New Review of Academic Librarianship, 21*(1), 1−3. Available from https://doi.org/10.1080/13614533.2015.1001229.

Walton, G. (2016). 'Digital literacy' (DL): Establishing the boundaries and identifying the partners. *New Review of Academic Librarianship, 22*(1), 1−4. Available from https://doi.org/10.1080/13614533.2015.1137466.

Ward, J., Bejarano, W., & Dudas, A. (2015). Scholarly social media profiles and libraries: A review. *LIBER Quarterly, 24*(4), 174−204. Available from https://doi.org/10.18352/lq.9958.

Wells, D. (2016). Library discovery systems and their users: A case study from Curtin University Library. *Australian Academic & Research Libraries, 47*(2), 92−105. Available from https://doi.org/10.1080/00048623.2016.1187249.

Williams, P., Nicholas, D., & Rowlands, I. (2010). E-journal usage and impact in scholarly research: A review of the literature. *New Review of Academic Librarianship, 16*(2), 192−207. Available from https://doi.org/10.1080/13614533.2010.503645.

Willinsky, J. (2018). The academic library in the face of cooperative and commercial paths to open access. *Library Trends*, *67*(2), 196−213. Available from https://doi.org/10.1353/lib.2018.0033.

Wong, A., & Partridge, H. (2016). Making as learning: Makerspaces in universities. *Australian Academic & Research Libraries*, *47*(3), 143−159. Available from https://doi.org/10.1080/00048623.2016.1228163.

Zhang, Y., Liu, S., & Mathews, E. (2015). Convergence of digital humanities and digital libraries. *Library Management*, *36*(4/5), 362−377. Available from https://doi.org/10.1108/LM-09-2014-0116.

Zhao, L. (2014). Riding the wave of open access: Providing library research support for scholarly publishing literacy. *Australian Academic & Research Libraries*, *45*(1), 3−18. Available from https://doi.org/10.1080/00048623.2014.882873.

The people side of change: Applying change management principles in academic libraries

3

Nel Duffield[1] and Jaime Royals[2]
[1]Information Technology and Digital Services, University of Adelaide, Adelaide, SA, Australia, [2]University Library, University of Adelaide, Adelaide, SA, Australia

3.1 Introduction

Academic libraries once had a captive audience. We were the primary owners and access providers to the books or journals our students needed to pass their courses. Students had no other viable options — they needed us. But the landscape has changed. The amount of information available online has grown in volume and quality. Users can now buy an article directly from an online provider rather than go through their academic library. They can, 'if they are so minded, single-handedly create and manipulate their own digital libraries' (Pugh, 2007, p. 4). Users do not have to modify their behaviour to fit in with us, to accept whatever we serve. Instead, we need to attract their business. Academic libraries are now one of many service providers working in an environment of market forces. We are operating in a competitive environment, pitching our services against commercial companies. As Knight (2017) explains, 'Access is simpler and cheaper, and a variety of service providers have begun to market directly to students. Users have become more self-sufficient and academic libraries no longer enjoy the monopolistic reign as the principal information provider'.

To compete in this new environment, academic librarians need to change the way we see ourselves and our users. It would be naïve to assume that universities will continue to fund academic libraries at the same level if user numbers drop. If students choose to purchase articles online themselves rather than use the library, that is a cost saved for the university. Of course, change is not a new concept to the academic library. We have moved from focusing on the selection, arrangement and maintenance of physical collections into the selection, arrangement and maintenance of online collections. We moved into the manual creation of subject guides, curating websites and recommending specific sources, then, when that became an outdated model, we stopped. We changed the focus of our teaching from 'how to search physical collections' to 'how to identify good material'. We moved into the collection, preservation and presentation of institutional datasets and into research data management.

Perhaps, the most significant new factor affecting libraries is the speed at which we need to change. Commercial companies operate at a staggering pace, updating their services and their user interfaces daily. They use machine learning to detect at

Technology, Change and the Academic Library. DOI: https://doi.org/10.1016/B978-0-12-822807-4.00003-8

scale what is working and what is not, then push out rapid, responsive updates, adjusting to user behaviour in a matter of hours. This may not be the natural world of the academic library, but it is of our students. To secure their business, we need to change what we do continuously. Our success is no longer built upon our stability as an organisation, but our agility.

To succeed, academic libraries must learn from the models of thinking applied in sectors more accustomed to operating within this highly competitive, volatile environment. We already have our toe in the water. A significant proportion of our business is already inextricably linked with information technology (IT), the driving force behind much of this change. A good many academic libraries are already part of the same organisational structures as IT, with the University Librarian reporting to the Chief Information Officer, or reporting upward to the same University executive. We are already exposed to much of the thinking and business practices that power IT, but it may benefit us as a sector to take up more of these. One clear example is change management. IT projects habitually employ a Change Manager to plan and execute the 'people side of change' to ensure the uptake of a new product or service.

Anecdotally, formal change management activities within academic libraries appear to be more common in large-scale projects involving significant investment. Large projects often have their own dedicated budget and hire an experienced or qualified Project Manager, who is more likely to be familiar with the advantages of effective change management, and accept that effective change management increases return on investment. The change management industry, admittedly not the most objective source, states that 'Data from over 2700 change practitioners showed that projects with "excellent" change management in place were six times more likely to meet objectives than those with "poor" change management – and even those using "good" change management were five times more likely to meet objectives' (Prosci, n.d.).

So, what is change management and how can academic libraries use it to their advantage?

This chapter gives a very brief explanation of change management and then discusses how change management can be implemented in the academic library sector.

3.2   What is change management?

Change management arose in the 1970s as a synthesis of ideas from business and psychology. The fundamental concept is that changes to systems or processes within a business can be more effectively implemented if people are ready and willing to support them. A project is considered to have three distinct aspects – people, process and technology – and good project management will address all three.

Historically, thinking about change in the business context focused more around top-down implementation of process change. For example, the Lewin model of 'Unfreeze. . .change. . .refreeze' (Mind Tools, n.d.) concentrates on activities rather than attitudes. This model argues that to effect change, a specific predefined activity must be dismantled, remodelled, then set again in the new configuration. For example, consider the implementation of a new digital repository. The first part of the change would involve analysing the ways that other library systems, such as the learning management system, integrate with the old repository, and discontinuing those processes (unfreeze). The systems would then be reconfigured to integrate with the new repository (change). Then the new process would be implemented and become business as usual (freeze). Although at first glance the model appears to only consider a very specific and mechanistic part of the change, for example it does not explicitly take into account 'the people side of change', it can be used in a variety of contexts and scales. It does, however, become harder to apply to a more fluid environment where situations are not necessarily easily replicated, and where a staff member has more autonomy in how a process can work.

In the 1990s, models of change began to focus more explicitly on the people side of change. The most famous model was developed by Kotter (1996), who in the seminal work *Leading Change* described an eight stage change process:

- Create a sense of urgency
- Build a guiding coalition
- Form a strategic vision and initiatives
- Enlist a volunteer army
- Enable action by removing barriers
- Generate short term wins
- Sustain acceleration
- Institute change

Effectively navigating these stages is intended to increase the likelihood of a change being implemented successfully. The Kotter model provides a roadmap for moving through a change and is flexible enough to be used to frame a strategy to implement specific changes in any sector or organisation, including academic libraries. Wheeler and Holmes (2017, p. 280) outline the use of the Kotter framework to implement a new vision in two US academic libraries. The authors explain that leveraging the eight-step Kotter model allowed them to 'quickly identify the necessary people and activities to empower the evolution of their libraries to be better positioned to meet the information needs of the future'. Kotter (1996, p. 44) provides a number of practical, tactical recommendations for every stage: activities and processes that are ultimately intended to counter or entirely prevent resistance. Recommendations include stopping management 'happy talk' and encouraging tough messages in senior management speeches and internal newsletters.

The model describes effective change management as a key responsibility of good leadership. This is a common theme in change management literature. For people to buy into a change and see it as worth supporting, they need to see that organisational leaders consider it important. In the Prosci model, which has become an industry standard more recently, a senior Project Sponsor plays a key role in implementing a change.

Similar to the Kotter model, the Prosci framework describes a number of specific stages that must be worked through sequentially to increase the likelihood of change being successful. These stages are described by the acronym ADKAR (Prosci, n.d.):

- Awareness − of the need for change
- Desire − to support the change
- Knowledge − of how to change
- Ability − to demonstrate skills and behaviours
- Reinforcement − to make the change stick

A significant difference from the Kotter model is that the ADKAR model assumes the allocation of an active 'change agent' to a project, whose role is to plan and execute change activities. The change agent role can take many forms. They can be a professional Change Manager, an expert in implementing successful change regardless of the local environment. A professional Change Manager will usually have some kind of formal certification, such as the Change Practitioner certification offered by Prosci. Professional change managers can move between banking, mining, and the tertiary education sector − any industry at all − and adapt their practices to the nuances of the sector. Alternatively, a change agent can be an existing staff member or member of a local project team, using the ADKAR framework to plan change activities. This is a more realistic model for an academic library which is unlikely to have the budget or appetite to employ a dedicated Change Manager. The ADKAR model has specific templates that a change agent can use at specific stages of the change, which means it is possible for someone less experienced to manage the change. This ensures that they consider a broad range of factors that will affect the success of a change implementation that may not otherwise be self-evident.

Regardless of how the change agent role is filled, in the ADKAR model the change agent remains behind the scenes 'stage managing' activities, as it is critical for local leadership to be seen as the face of change.

Theoretically, ADKAR can be applied to any project management methodology, but it lends itself more neatly to the waterfall style of the project with a set of distinct and linear stages − initiation, planning, execution and handover. As agile project management increases in popularity, lean change management is also becoming more common. Lean change management is designed to suit the iterative delivery cycles of agile, which focus on delivering value to the customer in continual, smaller releases rather than waiting to the end of the project to hand over a completed output. Lean change management focuses on generating conversations about the conditions needed for effective change, rather than creating detailed artefacts. There are a number of publicly available lean change management templates available for use.

These models are not mutually exclusive. An experienced change agent will often use a variety of techniques and have a suite of tools and templates synthesised from several models and adapted for the local environment. Some tools may work effectively in some industries with a specific culture and work less well in others.

In change management literature, there is a broad acceptance that 70% of change efforts fail (Stewart, 2019). Directly addressing the 'people' side of change can mitigate this risk, but it seems most academic libraries do not explicitly use change management practices. Anecdotally, there are a number of reasons for that. First, change management is not a part of the study librarians take to qualify. According to Stewart (2019, p. 30), it is not evident from examining the literature what proportion of library and information professionals receive change management training, noting that this study was undertaken in the United Kingdom. Whilst change management sometimes forms part of more generic business courses such as project management courses or an MBA, only a limited number of library staff hold an MBA or other business qualification. Second, library projects are often implemented by library staff in addition to their normal duties rather than by a formally qualified Project Manager. Staff are often chosen on the basis of their familiarity with the system being changed. They may not have the project management skills to recognise that successful implementation extends beyond technical or process changes. The 'people' side of project implementation, which is critical to successful change, will often be limited to sending out communications and providing system training. This may address the knowledge and ability aspects of ADKAR, but not the awareness, desire or reinforcement.

Of course, sometimes academic library staff instinctively use change management practices, even if they have not overtly identified them as such. Two significant foci cut across most change management methodologies, which allow a change to be considered from a number of different perspectives in order to maximise the likelihood of project success. They are a change impact analysis and a stakeholder assessment.

It is self-evident that a change agent needs to understand the nature of the change they are implementing. A systematic way to develop a detailed understanding is through a change impact analysis. By identifying requirements at a granular level, as early as possible in the change process, the project has the best chance of succeeding. The first step is understanding the 'as is' state of the process that is to be changed, and the desired 'to be' state. In the case of a small change, this is often done intuitively; however, in a large formal project, this is often conducted by business analysts who use process mapping techniques to fully understand the granular detail of the change. For example, an academic library decides to extend its opening hours. In the 'as is' state:

- Staff on service points work between 9:00 a.m. and 5:00 p.m.
- Students can access the library from 9:00 a.m. to 5:00 p.m.
- Complex queries are referred immediately to research librarians via a phone call
- The library café is open from 11:00 a.m. to 3:00 p.m.

In contrast, in the 'to be' state:

- Staff on service points to work between 9:00 a.m. and 9:00 p.m.
- Students can access the library from 9:00 a.m. to 9:00 p.m.
- Complex queries cannot be referred to research librarians after 5:00 p.m.
- The library café is open from 11:00 a.m. to 7:00 p.m.

The current and future states are compared side by side to draw out an understanding of precisely what will change. This is the change impact analysis. The change agent will then use this as a basis for planning their activities, to ensure affected staff are supported through the full ADKAR process from awareness through to reinforcement.

The change impact analysis can be used to inform a stakeholder assessment, a key tool for the change agent. A stakeholder assessment is exactly what it sounds like: a careful consideration of everyone who has a stake in the change.

The more detail that can be captured in the change impact analysis, the more specific stakeholder groups can be identified. For example, our change impact analysis has identified the referral of complex queries as a process that will need to be changed. There are two groups of library staff involved in this process: 'staff on service points' and 'research librarians'. We can now see there are two sets of needs and concerns to be addressed. The change agent can use this information to work towards analysing and meeting the specific needs of those groups. Of course, there are other groups and other concerns to be considered. The staff who need to work different hours are the obvious group; they may be pleased to be earning overtime, or displeased at having to go home after dark. Will the reshelvers work longer hours too, or will more need to be rostered in the morning to deal with a backlog of books? Will security staff need to be notified and will a cost be incurred for extra patrols? What does the current contract with the café say; can the library insist that they open longer hours or is it at their discretion?

A more detailed change impact analysis would have revealed these stakeholder groups and more. For example, within the broad category of 'students', there are many subcategories who may have different perspectives about the change, and so a different message may need to be crafted. Even if the message is the same, they may require communication in different forms. For example, the various subcategories − postgraduates, international students and so on − would require the same message 'the Library is now open for longer and these are the specific services you can access during these new hours'. However, the subcategories of students are more likely to receive this message if we contact them in bespoke ways. To target postgraduates, we may email a mailing list of supervisors, include the information in the postgraduate newsletter, and update the information packages that go to new postgraduate students. To target international students, we might put up posters in residential halls. The more students we reach, presumably the more will come to the library during our extended hours, and the more successful the change has been.

It is apparent that what seemed to be a relatively simple change had many ramifications which would ideally require direct remediation. Change management provides a straightforward framework to ensure that 'people' factors are identified and addressed, increasing the likelihood of a successful change.

3.3   Bringing the theory to life

Change management tools were used in a recent project at the University of Adelaide to redesign online student support guides. The purpose of the project was to review and improve the content, design, and wayfinding within the support guides, and to implement a continuous improvement process. The new model would significantly change the way online support material would be offered and would change the role of the Liaison Librarian in creating the guides. Knight (2017, p. 295) acknowledges that 'it is mandatory that academic librarians have the ability to deal with the complexities of change; recognise potential changes; and establish ways to engage the talents and energies of their environment', particularly given the drastic change in the information landscape and the need for libraries to provide a service that can compete with other information sources. As it was a relatively small project, the same staff member performed the roles of project manager and change agent. Anecdotal evidence suggests this is common practice throughout academic libraries.

Like many change initiatives, it was difficult to define what success would look like. Would it mean all the existing support guides were converted to the new format within a predetermined timeline? Certainly, that would be a component of a successful implementation. Would the project need to include some kind of measure around user numbers? This is more complex than it initially appears. It could be argued that increased user numbers mean the new guides are 'better', but if the guides are intended to teach students how to find resources themselves, ideally user numbers will decrease over time. Would decreased time spent by the Liaison Librarians on maintaining the guides be a measure of success? Yes. It would seem obvious to measure increased user satisfaction as an indicator of success, but whose satisfaction? Academics may be pleased the new guides encourage the students to find resources themselves, but the students may still yearn for the old versions, unaware or unconvinced of the benefits of the new versions.

This example demonstrates that measuring the success of a change is not an exact science. Even when it is clear within a change initiative what success will mean, it is still difficult to measure the effect that change management had upon the outcome. It is not possible to implement the change once with change management, then once without, and measure the difference. As Stewart (2019, p. 15) explains: 'Even if it was possible to introduce a similar change twice in an organisation, people's attitudes, fears and degrees of resistance could vary dramatically from one initiative to the other'. The idea that the effectiveness of change management is hard to measure is not an apocryphal view. Barends, Janssen, ten Have, and ten Have (2014) conducted a systematic review of 563 organisational change management articles published over a 30-year period. The authors identified a lack of repetition in studies in the field 'suggest[ing] that scholars and practitioners should be sceptical regarding the body of research results in the field of organisational change management published to date'. Regardless of the complexities, and in the interests of pragmatism, this project identified as its measures of success conversion of the existing guides to the new format, and customer feedback.

The first task of the project team was to thoroughly understand the nature of the change through a change impact analysis. The 'as is' state for library staff involved Liaison Librarians developing online content autonomously. The 'to be' state required content development to be guided by principles that described the required format and level of content. This was a significant change in both process and culture.

The change agent identified all the stakeholders in the project, worked to identify how they would be affected by the change, and determined the best means of communicating the changes to them. To do this effectively, the change agent needed to consider how best to communicate with stakeholders, as 'the term "agent" implies that the person undertaking the role is a conduit for communication' (Stewart, 2019, p. 25). They needed to consider whether it would be sufficient to inform a stakeholder of the change by email, or would several methods of communication, including face-to-face discussion and attendance at relevant meetings to promote the change, need to be utilised? The change agent also needed to consider whether they intended to inform, consult, involve or collaborate (International Association for Public Participation, 2014), and select a communication method accordingly. There are many engagement frameworks available that explain this process. In this specific project, students would need to be made aware of the new product, and shown how to find and use relevant guides. As this is considered 'informing', broadcast communications such as email, website notification and frequently asked questions were used. Lecturers would need to show students the guides, making it necessary to ensure academic staff were aware of the changes. They needed not only to understand what the changes were and why they were implemented, but to update all the references to the online support material in the learning management system.

As is demonstrated above, change management provides a structured way to initiate and build collaborative relationships with stakeholders. Change management methodologies which call upon the use of a 'subject matter expert' to advise on a project provide a means for librarians to engage with stakeholders such as researchers and teaching academics within a defined context. In a successful project implementation, this builds trust, professional respect and an acknowledgement of shared goals which can be the beginning of a more extensive 'knotworking' model described in Kaatrakoski and Lahikainen (2016):

> The notion of knotworking refers to a negotiated way of working in which representatives of different organisations or units work on a specific task, which is a shared object, and collaboratively analyse their work; the collaboration forms 'knots'. Compared to teams, knots are less stable and fixed, thus making it possible to adapt to change more rapidly.

Various teams of library staff were also affected by the change. The change agent needed to engage with staff to find out how they felt about the project. Why? The first reason is because staff who are resistant to a change are much less likely to do the work to implement it. And it has been acknowledged that 'rather than be champion[s] for change, academic librarians can and some often do resist change' (Knight, 2017, p. 295). In this specific project, it was the Liaison Librarians who maintained the online guides and would continue to do so in the future. However, they would now need to think differently about the content they develop. Previously, when the information was harder to find, these guides were used to store all content on a topic. Now that information is more abundant, only carefully selected key resources would be curated. This team needed to ensure that they adhered to the new guidelines regarding formatting and design, maintenance and continuous improvement. The messages from the project team needed to be tailored to address these potential areas of conflict. For example, the Liaison Librarians previously created guides that were bespoke for the students in their specific faculty, whereas the project was implementing a consistent look. Understanding how the affected staff regarded the change was critical to ensure messages from the project team addressed their key concerns. If the staff were largely supportive of the change, the project team could focus their efforts on communicating the benefits of the new approach to other stakeholder groups.

Client service staff, the front-facing library staff, also needed to be educated in the new model to ensure that they know what had changed, as well as why and how to use the new product. This would ensure that they communicate effectively with library users, drawing their attention to the guides in the appropriate situations and thus increasing their usage.

Change management is often discussed in the context of changes that effect external stakeholders, in this context academics and students. As previously explained, any change in services, like this change to online guides, also requires internal changes to processes or staffing. There are also changes that are entirely internal such as restructures or culture change initiatives. Using change management methodologies for these types of changes appears uncommon within academic libraries, and considered a luxury. However, there are examples when increasing staff capability is the specific focus of change management activities. A recent staff development activity at Flinders University Library concentrated on increasing the skills of staff, designed through a change management lens (Hall, 2015). It can be argued that the direct cost of change management offsets the cost of recruitment and retraining if unhappy staff decide to move on.

In this project, a thorough and explicit examination of the stakeholders, internal and external, made clear by understanding in detail the nature of the change, clearly led to better outcomes.

3.4   Conclusion

The informal application of change management techniques is a relatively effective approach for small or ad hoc initiatives. However, for more complex, higher-profile initiatives, academic libraries would benefit from engaging structured change management practices. Considering people at the beginning of a change, just as a project would typically consider process and technology, preempts any areas of resistance so that they can be addressed before they occur.

One way in which an academic library could mature its change management capability is for existing library staff to gain skills in change management through work-based learning: learning about change management whilst implementing a change. The risk with this method is that the change may not be implemented as effectively as it could be. However, this risk can be mitigated by coaching and mentoring from more experienced or external practitioners.

Other possible approaches to deepening change management expertise in library staff are to gain formal qualifications in change management, engaging external change managers for significant initiatives or utilising the skills of change managers already employed within their institutions in other business units, such as IT.

Although there is a cost implication for all of these approaches, the literature demonstrates that there is a measurable increase in the uptake of new systems when formal change management is used. When academic libraries need to implement change at an ever-increasing pace, applying change management techniques may give us the edge we require.

References

Barends, E., Janssen, B., ten Have, W., & ten Have, S. (2014). Effects of change interventions: What kind of evidence do we really have? *Journal of Applied Behavioral Science*, 50(1), 5−27. Available from https://doi.org/10.1177/0021886312473152.

Hall, L. W. (2015). Changing the workplace culture at Flinders University Library: From pragmatism to professional reflection. *Australian Academic & Research Libraries*, 46 (1), 29−38. Available from https://doi.org/10.1080/00048623.2014.985773.

International Association for Public Participation. (2014). *IAP2's public participation spectrum*. Retrieved from: https://www.iap2.org.au/wp-content/uploads/2019/07/IAP2_Public_Participation_Spectrum.pdf

Kaatrakoski, H., & Lahikainen, J. (2016). 'What we do every day is impossible': Managing change by developing a knotworking culture in an academic library. *Journal of Academic Librarianship*, 42(5), 515−521. Available from https://doi.org/10.1016/j.acalib.2016.06.001.

Knight, J. A. (2017). Academic librarians as change champions: A framework for managing change. *Library Management*, 38(6/7), 294−301. Available from https://doi.org/10.1108/LM-03-2017-0031.

Kotter, J. P. (1996). *Leading change*. Boston, MA: Harvard Business School Press.

Mind Tools (n.d.). *Lewin's change management model: Understanding the three stages of change*. Retrieved from: https://www.mindtools.com/pages/article/newPPM_94.htm

Prosci (n.d.). *Cost-benefit analysis of change management*. Retrieved from: https://www.prosci.com/resources/articles/cost-benefit-analysis-change-management.

Prosci (n.d.). *What is the ADKAR model?* Retrieved from: https://www.prosci.com/adkar/adkar-model

Pugh, L. (2007). *Change management in information services* (2nd ed.). Aldershot: Ashgate Publishing.

Stewart, S. (2019). *To what extent do library and information professionals actively manage change?: An investigation into organisations based in London and surrounding areas*. London: University of London (unpublished MSc thesis). Available from http://dx.doi.org/10.17613/4zsd-2t90.

Wheeler, T. R., & Holmes, K. L. (2017). Rapid transformation of two libraries using Kotter's eight steps of change. *Journal of the Medical Library Association*, 105(3), 276−281. Available from https://doi.org/10.5195/jmla.2017.97.

Section III

Case Studies

Developing massive open online courses

4

Susan Halfpenny and Stephanie Jesper
Information Services, University of York, York, United Kingdom

4.1 Context

Since 2014 the Information Services Teaching and Learning Team at the University of York has undertaken a range of projects to develop online digital literacy provision. The initial focus was to develop a skills hub, resulting in our Skills Guides.[1] We then sought to extend provision beyond information and digital skills, towards research-led educational resources, exploring the digital skills deficit and the social, political and economic impacts of digital technologies. Widening the coverage of our online educational resources provision would enable us to engage beyond our traditional user groups, enhancing our outreach and inclusivity.

Complementing this departmental vision, the broader *University Strategy* (University of York, 2014) stated a commitment to extend online learning provision, including the development of a pilot programme of massive open online courses (MOOCs) which aimed to:

- Enhance the University's reputation for innovation in teaching and the provision of a rich student experience
- Showcase the strength of York's programmes, with the potential to engage new and diverse audiences
- Support the University's objectives in demonstrating research impact and enhancing student recruitment
- Develop partnerships with other institutions, and identify potential commercial and scalable distance learning opportunities

These aims aligned to our own objectives.

For the pilot the University partnered with the MOOC learning platform FutureLearn in early 2016, agreeing to develop four courses within 2 years. Following calls for proposals, the Teaching and Learning Team were successful in their bids to develop two MOOCs: *Becoming a digital citizen: An introduction to the digital society* (2016) and *Digital Wellbeing* (2018).

4.2 Project implementation

With our proposal for the *Digital Citizenship* MOOC accepted, we assembled a small project team to coordinate, lead on development of course materials, and ultimately deliver the course. This proved a successful approach which we repeated for the *Digital Wellbeing* MOOC.

The *Digital Citizenship* MOOC had the ambitious launch date of 23 January 2017, with all content to be completed for FutureLearn's quality assurance checking by the end of November 2016. This gave less than 6 months to get the content written, filmed, and uploaded onto the FutureLearn platform. Not only would we have to write quickly, but, with no prior experience of developing MOOCs, we would also need to gain knowledge of best practice for online learning and ascertain how to use the FutureLearn platform.

Our first task was to write the course outline and promotional materials for FutureLearn[2]. This involved developing learning outcomes, storyboarding each activity and step across the 3-week course, scripting the promotional video, and liaising with the University's chosen film company about the brief. At the same time, we began developing our understanding of how the FutureLearn platform worked: learning the different types of steps (activities, discussions, videos, quizzes and tests) available; how to upload and edit content; and the markup and style used. With our later *Digital Wellbeing* MOOC, we had the advantage of familiarity with the platform functionality, making the development of the promotional content and course outline[3] more straightforward.

We initially took a linear approach to writing the first week of the *Digital Citizenship* MOOC, but writing this content gave us new insights and ideas, so we returned to our storyboard spreadsheet to rearrange weeks 2 and 3. This did not invalidate the planning we had done; rather it demonstrated its usefulness as a working document by keeping a log of what we had written and what needed doing, whilst allowing us to redraft our course structure and identify holes worth filling. When it came to planning the *Digital Wellbeing* course, we retained this spreadsheet storyboard approach (albeit simplified) and could again quickly reorder steps whilst retaining an overview, essential to our keeping within our deadline.

As we developed the *Digital Citizenship* MOOC, we sought feedback from FutureLearn on both content and approach, submitting week 1 for quality assurance at the beginning of October 2016. We found this useful. Not only did it reassure us we were doing things right, and provide direction on the remaining content, it also ensured we had a third of the content completed via the pressure of a midpoint deadline. The feedback was positive, including suggestions for further discussion points and questions. We incorporated these, resulting in lively learner contributions during the course run. For the *Digital Wellbeing* MOOC, we had more experience of what worked as successful approaches and logical structures, so did not submit for early feedback.

We knew early on that success hinged on academic contributions. They would provide validation and enable learners to engage with research. Such collaboration would be essential in an online course on a social science topic. Within Information Services (which includes Library, Archives and IT Services), we had the skills and knowledge to develop content on digital literacy, information literacy and the digital skills agenda. However, the course needed content beyond this to meet the learning outcomes and the objectives of the project. For learners to engage with practitioner experience and research conducted at the University of York, we needed to include academics and professional staff from other support services.

Collaboration and partnership would undoubtedly benefit Information Services, raising our profile as an educational provider within the institution by further communicating the breadth of learning and teaching we offer. It would also benefit our academic colleagues, enabling them to engage with new, diverse audiences about their research, demonstrating impact and further communicating their outputs. Our only concern was academic staff time, and whether our ambitious timeline of under 6 months would prove a barrier.

Of the staff we asked to contribute to the *Digital Citizenship* MOOC, all agreed to provide content. These included researchers from the Faculty of Arts and Humanities and the Faculty of Social Sciences, as well as participants from Careers and the Students' Union. Contributions predominantly took the form of a 'talking head' video, supported by a short commentary and links to open access content such as journal articles and press releases. We also solicited contributions from within Information Services, mostly in the form of articles and discussions.

The *Digital Wellbeing* MOOC proved a greater challenge. Partly this was the nature of what is a relatively new, underexplored topic, but a big impediment was our request that, to reduce video editing costs, contributors provide scripts before filming. We promptly learnt that it is easier to get a contribution from an academic if they can come without having to write something first. By changing our plans and accommodating this we were able to get contributions from academic colleagues across all three Faculties at York (Arts and Humanities, Social Sciences, and Sciences), plus professional services staff from our Open Door wellbeing team.

The scale of collaboration in both projects required a robust, streamlined process for receiving contributions. We asked for written contributions to be submitted as a Google Doc, enabling us to edit and collaborate on content before uploading to FutureLearn. One of us took sole responsibility for copy editing and uploading content, including sourcing images and cross referencing to other course steps.

We had a budget of £4000 (per MOOC) for the development of video content and the creation of the promotional video. Keen for as many contributions as possible, for the *Digital Citizenship* MOOC we organised two separate days of filming, a week apart, better enabling us to coordinate calendars and find times that suited our contributors (luck in this regard meant that we only needed 1 day of filming for the *Digital Wellbeing* MOOC). We employed a commercial film company, Digifish, to film and edit the content, including the promotional video.

4.3 Service delivery

The *Digital Citizenship* MOOC welcomed its first learners on 23 January 2017. On the start date, we had 3742 'joiners', increasing to 5953 by the end of the first run.

The course was designed to take place over 3 weeks (whilst FutureLearn makes all content available from the launch date, courses on the platform follow a suggested 'week' structure). Each week had an overarching theme and specific learning outcomes addressed by four themed activities incorporating video, article and discussion 'steps'. The weeks and activities were themed as follows:

- Week 1: Digital access and information inequalities
  - Activity 1: Introduction to the course
  - Activity 2: Digital society and citizenship
  - Activity 3: The digital divide and the skills gap
  - Activity 4: Finding information and critical appraisal
- Week 2: Digital identity and security
  - Activity 1: Digital literacies
  - Activity 2: Digital identities and personas
  - Activity 3: Information security and protecting yourself online
  - Activity 4: Challenges and responsibilities
- Week 3: Digital participation and ethics
  - Activity 1: Digital engagement
  - Activity 2: Online responsibility and ethics
  - Activity 3: Democracy and free speech
  - Activity 4: Becoming a digital citizen

The content of the 66 steps within these activities included 21 videos with supplementary text, 26 articles, 13 discussions, 3 quizzes and 3 end-of-week tests. The suggested study time to complete all content for each week was 3 hours, but following the first run we found 4 hours to be more realistic.

It was our initial intention for the *Digital Wellbeing* MOOC to be a shorter course. It would still take place over 3 weeks, but we wanted to reduce the weekly study time required. The diverse knowledge of the course educators and academic contributors meant we generated more content than planned, and the finished course was a similar length to its predecessor. Learners completed three activities per week although the number of steps varied, dependent on the necessary content for that week's topic (in the first MOOC we stuck with a consistent 21 steps per week across the four activities).

Throughout the 3 weeks each course ran, the course educators read comments and contributed to the discussions on a daily basis. We had a rota to ensure a member of the team checked and interacted with learners at least once a day. The expectation was to spend an hour a day checking progress and conversations, but this often took longer during the original run of the *Digital Citizenship* MOOC, as learner contributions were high. We have been pleased with the volume of contributions and the content across all the course runs. Learners shared links to other resources on the topics and responded to each others' points, fostering social learning and making the whole experience very collaborative.

4.4 Evaluation

Sign up for our first run of *Digital Citizenship* was 5953: a figure we have been unable to repeat, in part through less intense promotion (the University invested

Table 4.1 MOOC participation statistics.

	Digital citizenship		Digital wellbeing	
	23 January 2017	10 July 2017	15 October 2018	21 January 2019
Joiners	5953	2275	1999	997
Learners	3130 (52.6%)	1258 (55.3%)	1238 (61.9%)	686 (68.7%)
Active learners	2264 (72.3%)	875 (69.6%)	914 (73.8%)	460 (67.1%)
Social learners	912 (29.1%)	313 (24.9%)	309 (25.0%)	163 (23.8%)
>50% complete	766 (24.5%)	309 (24.6%)	346 (27.9%)	141 (20.6%)
>90% complete	591 (18.9%)	205 (16.3%)	240 (19.4%)	105 (15.3%)
Average steps visited	23/69 (33.3%)	22/69 (31.9%)	23/63 (46.5%)	23/63 (46.5%)
Average number of comments	10	8	8	6

more in marketing its first wave of MOOCs), but also because of changes to the platform. Sign up for our next two runs was around 2000 with the fourth only managing 997 (perhaps a consequence of being only 3 months after the previous run, and comparatively under-promoted). Completion rates were similar across all runs: the proportion completing over 90% of a course was between 15.3% and 19.4%. The average participant would make it to 23 steps in each case (22 for the second run of *Digital Citizenship*), equivalent to 1 week of the first MOOC and a little over that for the second (Table 4.1).

The fact that the later sign ups were never to the same scale as the first run was certainly disappointing, but even the participation rates for the later runs far exceeded anything we achieve with a face-to-face programme. Whilst our Skills Guides webpages typically receive around 5000 page views a month, such views are not sustained learning as part of a designed course.

One of our aims was to reach new and diverse audiences and we feel we achieved this. There was broad international participation on all four runs. Charts 4.1 and 4.2 show how *Digital Wellbeing* was most popular in the United Kingdom, whereas *Digital Citizenship* had a more global appeal. Participants have come from a diversity of backgrounds, professions and age groups which has greatly contributed to the success of the social learning aspects of the course. Our impression (to an extent supported by the figures) is that the volume of discussion in the courses has had a positive impact on retention.

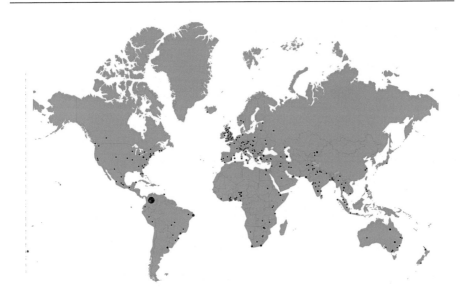

Chart 4.1 *Digital Citizenship* learners nationality.

Chart 4.2 *Digital Wellbeing* learners nationality.

In terms of participant feedback, 48% of the 100 respondents to the closing survey rated the *Digital Citizenship* MOOC 'Excellent', and a further 40% called it
'Good' ('OK', 10%; 'Poor', 2%). The *Digital Wellbeing* course used a different
feedback mechanism and the responses are outlined in Table 4.2. The course met or

Table 4.2 *Digital Wellbeing* postcourse feedback.

		15 October 2018 (n = 86)	21 January 2019 (n = 51)
Did this course meet your expectations?	Better	35 (40.7%)	29 (56.9%)
	Met	45 (52.3%)	19 (37.3%)
	Worse	3 (3.5%)	1 (2.0%)
	Not sure	3 (3.5%)	2 (3.9%)
Did you gain new knowledge or skills by taking the course?	Yes	74 (86.0%)	48 (94.1%)
	No	3 (3.5%)	2 (3.9%)
	Not sure	8 (9.3%)	1 (2.0%)
	No answer	1 (1.2%)	–
Since starting the course, have you applied what you learned?	Yes	63 (73.3%)	35 (68.6%)
	No	13 (15.1%)	9 (17.6%)
	Not sure	9 (10.5%)	7 (13.7%)
	No answer	1 (1.2%)	–

exceeded the expectations of over 90% of the respondents, with the vast majority gaining new knowledge or skills in both runs (86% and 94.1% respectively), and a majority also having been able to apply that learning at the point of the survey (73.3% and 68.6%).

These numbers are from small samples, typically of those who completed the course, so do not hold much weight, but it is still 100 people who went out and applied what they had learnt from an online course that we put together. Again, when compared to an internal course, these numbers are significant.

In writing the content there was always the intention to reuse it elsewhere. In total we now have 27 videos that detail teaching and research at the University of York, as well as a large collection of articles. Not only were these available to the learners on our MOOCs, they can also be re-used and resurfaced on other platforms (such as our Skills Guides[4]) or as part of stand-alone projects.[5]

As a means of stimulating new material, the pressure of a MOOC was undoubtedly effective. However, there were other benefits: the self-discipline of the medium; the experience for those who took part; the collaborations involved. The latter proved particularly successful and we were able to forge new contacts across departments and make new friends. This, with the MOOC itself, has raised the profile and reputation of our team. We believe the collaborative aspects of the project contributed vastly to our ability to showcase the strength of York's programmes and demonstrate research impact, thereby meeting the University's objectives for the MOOCs.

4.5 Lessons learned

The biggest lesson learnt was, inevitably, how to write a MOOC. Writing a MOOC, it transpires, is not quick. There is much to write, much to research. Even finding illustrative images for each step takes time. And then, there is the time required to facilitate a MOOC: time to moderate conversations and spark discussions.

Time posed the greatest difficulty and risk to completing the project. Members of the core project team were not solely employed to develop MOOCs. The content creation, research and coordination had to fit around business-as-usual and other service development initiatives. Much of the first MOOC's creation took place during the Autumn term, our busiest time for teaching, inductions and enquiries support. Finding time to write the content was, therefore, problematic. We learnt from this for the second course where development predominantly occurred during the summer.

A number of changes in circumstances made for a heavy workload even before factoring in the writing. This was true for both courses. In each instance, we assumed that one of us would be able to provide a central core of content from which the rest might extrapolate, but in each instance circumstances intervened. The extrapolations had to lead the narrative, forcing us to approach the week structures anew, often with a large shift in focus as new ideas led off in new directions.

The platform provided limitations. We initially intended a greater amount of interactivity and flexibility of structure than was possible on FutureLearn, whilst other kinds of interactivity were imposed upon us by their need for weekly tests. We struggled to find appropriate questions for these, given the topics we were covering (our courses were not really about wrong and right answers). The pressure was even higher after the first run, when a change in subscription model meant people were paying specifically to be able to do the tests. Doing justice to this element of the course was particularly difficult.

The topics of digital citizenship and digital wellbeing are constantly evolving in an environment of exponential technological change. Consequently, our course content has a short shelf life. We have been able to get two runs of the courses with only minor changes to content. However, a rerun of the *Digital Citizenship* course would require a complete restructure and review of the content, including new videos to cover the current research in this area. There is potential for a third run of the *Digital Wellbeing* MOOC, but not for much longer.

A lot of what we learnt doing the first MOOC informed how we conducted the rerun and how we went about our follow-up MOOC (factors like allowing more time to facilitate, or to write and source video content). Whilst there are other ways to facilitate an online course that could be more inventive, there is not much scope for reinvention within the platform being used. Given such bounds, there is little we have sought to do differently.

The development of the MOOCs gave opportunity for professional development in a range of areas. We already had experience of online educational resource development and face-to-face teaching and have postgraduate teaching qualifications, but neither of us had previously developed an online course that would require participants to engage with materials over an extended period of time. Development of the materials required pedagogical understanding and the ability to translate complex concepts in an accessible way to a general audience. We needed to be creative in our approach to the topics to ensure that the content was engaging and to encourage active participation throughout the 3-week runs. Development of the courses required us to take a different approach to our traditional teaching. We needed to pose questions that would allow social learning rather than provide answers. We were grateful for the support of the University's MOOC project lead as they were able to offer us advice on course design and what approaches work best for this type of course delivery.

4.6 Final reflections

Overall, we found making MOOCs both an enjoyable and beneficial service development initiative. Partnering with FutureLearn, an established platform, enabled us to engage with their existing audience – a new audience to us – and adopt a practiced approach to online course delivery. The project has raised the profile of the team both within the institution and beyond, allowing us to work with new academic and professional partners, and to reach new and diverse learners. We have subsequently been contacted by organisations and researchers about content reuse.

The two courses have greatly extended the coverage of our learning and teaching resources and support. As a team our knowledge has grown massively: not only in terms of online course design, but also our understandings of digital literacies, technological change and digital society. We feel the courses offer new and unique content on the topics of digital citizenship and digital wellbeing.

The development of the course enabled us to undertake research in a range of ideas, to inform the course content and also build our knowledge of the digital society. We needed to engage with academic collaborators to draw in their expertise, which required negotiation and persuasion to ensure the work could be completed within the ambitious timescale. Although at times it seemed that the task we had set ourselves was too ambitious, we were really pleased with the results of the service development and the opportunities it presented to us. Many of the skills and behaviours that were required to deliver this project were those that are core to any librarian role: research skills; relationship and partnership management; curation of content; and determination.

Despite the drop in learner numbers since the first run of the *Digital Citizenship* MOOC, we still feel there is a great benefit to creating online courses in this format. In the future we hope to re-run the *Digital Citizenship* MOOC, following an update of the content, enabling a new cohort of learners to interact with this course. We are also exploring other potential topics for completely new MOOCs. We see this as an area of expansion, one we feel worthy of further and future resource.

Acknowledgements

We would like to take this opportunity to acknowledge the following academic and professional services staff who contributed to the success of these initiatives: Tom Banham, Iain Barr, Millie Beach, David Beer, Alice Bennett, Michelle Blake, Thom Blake, Siobhan Dunlop, Mike Dunn, Laila Fish, Heidi Fraser-Krauss, Philip Garnett, Lina Gega, Alison Kaye, Chris Kyriacou, Jo Iacovides, Brian Loader, Lindsey Myers, Sara Perry, Ned Potter, Kirstyn Radford, Darren Reed and Tom Smith.

Endnotes

1. University of York Skills Guides: https://subjectguides.york.ac.uk/skills.
2. FutureLearn. *Becoming a digital citizen: An introduction to the digital society.* Course outline and promotional materials: https://www.futurelearn.com/courses/digital-society.
3. FutureLearn. *Digital Wellbeing.* Course outline and promotional materials: https://www.futurelearn.com/courses/digital-wellbeing.
4. University of York, Skills Guides. Online safety: https://subjectguides.york.ac.uk/skills/safety.
5. Inspiring Minds, a blog from Information Services at the University of York: https://informationdirectorate.blogspot.com/search/label/Digital%20citizenship.

Reference

University of York. (2014). *University Strategy 2014−2020.* Retrieved from: https://www.york.ac.uk/media/abouttheuniversity/governanceandmanagement/documents/University-Strategy-2014-2020-revised-June-2016.pdf.

Implementation of a Leganto Reading List service at Curtin University Library

5

Linda Sheedy, David Wells and Amanda Bellenger
University Library, Curtin University, Perth, WA, Australia

5.1   Background

Curtin University is a public teaching and research university based in Perth, Western Australia, and delivers teaching programmes in Perth, at locations in regional Western Australia, and at campuses in Malaysia, Singapore, Dubai and Mauritius. The University also serves a large cohort of online students. With a strong focus on the electronic delivery of library resources, the University Library has more than 55,000 clients worldwide (Curtin University, Office of Strategy and Planning, 2018).

In 2002, amendments to the Australian copyright legislation led Curtin University to centralise the management of copyright obligations. It was mandated that all resources copied by the University in reliance on the Statutory Licence as defined in the Copyright Act would be handled by the Library, and the E-reserve service was established to implement this decision.

The E-reserve service's core business was to use its own in-house infrastructure to digitise print resources and facilitate their communication to students, ensuring that they were compliant with the Statutory Licence (Tang & Hanlon, 2005). The model developed managed the records for these resources in the library management system operating at the time and made those records discoverable through the library catalogue, alongside books and other materials owned by the Library, and linked them to particular teaching units (courses). Although this worked well, there were two major shortcomings to this approach. One issue was that to group the E-reserve readings together appropriately in the library catalogue the resources needed to be catalogued. To achieve this, significant staffing resources were required. Second, it was not possible to provide any context to those records, apart from instructor name and unit title, and, therefore, students needed other curation resources, such as unit outlines and the University's learning management system, to know what the resources for each unit were and when to read them. This required significant additional effort for instructors who created this information. It was a major weakness in the provision of the E-reserve service that it was not integrated with Blackboard, the central learning platform for student learning.

Technology, Change and the Academic Library. DOI: https://doi.org/10.1016/B978-0-12-822807-4.00005-1

In replacing E-reserve with Leganto, the Library facilitated a reconceptualisation and expansion of a key library service, thus assuring the Library's centrality to the University's learning and teaching endeavours.

5.2   Establishing the project

When the implementation of Leganto as the new reading list software was first proposed, the articulated aims were: to enrich the student learning experience through a single user interface; to automate copyright management; and to integrate with the University's Blackboard learning management system via an LTI (Learning Tools Interoperability) link. It was also anticipated that Leganto's integration with the Alma library management system would lead to greater process efficiencies, including improvements in acquisitions, digitisation and copyright management.

Ex Libris announced the launch of the Leganto product in 2015 and made a call for expressions of interest from within its existing customer base to work alongside them on its development. Not long afterwards, Curtin University Library was announced as a participant in the Ex Libris Leganto Early Adopter Program. The purpose of joining this program was to benefit from the extended development lead time and take advantage of the opportunity to contribute to the development of the product through early consultation with the vendor.

The Library formed a working group comprising experts from a number of key areas including senior library managers, E-reserve staff, library systems analysts, the University Copyright Officer and librarians from across the Library, who assisted with testing and worked with the Faculties to roll out the new product. Outside the Library, Curtin Information Technology Services (since renamed Digital and Technology Solutions) assigned both Blackboard staff and a system developer to provide the support required to integrate with other University systems. Project sponsorship was provided through the overarching Transforming Curtin IT program − Curriculum Management project. Ex Libris contributed a dedicated Ex Libris Leganto development team based in Israel, with whom fortnightly webinar meetings were conducted.

To mark the transition from an in-house digital copyright solution, the service was renamed 'Reading Lists' to reflect the more comprehensive service that it represented, allowing instructors and students to access the Library's physical and electronic collections as well as web-based resources seamlessly through the Leganto interface.

5.3   Implementation of Leganto

The initial implementation of Leganto required testing of the product, configuring integrations, and considering stakeholder requirements. Experience gained through these processes drove several key decisions regarding the University's overall approach to the Reading List service. Most importantly, we agreed to the principle that instructors would use the Leganto interface directly and that they, rather than library staff, would populate the software with citations. However, at the time of the Leganto implementation, a number of other systems were being rolled out across the University that were also designed to be used by the end user. There was, therefore, a concern that Leganto, together with these other systems, would be seen as adding to academic workloads. System rejection by end users was thus a major risk to the implementation. In the project's favour, however, was the understanding that academic staff members would have an uncontested curatorial responsibility for their units' readings. The project team felt that to harness the power of Leganto, it was necessary to tap into their specialist knowledge and that this could be best achieved by giving teaching staff access to the Leganto interface. Whilst this also assisted with moving components of the workload away from the Library, its most advantageous outcome was the accuracy and completeness of the reading lists, when created by the staff closest to understanding the unit content.

In June 2016, Leganto was rolled out in a soft launch to interested teaching staff who wanted to use the product and in February 2017, the commencement of the new teaching year, the Reading List service, with Leganto, became the mainstream service for the University's reading list and copyright compliance needs.

From 2002 until 2013, the E-reserve team had been part of the Library's circulation service. However, in 2014, with the migration to Alma, the team was organisationally aligned with the Collections team, which was also responsible for collection development, maintenance of the library catalogue, and resource acquisition. This meant that the service was moved from a primarily client-facing team to a team which had traditionally largely operated behind the scenes. The day-to-day running of E-reserve had been managed with one Technician (level 4/5) and five Library Assistants (level 3). In the new structure, the Reading List service, with Leganto in place, was initially staffed with one Coordinator at level 7 (who also has other duties), one Technician and 1.5 (full-time equivalent) Library Officers (level 4). This change in number and level of staff is, on the one hand, an acknowledgement of the increased complexity of the work required, with staff taking on more responsibility for the management of the system and the service, but, on the other hand, also reflects a decrease in the volume of straightforward processing. Challenges came from both the organisational and the workflow change, which required staff who had not previously worked directly with academics to become confident in customer service. Moreover, staff were used to traditional collections-centric activities and needed to adjust to taking on a role that was dynamically different in style and approach. Further, the new Leganto workflows marked a significant change from how the previous system worked and this resulted in many Library staff feeling disconnected from the now unfamiliar service. Cultural adjustment and training were required both to acclimatise Collections staff to their new roles, and to redefine the way circulation services staff were able to support the new service.

Under the old model the E-reserve team, operating a service which was embedded in the Library's management and discovery systems, had relied on the work of other library staff in a number of respects. The team did not, for example, need to maintain the library catalogue to facilitate the discovery aspects of the E-reserve collection. Now, the Leganto user interface is wholly managed within the team. Furthermore, bringing Leganto into the library environment as a distinct system meant absorbing some additional work. For example, the ongoing work of Ex Libris to develop the Leganto product means monthly development releases, which have to be assessed and implemented as appropriate. Where this has meant significant change to work-flows it no longer only impacts on Library staff but must be communicated to all users across the University, a considerably more complex exercise.

The implementation of Leganto also led to increased engagement with instructors. The Reading List Coordinator, for example, is responsible for delivering training to instructors as well as creating effective online instructional materials. Furthermore, to ensure the Leganto model is successful, Library staff are careful not to undertake tasks that instructors can do for themselves through the Leganto interface. This means that the entire team needs to be much more directly accessible to instructors in a sup-port capacity so that instructors are enabled to use the software to achieve their objec-tives. Accordingly, the changeover of systems needed both to respect the steep learning curve presented to teaching staff and to unashamedly pursue implementation to ensure a smooth and rapid transition from the old to new service.

There is also an increased responsibility to be a good citizen within the Leganto cus-tomer community. This has included the Reading List Coordinator becoming a member of the Leganto Product Working Group, and contributing to the NERS (New Enhancements Request System) process for Leganto enhancement. Curtin University Library is also collaborating with Ex Libris on the 'Predicting Students' Success with Leganto' project and contributing to a Leganto Focus Group on tighter integration with the Alma purchase request workflow. This collaboration has resulted in several Leganto-focused presentations at conferences (Bedford, Donelly, Sheedy, & Mooi, 2017; Green, Darom, Katz, & Lewis, 2019; Sheedy & Green, 2019a; Sheedy & Green, 2019b).

It was clear from the beginning that the change to Leganto would result in a move away from the traditional E-reserve workflow model. First, it meant that all of the work to populate the system was now directly handled by teaching staff. For Library staff this has meant letting go of the types of controls that they had previ-ously, such as control over citation quality. Where Library staff had previously cre-ated all of the citations, they now create less than 1%. With instructors now driving both the volume of work and its timing, this presents a challenge in a significantly smaller staffing model to be able to manage workloads within given deadlines. Leganto was configured to automatically approve most of the citations, reducing the number that required manual intervention from Library staff to a much smaller subset, containing, for example those requiring copyright management and resource acquisition. Leganto's ability to process citations, for both resource fulfilment and copyright/licensing compliance on a 24-hour basis, is directly linked to increased satisfaction with the service.

An example of the impact of changes in volume and timing can be seen in the initial implementation of the Reading List service in 2017. The Friday before the system was due to be used by students for the first time we realised that even though Library staff had worked hard on the incoming reading list processing, the rapid take up of Leganto meant that there were still approximately 3500 citations which had not been set to 'complete', a requirement for the students to be able to access the resources. It would not have been possible for Library staff to open all of the citations in time. Fortunately, Ex Libris staff were able to complete the task programmatically over the weekend, making the first day a great success and enabling the Library to hold faith with both the instructors and the students.

Library staff also immediately needed to acquire a broader knowledge of University systems such as Student One and Blackboard with which they had no previous experience. Library staff do not have direct access to Blackboard, although it is necessary for a Leganto Reading List to be associated with a particular Blackboard instance. Consequently, the Reading List team is reliant on instructors, who have access to both systems, to do this work correctly. Another challenge for the Library is the dependence on teams external to the Library to maintain these and other systems, to be cognisant of any changes that might impact on Leganto and to act on the Library's behalf to ensure the service is not affected. Beyond this was also the need to convey the transformative nature of the technological change to other staff in the Library and across the University.

5.4   Outcomes

At the retirement of the E-reserve model at the end of 2015, the service's engage-ment with the University totalled 1630 active reading lists comprising 15,340 cita-tions. The service had taken 13 years to achieve this level of embedding into the University environment. The move to Leganto allowed the use of records from a number of sources that did not need to be catalogued into Alma, and the scope of Reading Lists is far greater than that of the E-reserve model. It includes not just digitised content made under the Statutory Licence, but also content copied with permission, content directly licensed with publishers and openly licensed content, and the citations can originate from a broad range of sources. In 2018 teaching staff contributed 2308 active reading lists, adding 42,000 citations in this year alone. Moreover, in 2018 Leganto reached over 28,595 students and generated 778,935 full-text uses of electronic resources. The rapid increase in uptake by both teaching staff and students demonstrates that Leganto increased the use of reading lists and met student expectations for access to resources, making it easier for teaching staff to request new acquisitions and the digitisation of resources and manage copyright. At the same time, it significantly reduced workloads for both Library staff and for instructors involved in the curation of reading list documentation.

There are several factors that contributed to the successful implementation of Leganto. First, as the Reading List service is a replacement for the traditional E-reserve service, the new service continued to be the mandatory copyright compli-ance reporting mechanism, and instructors who needed this service had to transition to the new product. This provided an immediate client base with which to work in establishing the new service. This was assisted by exposing the existing reading lists into Leganto, which meant instructors could continue with little disruption. Second, the Leganto implementation was part of a wider University programme for system improvements. The link to a major project supported at high levels in the University provided the required impetus for staff to prioritise a universally adopted reading list solution and greatly assisted the implementation.

Before the formal introduction of Leganto in 2017, the soft launch in 2016 had already attracted the attention of a number of teaching academics and professional support officers across the University which helped to mitigate some of the risks associated with the implementation of the new system. These staff recognised the potential for Leganto to relieve some of their pain points and they actively championed the implementation within their respective Faculties. This proved to be crucial through the opportunities made available, such as invitations to Library staff to deliver training and present at key Faculty meetings, and the formation of ongoing relationships that support the embedding of the service within the University.

The Library's approach to the implementation has been well received by the University, as evidenced by the strong uptake of the new service and the positive feedback it has received from teaching academics and support staff. Although it was mandatory to use the Reading List service for copyright compliance, the service itself was more broadly supportive of teaching staff in achieving their teaching outcomes. Teaching staff were not required to undo their existing learning resource arrangements to comply with the new product, but were gently encouraged to migrate from their current arrangements into the new service. The Library's flexibility in working with instructors at their point of need assisted staff to see the service as a welcome support for their teaching. A partnership between the University Copyright and Reading Lists teams formed a mutually beneficial relationship. For example, when assisting teaching staff with copyright matters, the Copyright team directs instructors to the Reading List service. In return, the Reading List service assists instructors to engage with the Copyright team where appropriate. In this way, both services have to been able to contribute at a higher level to the University's success on matters of library resource provision and copyright/licensing compliance.

All of these elements combined to create an environment that allowed the Library's E-reserve service to be transformed into a holistic and well-used service that effectively achieved the original project objectives on time and on budget.

One ongoing challenge for management will be the question of identifying appropriate ongoing staffing for the fully implemented and embedded Reading List service. At present, there are a number of discrete Leganto tasks which need to be fulfilled: support for instructors; reading list processing; and monitoring of systems. Over time the balance of work is likely to change. Technological developments affecting the Reading List service may include, for example, the increased availability of resources in electronic formats, and this may reduce the need for digitisation of print resources. The Reading List service may thus come to focus more on the acquisition of resources and there may be a correspondingly reduced need for other types of work. Further developments with Leganto will also include the automation of the acquisition process, automated copyright approvals and reporting, and greater improvements in digitisation workflows.

The Leganto system allows for the collection of management data previously unavailable to Curtin University Library. This includes instructor and student usage data as well as technical data about the reading lists themselves. Reports are directly available to instructors through the Leganto interface and to Library staff through Alma Analytics. The use of this data in initiatives like the 'Predicting Students' Success with Leganto' project, will help enhance the effectiveness of reading lists for learning and teaching. By facilitating this type of analysis, Leganto will release Library staff to focus on a more value added role central to assisting the University with both its student success and retention objectives.

5.5 Conclusion

The technological advances made by the introduction of Leganto into the University learning and teaching environment have led to improved workload management and end user satisfaction. Leganto has refocused the workload for Library staff from data entry to providing value added services and has opened up even greater opportunities to engage with the University's teaching community. Continued development will have an impact on how these types of services are delivered and what gains can be made with regard to the efficiency of workflows, contribution to support for teaching, and student success. These changes were facilitated by integration with multiple systems, enabled by University collaboration and required significant organisational and workflow transformations.

References

Bedford, K., Donelly, T., Sheedy, L., & Mooi, M. (2017). *Leganto panel: Letting go with Leganto − four Australian universities reflect on implementing a new course resource list solution.* Paper presented at ANZREG 2017, Monash Law Chambers, Melbourne, VIC, Australia.

Curtin University, Office of Strategy and Planning (2018). *Curtin University student statistics 2012-2016* Retrieved from: https://planning.curtin.edu.au/stats/students2012-2016.cfm

Green, P., Darom, G., Katz, T., & Lewis, D. (2019). *Predicting students' success with Leganto: A proof of concept machine learning project.* Paper presented at THETA 2019: The tipping point, Wollongong, NSW, Australia.

Sheedy, L., & Green, P. (2019a). *Predicting students' success with Leganto: A proof of concept machine learning project.* Paper presented at IGeLU 2019: Driving change, creating value together, Singapore.

Sheedy, L., & Green, P. (2019b). *Predicting students' success with Leganto: A proof of concept machine learning project.* Paper presented at ANZREG 2019, Bond University, Gold Coast, QLD, Australia.

Tang, K., & Hanlon, J. (2005). E-reserve as a solution to digital copyright management at Curtin University of Technology. In A. Huthwaite (Ed.), *Managing information in the digital age: The Australian Technology Network Libraries respond* (pp. 101−116). Adelaide, Australia: University of South Australia Library for the Librarians of the Australian Technology Network.

Transforming information advisory services in university libraries: A case study at the University of Sheffield, UK

Alison Little[1], Alison Morton[1] and Lynn Sykes[2]
[1]University Library, University of Sheffield, Sheffield, United Kingdom,
[2]Formerly University Library, University of Sheffield, Sheffield, United Kingdom

6.1 Case context

Academic libraries are increasingly required to monitor their environment for nascent changes to student needs and expectations. Subsequently, academic libraries have become 'strategically agile' in their operations (Doz & Kosonen, 2008) as they strive to keep up with rapidly changing trends in contemporary technologies, particularly those favoured by students, such as web 2.0 and social media platforms. Such change by academic libraries, in being active in the adoption of new tools and practices, is widely recognised. This includes recognition by SCONUL, who emphasise that 'in recent years UK HE libraries have been at the forefront of the move into digital resources' (SCONUL, 2017).

Established by Royal Charter in 1905, the University of Sheffield is a large urban university with approximately 27,000 students enrolled on undergraduate and postgraduate courses (academic year 2016/2017). As a member of the Russell Group, it is one of 24 leading research-intensive UK universities. The University of Sheffield Library is a member of RLUK (Research Libraries UK), a consortium of the most significant research libraries in the UK and Ireland. The Library is a destination; being a place of discovery, enquiry, collaboration and knowledge creation and consists of four main sites: Western Bank Library; the Information Commons; the Health Sciences Library; and the Diamond. It has been committed to being a leader in adapting to contemporary digital library practices, and has made a significant investment in digital content and services in recent years. Digital tool adoption has been a central driver as part of the Library's strategy to be positioned to deliver 24 hour services to students and staff, regardless of their location. This has been demonstrated through 24 hour, 365 days a year access to the Information Commons, and through adoption of digital help and enquiry tools accessible to students in any geographical location. This element of the Library's strategy is emphasised in its vision statement to 'offer engaging experiences with people and content that enrich the University's learning and research communities in both physical and

Technology, Change and the Academic Library. DOI: https://doi.org/10.1016/B978-0-12-822807-4.00006-3

digital spaces' (University of Sheffield Library, 2015). As part of this strategy, the University Library has also made increasing investment in new digital technologies and practices to support its enquiry management, as part of a long-term strategy to transform advisory services.

6.2 Literature review: digital tool adoption for enquiry management in academic libraries

The adoption and embracing of digital tools by libraries, including those in academia, has been a varied and, at times, slow process. This has been driven by the traditional view held by some that digital adoption goes against the purpose and tradition of libraries as institutions (Borgman, 2007). This is well positioned by the belief of some that 'if a library is a library, it is not digital; if a library is digital, it is not a library' (Greenberg, 1998, p. 106).

Despite the adoption of contemporary technologies and practices being rejected by some libraries and librarians, others have embraced change in line with the potential for improving library functions and services, and the changing information-seeking behaviour of library users (Keralapura, 2009). Academic libraries have been at the forefront of digital tool adoption and innovation, in line with having to adapt services in an agile manner to the changing needs and demands of student populations (Doz & Kosonen, 2008; Lukasiewicz, 2007). Indeed, academic libraries have evolved in a relatively short space of time from focusing on the management of physical resources and related services towards transforming resources and services into new and changing digital formats, in the support of learning and teaching, and research (Choi & Rasmussen, 2009; Raju, 2014). This includes changes in products offered by libraries, including digital reading materials, online learning resources and subject-specific portals (McCarthy, 2005). This has also led to the repurposing of academic library spaces (Matthews & Walton, 2013), and a focus on enabling spaces for computers and self-service, open spaces for personal study and virtual spaces to facilitate changes in the learning process (Hockey, 2016; Raju, 2014).

Whilst the adoption of contemporary technologies in academic libraries has become near ubiquitous (O'Connor & Au, 2009), one pertinent challenge has been to ensure that they remain competitive and congruent with the rapid changing field of technologies, and associated knowledge and skills, and adapt accordingly in line with changing customer behaviour and expectations (Lukasiewicz, 2007; Orlikowski, 2007; Raju, 2014). Such challenges have been seen in the approach by academic libraries to enquiry and advisory services, where traditional physical enquiry desks are no longer appropriate or sustainable for students and staff, whose expectation is to be able to interact with library enquiry teams through a more dynamic range of IT-driven solutions (Hockey, 2016; Matthews & Walton, 2013). However, physical desks remain a 'sacred cow' in many academic libraries (Hockey, 2016, p. 128), where they are yet to consider moving away from this prevailing symbol of librarianship and traditional library service (Arndt, 2010), and towards adoption of virtual services, such as live chat (Hockey, 2016) and web 2.0 platforms (Dawson, 2011). Whilst service desks still represent a sizeable means of enquiry management in academic libraries, it is increasingly seen that libraries are complementing this service with digital tools (Dawson, 2011). Ultimately, despite such insights, there still exists a major challenge for libraries to take more significant steps away from the enquiry desk, and towards predominantly digitally driven enquiry services (Hockey, 2016).

6.3 Methodology

This paper follows a qualitative, longitudinal case study method, with secondary planning documentation the central form of data utilised. In addition, a number of primary data sources are drawn upon, such as staff surveys, and first-hand reflective diaries, which are used here to document and develop a narrative regarding the University Library's key processes of enquiry management implementation.

6.4 Developing a cohesive information and enquiry management strategy

The first aspect of digital tool adoption explored in this chapter relates to knowledge sharing. We detail the creation and curation of a dynamic staff knowledge base and how this has evolved over several years to underpin the delivery of an integrated enquiry service (Fig. 6.1).

In 2010, we initiated an enquiry management project to review how library enquiries were dealt with across sites and services. A major outcome, resulting from the

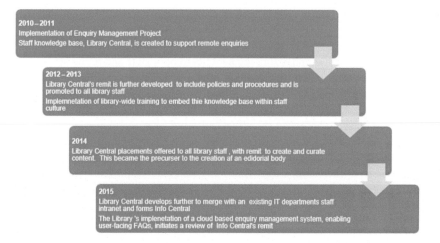

Figure 6.1 Creation and development of a dynamic staff knowledge base using Google Sites.

project findings, was the creation of a dynamic knowledge base to enable staff to explain confidently library policies and procedures, ensuring quality and consistency. The University had adopted Google Apps for Education, and, in November 2011, after rigorous testing with key members of library staff, the first steps were taken on the Library's new digital transformation journey with the adoption of Google Sites to provide the basis for the staff knowledge base. Google Sites was chosen as it:

- offered a cost-effective platform with a user-friendly interface
- had dedicated navigation features
- provided a centralised cloud-based system eliminating concerns around updates and version control

The initial 2011 version of the knowledge base was limited to supporting staff dealing with remote enquiries. However, it soon became evident that customer-facing staff at information desks across the University's library sites would benefit from the information curated within. The site was aptly named 'Library Central', emphasising the intended centralised nature of the knowledge base (Desouza & Evaristo, 2004).

To launch the Library Central knowledge base to all library staff and obtain staff buy-in, a number of library training events were hosted throughout 2013 to showcase the site and obtain feedback. To engage staff and enable them to recognise the site's value, Library Central was actively promoted as the quickest, most efficient and effective way to access resources. A series of 'quick link' icons were added to the platform to allow instant access to key systems and web pages, such as the University's Library Management System (LMS), the Library's discovery platform (catalogue) and status information regarding e-resources. Regular email updates were generated to promote new content, and staff were encouraged to openly suggest improvements for the knowledge base via an integrated Google Form. Uptake was slow, and staff were unsure of the relevance and value that the platform offered to their various roles, an issue often noted with the uptake of knowledge sharing processes (Nonaka & Konno, 1998), and new workplace technologies and knowledge systems (Orlikowski, 2007; Siakas, Georgiadou, & Balstrup, 2010). The challenge at this early stage of the library-wide implementation was ultimately to nurture a culture of knowledge sharing, emphasising the benefits to both staff and to the service.

On reflection, we underestimated the impact that the new system would have on staff. We had envisaged that staff would welcome this collaborative digital tool and knowledge base. However, instead, we found that we had saturated them with information and failed to appreciate the effect this would have.

To look at the issues around limited staff engagement, we utilised the embedded Google Analytics functionality to monitor usage and detect areas of the site that showed steady or increased usage. Analysing this data empowered the development team to understand how Library Central was being used. Ultimately, this led to targeted promotion of site content and updates in relation to the resolution of enquiries.

In 2013, a major opportunity for establishing the knowledge base occurred when the Library moved to a new LMS. It was decided to use Library Central as a dedicated training and documentation hub, guiding staff during and after implementation.

One rationale here was the increasing need to keep staff across sites informed of system updates and issues, together with current status problems regarding e-resources. In addition to the knowledge base, we created a Google + community, 'Library Latest', to disseminate transient information quickly and effectively, embedding it into Library Central to further emphasise the importance and relevance of this shared resource. The gradual change in the culture of customer services staff in relation to adopting the knowledge base, in addition to an express need to use it, resulted in the value of both these collaborative tools being recognised by a growing number of staff across library sites and teams. Overall, there was a realisation that the digital technology opened up immediate access to information for their work and in supporting students and other library users at the point of need.

However, obtaining unilateral buy-in from staff at this point in our journey was still an aspiration rather than a reality. We had underestimated how change was perceived, especially the length of time required before new initiatives became embedded within the culture of the library. Future iterations of the knowledge base would centre around staff focus groups, acknowledging and embedding staff suggestions and concepts.

In 2014, we offered a number of placements to staff to create and curate content within the knowledge base. The brief was to develop specific areas in Library Central and autonomy was given to staff on the placements regarding the format of areas and the content within. However, it became evident that this approach was unsustainable. The content had no unified look and feel, which impacted on the potential usability of the knowledge base, and it was unclear as to the validity and the source of the information held. As such, this raised concerns amongst staff regarding the integrity of the knowledge base. Ultimately, the outcomes from these placements would provide the impetus to create strategic guidelines and implement an editorial body for Library Central.

2015 saw a review of the Library's customer-facing advisory support offer. There was particular consideration of how new tools and practices might help bring about a more contemporary approach to enquiry services across the University's different library sites. At this time, queries were being answered using an IT technical support software package, administered by the University's IT department. However, it was deemed to be no longer fit for library purposes for a number of reasons:

- It was not available to library external members.
- Staff were unable to monitor enquiries referred to specialist teams as there was no visible audit trail available within the software.
- As all analytics and enquiry profiles were created by the IT department, the Library had no autonomy to create or extract data or to make any developments to the service.

There was an evident need to begin scoping out potential enquiry management software providers. A clear remit was outlined: the software should be user-friendly; it should enable library staff to respond and effectively refer enquiries; and the platform had to include the facility to create a dynamic bank of customer-facing FAQs, whilst supporting an embedded live chat service accessible to all library users. After consultation, and reviewing the pros and cons of available software packages, it was decided to trial Springshare LibAnswers during Summer

2015. In theory, the software addressed all aforementioned criteria, and in practice it soon became evident that the Library could adopt the software across all key teams to deliver a more holistic approach to enquiry management. Soon after this, the requirement for a designated virtual advisory service was identified as a priority in response to student needs and expectations.

Alongside the implementation of LibAnswers came the evolution of Library Central into its second iteration in 2016. This arose from concerns over the potential for duplicated and, perhaps more critically, conflicting information between information stored on separate Library and IT knowledge bases. Library and IT staff collaborated in the development of a joint knowledge base which addressed the needs of both of these distinct front-line services in delivering a highly efficient and effective mutual service. This was branded as 'Info Central' to reflect the fact that the knowledge base now contained Library and IT support. A content review of both resources was implemented and focus groups were held to ensure staff across both departments had the opportunity to offer feedback. On reflection, we approached the integration of the two knowledge bases without considering the strength of ownership that the IT team had towards their knowledge base. In retrospect, we would have applied true collaboration and influence to ensure a positive outcome and to avoid conflict. The insight gained from this process became a key point of learning when we moved on to develop future iterations of the newly devised Info Central.

To ensure the integrity of the newly merged site, we instigated a systematic review of the platform's content. Areas belonging to specific teams were clearly identified, and a policy that all content would be created by specialists and subsequently curated by a designated editorial team (consisting of both Library and IT staff) was agreed. The editorial team would also be responsible for the consistent look and feel of the site, the promotion of new content, and the liaison with specialists to ensure integrity and sustainability. Additionally, and to ensure an audit trail of updates, all content clearly showed the date it had been created and this occurred at the point when content was updated with additional details of its authorship. In hindsight, the concept of an 'open' approach to adding content was somewhat idealistic and, as information professionals, we should have identified that an editorial structure was imperative.

Spring 2016 saw both the knowledge base and enquiry management platforms on their way to becoming well established in the Library's plethora of support tools. The relevance of an information and enquiry management structure was incorporated within the Library's strategic project which was looking more widely at the delivery of services (Fig. 6.2). Specifically, this project explored how the Library might develop flexibility in service models to respond to changes in the way that students learn and to reach them in all their spaces (both physical and digital).

The strategic project helped to give legitimacy to both the staff knowledge base and the virtual advisory services, and clear project objectives enabled both areas to develop significantly over a relatively short space of time.

In tandem with the strategic project, the Library explored and developed a range of student enquiry channels, including email, live chat, phone, tweets and SMS (text messaging). During busy periods, these channels can generate several hundred enquiries each day.

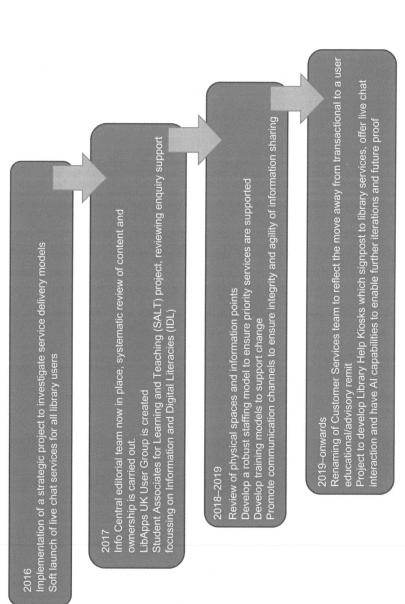

Figure 6.2 Strategic review of service delivery moving forwards.

A team of Student Associates for Learning and Teaching (SALTs) worked alongside the Library's Virtual Advisory and Help Service, and in collaboration with the Library Learning Services Unit, to develop support for information and digital literacy advice. This was delivered via the use of screen sharing software, screencasting, web conferencing, online tutorials and video, with the aim to create high quality and targeted resolutions to information and digital literacy queries.

The SALTs project proved successful in identifying common themes in student enquiries, and explored potential solutions by which the Library could better address these queries. It was established that existing library resources already matched the needs of students and, therefore, the 'action research' approach taken enabled the project to follow an alternative, more appropriate path. Instead of creating new resources, the project suggested that the development of the library services would require an improvement in the visibility of existing resources, embedding them in accessible places and integrating them on a faculty level, such that they are reinforced to students and can be easily utilised at point of need.

The findings of the SALTs team legitimised the Library's earlier initiative to embed a live chat widget within its high discovery platform, and subsequently the number of chat enquiries increased by 790%.

Ultimately, the development of different practices, and associated adoption of new tools to aid virtual enquiry management, have been essential to enabling a range of contemporary new services to meet the evolving needs of library users (Table 6.1).

Quality control remains an ongoing concern, and a long-term goal for the Library is to improve the service experience through continued use and development of self-help services such as FAQs, and via responses to specific enquiries through the variety of enquiry tools being adopted.

As we move beyond 2019, we have found that the analytics captured within the enquiry management system has been instrumental in creating user FAQs and tutorials, together with staff training programmes. In September 2019, we added the Reference Effort Assessment Data (READ) scale to our existing analytics to capture qualitative data, which, alongside the data already being captured, will measure the impact our enquiry service has during the student lifecycle. This six-point scale was developed to measure the processes, activities, effort, skill, knowledge and teaching skills utilised by library staff during a reference enquiry (Gerlich & Berard, 2007). We also aim to take this a step further, by utilising the READ scale to measure impact using a case study technique.

6.5 Discussion: the evolution of effective enquiry management over time

In discussing the adoption of new tools in the Library, the discussion focuses on how the two main elements detailed here have come together to complement each other in forming an effective enquiry management service. In doing so, what we

Table 6.1 Service model delivery outcomes – February 2018.

The core Virtual Advisory and Help Service (VAHS) fully established with a team of advisors to support staff dealing with the growing number of complex enquiries arising from the integration of live chat in the library catalogue. VAHS staff are responsible for knowledge management and quality assurance. Live chat fully established, following a soft launch and is now the most preferred mechanism for the resolution of queries. Numbers have increased since its implementation by 790%.
Enquiry skills training is developed to support staff and ensure consistency and quality of service. > Enquiry cafes using actual, anonymised enquiries and responses provide a forum for discussion on best practices and alternative approaches to problem solving. > Q&A sessions are delivered by specialists across the library service to inform and raise awareness of how the different specialists can support enquiries. > Continuing professional development (CPD) interactive workbooks focus on reflection regarding specific aspects of the student journey, ensuring staff are proactive rather than reactive to queries that arise at certain points in the academic year.
As a result of the action research project with Student Associates for Learning and Teaching, FAQs are now being systematically reviewed with the objective of adding screencasts and videos to the best effect. Effective enquiry management alongside qualitative and quantitative data now enables the Library to measure the impact of this service. In collaboration with subject librarians and academic departments, the Library offers 'pop-up' library services across the University campus to improve the visibility of the Library's offer.

emphasise as particularly important is enabling the evolution of the service over time. Two main factors are considered here and in our conceptualisation (Fig. 6.3): first, the support offered by the knowledge base for staff to enable effective enquiry management; second the support offered to students as new virtual advisory practices are adopted.

As was demonstrated through the narrative of our case, the knowledge-sharing platform was particularly important as a means of bringing about effective enquiry management in the library sites by ensuring key staff were supported through the adoption of an online knowledge base. More specifically, the platform has been particularly useful as a means of ensuring staff have up to date, consistent and accurate information to help with managing enquiries. Over time, Info Central has evolved to become a knowledge base which incorporates core library policies and procedures and supports training and professional development initiatives. Further, the platform has been extended to use in the University's IT department, integrating key information which can be leveraged strategically by staff across different Library and IT teams.

Thus, in summarising our discussion, the adoption of new enquiry management practices to support both staff and students has been central to the University Library's strategy for enquiry management and the development of advisory services.

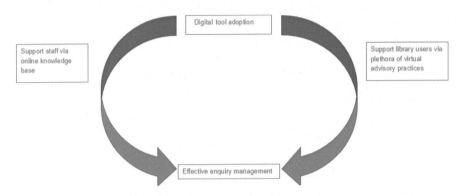

Figure 6.3 Digital tool adoption leading to an effective service delivery model.

6.6 Implications and conclusion

In conclusion, a number of key implications are derived from this study, both empirically and for practice.

Empirically, and for theory, this work contributes to the existing literature on digital tool adoption, particularly in library settings, and offers a longitudinal account of tool development and implementation for enquiry management through which a conceptualisation of effective enquiry management using digital tool adoption is conceived. Relating this to the practical implications of our work, the case narrative here is perceivably of value to practitioners, particularly academic librarians adopting contemporary practices for enquiry management. The development of enquiry management we present also offers a detailed narrative for different stages of implementation and explicates how this evolved over time. It can provide a useful guide for managers.

Overall, the implementation of a strategic project looking at our service models, our physical and virtual spaces, has given legitimacy to our information and enquiry management tools and services. As some transactional elements of our service offer are declining, the project looked at how it could support an expanding virtual advisory service. In conclusion, this case study sets out how the two elements of contemporary tool adoption have complemented each other over time, and come to support and enhance library services from both a staff and customer perspective. It explores the implications and benefits for staff as practitioners, whilst acknowledging potential challenges in the adoption of new tools and practices in academic libraries, based on experiences at the University of Sheffield. We hope the case presented here is of interest to others working in academic libraries and enquiry management.

The implementation of new tools has been pivotal to rebuilding our conversation with customers away from the traditional 'information desk', ensuring that help is available at the point of need. In particular, the narrative emphasises the use of self-help tools combined with chat, email, phone and social media to enable engagement, promotion, support and development of services. The recently added use of screen sharing and screencasting has provided another inclusive element to our virtual interactions.

References

Arndt, T. S. (2010). Reference service without the desk. *Reference Services Review*, *38*(1), 71−80. Available from https://doi.org/10.1108/00907321011020734.

Borgman, C. L. (2007). *Scholarship in the digital age: Information, infrastructure, and the internet*. Cambridge, MA: MIT Press.

Choi, Y., & Rasmussen, E. (2009). What qualifications and skills are important for digital librarian positions in academic libraries?: A job advertisement analysis. *Journal of Academic Librarianship*, *35*(5), 457−467. Available from https://doi.org/10.1016/j.acalib.2009.06.003.

Dawson, P. H. (2011). Are science, engineering, and medical libraries, moving away from the reference desk?: Results of a survey of New Jersey libraries. *Science & Technology Libraries*, *30*(4), 343−353. Available from https://doi.org/10.1080/0194262X.2011.626337.

Desouza, K. C., & Evaristo, J. R. (2004). Managing knowledge in distributed projects. *Communications of the ACM*, *47*(4), 87−91. Available from https://doi.org/10.1145/975817.975823.

Doz, Y., & Kosonen, M. (2008). *Fast strategy: How strategic ability will help you stay ahead of the game*. Harlow: Pearson Education.

Gerlich, B.K., & Berard, G.L. (2007). Introducing the READ scale: Qualitative statistics for academic reference services. Georgia Library Quarterly, 43(4), 7−13. Available from: https://digitalcommons.kennesaw.edu/glq/vol43/iss4/4/.

Greenberg, D. (1998). Camel drivers and gatecrashers: Quality control in the digital research library. In B. L. Hawkins, & P. Battin (Eds.), *The mirage of continuity: Reconfiguring academic information resources for the 21st century* (pp. 105−116). Washington, DC: Council on Library and Information Resources and the Association of American Universities.

Hockey, J. M. (2016). Transforming library enquiry services: Anywhere, anytime and any device. *Library Management*, *37*(3), 125−135. Available from https://doi.org/10.1108/LM-04-2016-0021.

Keralapura, M. (2009). Technology and customer expectation in academic libraries: A special reference to technical/management libraries in Karnataka. *International Information & Library Review*, *41*(3), 184−195. Available from https://doi.org/10.1080/10572317.2009.10762812.

Lukasiewicz, A. (2007). Exploring the role of digital academic libraries: Changing student needs demand innovative service approach. *Library Review*, *56*(9), 821−827. Available from https://doi.org/10.1108/00242530710831275.

Matthews, G., & Walton, G. (Eds.), (2013). *University libraries and space in the digital world*. London: Routledge.

McCarthy, J. (2005). Planning a future workforce: An Australian perspective. *New Review of Academic Librarianship*, *11*(1), 41−56. Available from https://doi.org/10.1080/13614530500417669.

Nonaka, I., & Konno, N. (1998). The concept of 'ba': Building a foundation for knowledge creation. *California Management Review*, *40*(3), 40−54. Available from https://doi.org/10.2307/41165942.

O'Connor, S., & Au, L. (2009). Steering a future through scenarios: Into the academic library of the future. *Journal of Academic Librarianship*, *35*(1), 57−64. Available from https://doi.org/10.1016/j.acalib.2008.11.001.

Orlikowski, W. J. (2007). Sociomaterial practices: Exploring technology at work. *Organization Studies*, *28*(9), 1435−1448. Available from https://doi.org/10.1177/0170840607081138.

Raju, J. (2014). Knowledge and skills for the digital era academic library. *Journal of Academic Librarianship*, *40*(2), 163−170. Available from https://doi.org/10.1016/j.acalib.2014.02.007.

SCONUL. (2017). *The value of academic libraries*. Retrieved from: https://www.sconul.ac.uk/page/the-value-of-academic-libraries.

Siakas, K. V., Georgiadou, E., & Balstrup, B. (2010). Cultural impacts on knowledge sharing: Empirical data from EU project collaboration. *VINE*, *40*(3/4), 376−389. Available from https://doi.org/10.1108/03055721011071476.

University of Sheffield Library. (2015). *Our library. Our information future: The University of Sheffield Library Strategic Plan* Retrieved from: http://librarysupport.group.shef.ac.uk/strategicplan/.

Accelerating student learning in communication and research skills: the adoption of adaptive learning technologies for scenario-based modules

Katie Mills[1], Ferg Roper[2,3] and Sarah Cesare[1]
[1]University Library, University of Western Australia, Perth, WA, Australia,
[2]South Metropolitan TAFE, Perth, WA, Australia, [3]Formerly Capability Development, University of Western Australia, Perth, WA, Australia

7.1 Introduction

Communication and Research Skills (CARS) is a compulsory, introductory online unit for all undergraduate students at the University of Western Australia (UWA). It assists students to develop basic communication and research skills such as working in teams, delivering an oral presentation, finding evidence and writing their assignments in an academic context. The unit was originally created by the University Library and the University's Academic Skills Centre, STUDYSmarter, in 2010. Apart from updates to the content and a platform change in 2015, there had not been any major reviews or updates until an institutional-wide review of the unit was conducted in 2017.

7.2 Aims and objectives

The institutional-wide review identified that the varying levels of students' prior knowledge and educational experiences highlight 'the difficulty of providing uncontextualised, introductory information, as students with more advanced skills may find the content too basic and thus less valuable'. The review's three main recommendations focused on this challenge and emphasised the need to contextualise and customise the content, delivery and use of the unit. As a result, the objectives of the redesign project were to update CARS content to focus on practical skill development in a variety of academic and professional contexts and deliver it on a platform that would allow for the customised delivery of this content. The project commenced in August 2018 with the aim of launching to commencing students in late February 2019.

Technology, Change and the Academic Library. DOI: https://doi.org/10.1016/B978-0-12-822807-4.00007-5

7.3 Methodology

The UWA Library's project management approach is based on Prince2 methodology and the project was established with a project manager, project board and project team. The project team included representatives from the Library and STUDYSmarter, who were later joined by a learning designer and educational technologist from the University's Educational Enhancement Unit. Each team member provided a different perspective to support the Library's development of CARS:

- Librarians managed the project, designed the branching scenarios and developed the modules in Articulate Storyline 360.
- Learning skills advisors also designed branching scenarios and wrote content for the modules relating to effective study techniques, writing, communication and research skills.
- Learning designers provided advice and support around learning principles and strategies, including design for branching scenarios.
- Educational technologists established the technology requirements such as the virtual learning environment, software and templates.

The project was mapped out in stages, which included the following:

- Assessment and selection of available learning platforms
- Storyboarding of content and activities
- Development of a communication plan
- Design of assessments
- Development of modules
- Testing
- Development of an ongoing management plan

These stages were not as linear and standalone as initially expected, due to the way the team dipped in and out of stages by storyboarding and developing prototypes, testing ideas and redeveloping modules based on feedback.

7.3.1 Review of available learning platforms

The original CARS unit was built in Adobe Captivate 8 and deployed via two platforms: as a package within the virtual learning environment (Blackboard Learn) for students currently enroled in the unit, and openly available as HTML5 content on the CARS web page. The CARS review identified 12 functional requirements that would need to be met by a replacement platform to address student experience, sustainability and technology needs. Being able to create a 'choose your own adventure' personalised delivery style and incorporate gamification principles were two of these requirements that focused the platform review on adaptive learning technologies.

The team's investigation of adaptive learning technologies led to a meeting with an educational technologist from the University's Educational Enhancement Unit who recommended attending a unit design workshop. Unit design workshops are based on 'Carpe Diem', a process of learning design through teamwork and collaboration (Salmon, 2016). These workshops consist of a team of professionals (namely, learning designers, educational technologists and librarians), who specialise in different areas of education support coming together for a day to assist a unit coordinator to reconsider the design of their unit with a particular focus on effective and innovative learning and assessment strategies. Although CARS is not a traditional credit unit, the same principles applied in mapping out the unit to get to the core of its teaching goals. In hindsight, the decision to start the project with a focus on the technology was premature as it was important to understand initially the purpose of the unit, the pain points for students, and what their CARS experience should look like.

7.3.2 Storyboarding and rapid prototyping

Through taking part in the unit design workshop, the team realised that the ultimate goal of CARS should be to foster behavioural change and the development of skills rather than simply the retention of information to pass a final quiz. Students should feel more prepared for university and confident in applying the skills in real life as a result of completing the unit. Early in the development phase, it was determined that a traditional approach to learning design would not be suitable for CARS. The modules had to be self-paced, interactive and provide feedback, without intervention from an instructor. Another aim of CARS was to provide a resource that was not simply recreating content that was readily available online. As such, an action mapping approach to learning design was used (Moore, 2017). Action mapping focuses on first developing goals that solve real-world problems, and then the subsequent actions required to do so. This approach switches the emphasis from memorising decontextualised knowledge related to a topic, to what the learner actually needs to do to solve a problem. The final steps of action mapping include practising behaviours and decisions whilst accessing information resources and 'task aids' at the point of need.

Inspired by best practice examples such as Connect with Haji Kamal (World Warfighter, 2010) and Arcade Intern (Dalmady, 2015), the team began exploring a scenario-based approach to the future delivery of CARS. This involved replacing previously static content with scenarios that would encourage students to make decisions and apply skills as they navigate through the unit, mimicking realistic and interactive situations that they are likely to encounter in their studies (Moore, 2017). For example, in the module on teamwork, a team of student characters are shown discussing their group assignment and the user is asked to make decisions to guide the team's experience. The success of the team depends on the decisions made and the user is given feedback at the end of the module. In another module, the user makes decisions about search strategies, referencing and the most reliable sources to use in their character's assignment (Figs 7.1–7.3).

Several software solutions were considered for the development of CARS, including Twine and Articulate Storyline 360. Twine, an open-source, text-based interactive storytelling tool, was used to create prototypes to introduce the project team to the concepts behind adaptive learning and branching scenarios. Twine was developed for online 'choose your own adventure' stories and can incorporate conditional logic, variables and images, which are published in HTML. Twine is easy

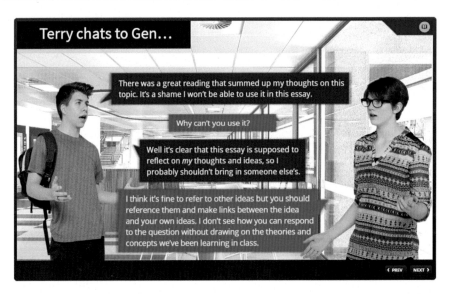

Figure 7.1 Screenshot from *Module 2: Writing your assessment* showing character dialogue from a reflective essay scenario.

to use, with simple text-based commands and markup that allows for rapid proto-type testing and scenario mapping. Developing the modules in Twine enabled early testing of the pathways for each of the CARS modules, along with the creation of a visual map for each scenario (Fig. 7.4).

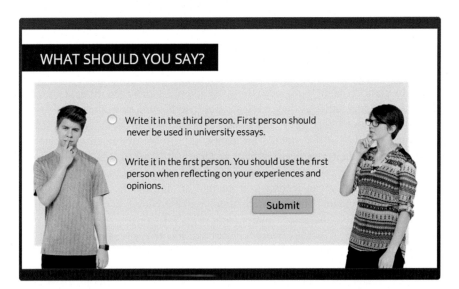

Figure 7.2 Screenshot from *Module 2: Writing your assessment* showing the realistic decisions that the students have to make to proceed through the scenario.

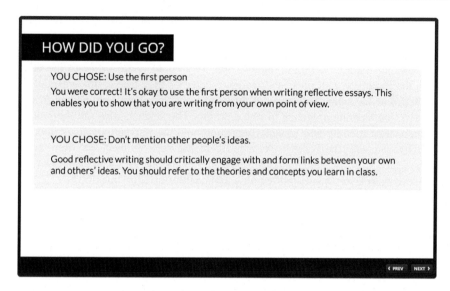

Figure 7.3 Screenshot from *Module 2: Writing your assessment* showing the adaptive feedback presented to the student at the end of the module based on their decisions throughout.

Whilst Twine proved to be an efficient way to test ideas and prototype learning scenarios, it was ultimately decided that the final product needed to have the capability for greater customisation of the graphical interface and user experience. To investigate another option, two project team members built a working prototype of one of

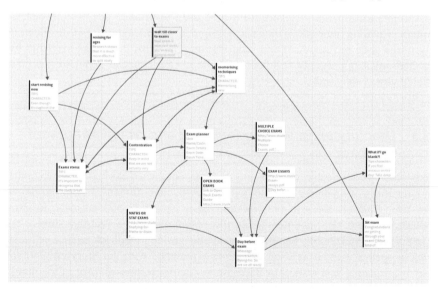

Figure 7.4 Screenshot showing a branching scenario prototype developed in Twine for *Module 1: Starting your assessment and finding evidence.*

the modules in the trial version of Articulate Storyline 360, despite having had no previous experience in the software or adaptive learning technologies. The prototype module was tested by 18 current students who were asked to compare it to the equivalent existing module. Overall, students felt they could relate better to the content within the prototype as it presented realistic scenarios they face as students and demonstrated how to apply skills and put them into practice. They commented that they preferred this learning approach to rote learning. The students also felt the prototype was more user friendly and visually appealing, and the interactivity made them feel more engaged with the content. As a result of the positive feedback from students and the successful assessment against functional requirements, the decision was made to proceed with a scenario-based learning approach using Storyline 360.

7.3.3   Development, stakeholder feedback and usability testing

Starting the learning design process with action mapping naturally led to the scenario development for the modules. Each scenario had major decision points that provided students with the option to go down different pathways, where they had to make realistic decisions with consequences and adaptive feedback built in. This required programming variables and triggers into Storyline 360 so that the software would take learners down their chosen pathway, and also remember their choices. Triggers allowed the user to take particular actions depending on what they clicked on, such as taking them to another slide, opening a layer, or revealing feedback. Variables were used to store choices the learners made in Storyline 360, such as the buttons they clicked on, or the slides they went to on a particular pathway. By storing variable information, triggers were then used to provide adaptive feedback to learners. Creating multiple pathways required a significant time investment, not only in the slide development and programming, but also in making sure that learners had equal opportunity to understand the CARS concepts required, no matter which pathway they took.

7.3.4   Usability tests, written feedback and crowd-annotated feedback

Stakeholder feedback and usability testing was conducted during the development using a variety of methods. One method used Articulate Review 360, an online platform which allows users to preview and share Storyline 360 projects, to gather feedback on the CARS modules. Using this online platform meant that subject matter experts and stakeholders could annotate changes and feedback against particular slides or scenes without needing any prior experience with the Storyline 360 software or a separate spreadsheet or database to capture responses. Due to the number of pathways and different combinations in a scenario-based module, this approach ensured rigorous crowdsourced testing to ensure all pathways worked and dead ends were avoided (Fig. 7.5).

Figure 7.5 Screenshot from Articulate Review showing contextual stakeholder feedback from the usability testing phase.

The usability testing involved project team members observing students and staff as they worked through the modules. The users were encouraged to 'think out loud' and share their thoughts and expectations about the experience. This proved to be a useful way to test assumptions about the technology, especially around topics such as navigation, functionality and design.

Navigation had been discussed by the project team a great deal during the development before the decision was made to provide minimal instructions and aim to design the experience in a way that was intuitive enough that they were not needed. Despite this, usability testing showed that the vast majority of users overlooked the tips and guides icons that linked them to the contextual task aids at the top right of the screen. As a result, the team added an introduction slide detailing how to navigate the module (Fig. 7.6).

The modules were originally designed with feedback only presented upon completion of the pathways. Feedback from some of the students during the usability testing indicated that they had forgotten their choices by the time they reached the end of the module and that they would prefer to receive the feedback in context. This became a delicate balancing act to try and present a realistic story and pathways, whilst ensuring feedback was timely and relevant. This impacted on the design of some modules, with longer modules being split so that feedback could be presented at the halfway point, as well as immediate feedback being added for any interactive activities such as 'drag and drop' and other matching activities. Another observation from the usability testing was that students felt they might have missed important information due to the pathway they went down. The ability to jump backwards in a module and reset any previous choices and completed activities required further experimentation with the software and an extension of the triggers and variables.

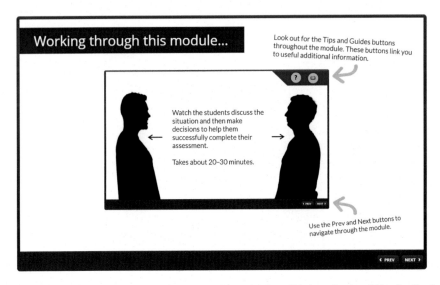

Figure 7.6 Screenshot showing the redeveloped introduction slide based on usability feedback.

7.3.5 Accessibility

It was important that CARS be fully accessible so all students receive the same learning experience. The software chosen needed to meet web accessibility standards and requirements and this was one of the core functional requirements during the review of learning platforms. At the time, it was noted that Storyline 360 supported WCAG (Web Content Accessibility Guidelines), including screen reader support. However, after testing the modules with a student with a visual impairment and using the JAWS screen reader program, the project team discovered the importance of tab order within the screens and adding alternative text to all images, activities and links. This emphasised the importance of testing the tools and resources with a screen reader rather than assuming the software is accessible straight out of the box.

7.4   Outcomes and impact

The redeveloped CARS unit was launched to commencing students at the beginning of Semester 1 in February 2019. Enroled students were given access to the unit via a link to the HTML5 version from the University's Blackboard VLE (virtual learning environment). In addition, the HTML5 version was linked from a web page to provide open access to the unit for unit coordinators and the wider community. As of June 2019, 3519 students had completed CARS.

Student feedback was gathered throughout the semester via a survey embedded into the CARS LMS unit, and additional interviews were conducted with a selection of students who had completed CARS. The students were asked to share their experiences on the content, activities, dialogue, format and usability of CARS.

Generally, students enjoyed the scenario-based format and felt it offered a better learning experience than simply reading information and memorising. They also reported that the unit was user friendly and easy to navigate across modules, although a small group of students did encounter issues when viewing CARS on mobile devices as it did not display well on smaller screens.

Several students shared that they found CARS useful for gaining an understanding of the expectations at university and that they could relate to the information in CARS as it reflected their own early experiences at university. Students found the content relatable, mimicking the way they would think and react if they were actually doing the assignment.

Students liked the activities embedded into the modules as it was an opportunity for them to test their knowledge. However, a number of students stated that they would have liked to have the choice to skip an activity, yet they were unable to do so. Additionally, when they got an activity incorrect they did not receive detailed feedback, so they did not always know how to improve. Despite the addition of an introductory navigation slide as a result of the usability testing, none of the students interviewed noticed the tips and guides icons embedded into slides.

As a result of student feedback and testing, a number of updates and changes have been made to the CARS modules for Semester 2, 2019. These changes included reviewing all activities embedded into the modules to ensure they provide targeted constructive feedback, adding the functionality to enable users to skip an activity if desired, carrying out further cross-device testing to improve user experience on mobile devices and creating an additional creative assessment type pathway. The tips and guides icons were also made more prominent throughout the modules so that students have the opportunity to learn in more detail about the content they are working through on the slide.

An ongoing development and management plan was the last product to be delivered as part of the project. A team was established to provide operational support and management for the administration, development, maintenance and promotion of CARS. This operational team will carry out a biannual review of CARS to ensure the content remains up to date and any technology changes are addressed.

7.5 Conclusions and recommendations

The CARS project was the Library's first experience with adaptive learning technologies and case scenarios, and one of the first examples of this approach used at UWA. There were risks involved due to students potentially not being familiar and/ or receptive to this approach and the reach and profile of the unit should it have been unsuccessful. The project benefitted from a supportive project board that encouraged experimentation and innovation, and validation in the early stages from stakeholder feedback about the prototype.

The project gave the librarians involved the opportunity to develop new and unique skills, especially around storytelling and scenario writing. In developing the scenario branches, the project team identified behaviours or common mistakes made by students in the context of a situation, setting or problem at university to determine the decision points. Storyboarding and branching, developing realistic plots and writing the scenarios around these decision points were a new experience for all involved and a different approach to thinking about user behaviour and library instruction. The team also developed new skills in prototyping, usability testing and accessibility testing which will be valuable transferable skills for other Library projects and activities.

UWA Library is already exploring how adaptive learning technologies could be used beyond CARS. Librarians were recently trained in Articulate Storyline and worked in pairs to develop short, standalone learning objects to be made available in the University's LMS for reuse by unit coordinators. Other parts of the University have also been exploring adaptive learning including the development of a 'Health and well-being at UWA' pilot programme.

Based on the CARS experience, seven recommendations for other libraries considering incorporating adaptive learning methods and technologies into their information literacy instructional design are listed below:

- Start with the content and learning experience, not the technology. Do not let the technology dictate the learning design.
- Partner with colleagues from other areas of the university to bring together expertise and different ways of thinking.
- Carry out rapid prototyping and testing. Do not wait for the content or design to be 'perfect' before asking for stakeholder feedback.
- Be careful not to overcomplicate your design. Branching scenarios can expand very quickly as each scenario-based activity you add requires additional pathways and multiple learning paths. These can be time consuming to build and add.
- Start with a design template to ensure your modules have a consistent look and feel.
- Take the time to make the content accessible. Do not assume the software is fully accessible simply because it states it supports assistive technologies.
- Do not underestimate the time commitment in planning, storyboarding, building, consulting with stakeholders, and testing.

This project demonstrated that adaptive learning technologies can provide new opportunities for libraries to enhance their online literacy instruction by contextualising learning using real-world scenarios with adaptive feedback.

References

Dalmady, A. (2015). *Arcane Intern*. Retrieved from: <http://astriddalmady.com/ArcaneIntern.html>.

Moore, C. (2017). *Map it: The hands-on guide to strategic training design*. Montesa Press. (n.p.).

Salmon, G. (2016). *Carpe Diem learning design: Preparation & workshop*. Retrieved from: <https://www.gillysalmon.com/uploads/5/0/1/3/50133443/colour_carpe_diem_planning_process_workbook_version18_junc2016.pdf>.

World Warfighter. (2010). *Connect with Haji Kamal*. Retrieved from: <https://www.worldwarfighter.com/hajikamal/activity/>.

Developing an online book finding tool for a university library

David Bennett and Colin Work
University Library, University of Portsmouth, Portsmouth, United Kingdom

8.1 Introduction

An important part of library education is to help users find information independently and efficiently. Surveys suggest that many students still prefer to read printed books than e-books, particularly when reading large amounts or consulting images and complex diagrams (Bowman, 2013, p. 49; Wilders, 2017, p. 387). Academic libraries can, therefore, expect to retain significant printed book collections for the foreseeable future.

Consulting focus groups of library users at the University of Portsmouth Library suggested that many library users struggled to relate two-dimensional (2D) floor plans to the building layout and were even confused by three-dimensional (3D) floor plans that were complicated with extraneous information. Many users reported resorting to using shelf end signage to find books and other items and that this method was particularly slow and laborious. Huang, Shu, Yeh, and Zeng (2016) similarly found fixed signage and handouts to be useful only to library users already familiar with the layout of a library and who had above average navigational skills. They argued that library users needed to be shown the location of books on a realistic representation of the library, complete with directions, that they could carry with them and use to locate books or services.

8.2 Previous attempts at internal library navigation

Large institutions, from supermarkets to museums and libraries, have long been interested in finding ways to develop effective mobile navigation tools that will work indoors to help users navigate collections and locate service points (Fitzmaurice, 1993; Xiao, Chen, Li, Chen, & Wu, 2018, p. 2229). GPS-based systems allow accurate positioning and navigation information outdoors but cannot operate indoors. There is no standardised or fully applicable system for indoor positioning and navigation yet (Xiao et al., 2018, p. 2229). Scattering and blocking of signals by shelving, walls and other surfaces, differences in mobile phone chipsets, and a higher required level of accuracy as people navigate much more tightly packed spaces make indoor navigation a significantly harder problem to solve (Ma, Poslad, Bigham, Zhang, & Men, 2017; Pearson,

Technology, Change and the Academic Library. DOI: https://doi.org/10.1016/B978-0-12-822807-4.00008-7

Robinson, & Jones, 2017; Xiao et al., 2018, p. 2230). Even after Ma et al. (2017) corrected for variations in mobile phone chipsets, their results were still only correct to 0.87 m, an error large enough potentially to create confusion when trying to identify on which shelving unit an item is shelved. Many systems rely on wi-fi sensor or Bluetooth beacon nets but with so much shelving and other surfaces, libraries require many signal emitting beacons to operate such systems effectively, and so, despite the low unit cost of individual devices, the infrastructure and maintenance costs of such systems remain considerable (Hashish et al., 2017; Pearson et al., 2017, p. 24). These technologies show promise but are not yet ready for use.

In an attempt to provide start to finish directions that did not rely on indoor positioning, Pearson et al. (2017) proposed that users searching the library catalogue or other resource discovery platform for printed resources first scan the barcode of a randomly selected book on a nearby shelf with their smartphone. This allowed the system to plot its presumed location based on the classmark of the book just scanned. The system would then mathematically plot the shortest available route from the location where this book should be shelved to the expected location on the shelves of the book being sought, with overlaid directions onto a digital floor plan and displayed on the user's mobile phone (Pearson et al., 2017, p. 26). This system overcame many of the problems associated with other internal navigation systems, but it relied on the book the user has scanned to identify their starting location being correctly shelved to locate their starting position in the library accurately and give meaningful directions. It also relied on users being able to navigate using a 2D plan view map that, it has already been established, many users find it difficult to use.

8.3 Framing the problem

The University of Portsmouth Library poses complex problems for stock location:

- An unusual building layout with three floors, divided into eight separate areas
- Books arranged to maximise study space rather than in an intuitive sequence
- 24/7 opening during term-time and the Easter vacation, during which time the library is staffed only half the time that it is open
- Widening participation has meant that support is provided for an increasing number of users with autism and ethnic minority groups, both groups being sometimes more reluctant than others to ask for help (National Autistic Society, 2017; National Union of Students, 2011; Stevenson, 2012, p. 10; Wong & Chiu, 2019)
- Concern over the ongoing maintenance costs of maintaining an accurate representation of classmark locations at any useful level of detail, whilst books were frequently being moved to different shelves and even different floors following a recent refurbishment, changes in teaching interests, and weeding to accommodate more study space
- Any solution had to be an instantly responsive client-side web script, as many users visit the library infrequently and would not necessarily be interested in downloading a library app (Mansouri & Soleymani Asl, 2019, p. 58; Pope, 2018, p. 23)

8.4   Innovation and solution

8.4.1   Producing the first 3D floor plans

The map librarian first generated a 3D image of existing 2D floor plans using Google SketchUp. The 3D model was clearly better at helping users orient themselves because it offered an isometric view of spaces, rendering walls, columns and other structural features as they appeared when stood on the floor. However, the bitmap files produced by SketchUp had certain limitations:

- They were bitmapped images that could not easily be scaled to different sizes of screen or poster without loss of resolution, impacting in particular on the readability of text (a particular problem for images such as these with a high level of detail).
- Any substantive changes would require an entire floor plan to be redrawn within SketchUp.
- Custom versions of floor plans to highlight specific features or directions would also require the floor(s) in question to be redrawn.

8.4.2   Moving to a sustainable format

The web developer saw the potential in having 3D floor plans and sought a more practicable and sustainable implementation. Using Adobe Illustrator, he produced 3D copies of the existing images, saved as vector image files. These vector-based master files could be resized with no loss of resolution, supported more detail and surface textures, such as glass, metal and foliage, that resulted in a more realistic rendering, and most importantly were easy to maintain. Reuse of drawn elements saved time producing these maps. For example, a single shelving unit was drawn and then copied around 150 times, Illustrator making it simple to subsequently adjust size, lighting and light direction for each block.

To allow different features to be emphasised by hiding, adding or moving layers or changing the perspective of the floor view, each element (walls, bookshelves, furniture, etc.) was included as a separate layer in the file. This also meant that when an object was replaced or moved, the change could be easily reflected by simply modifying the appropriate layer. The use of multiple independent layers also allowed different versions of the same floor plan to be produced showing only selected layers to produce simple maps for other purposes, including wall-mounted printed maps (Fig. 8.1).

Distorting the perspective of all three individual floor plans even allowed a composite diagram of all three floors to be produced in a single image. This was useful for representing facilities available on more than one floor, such as toilets (Fig. 8.2).

Vector files are not generally viewable within web pages, and so the completed vector images were mechanically converted into JPEG and PNG bitmapped formats for use on the web.

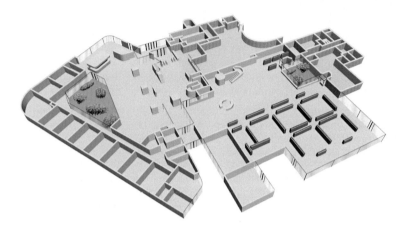

Figure 8.1 Ground floor 3D library plan without labels.

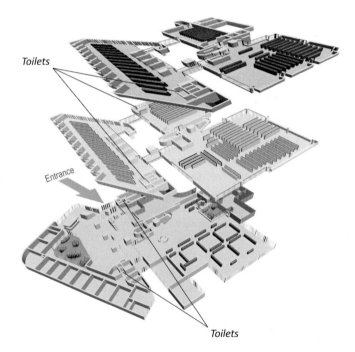

Figure 8.2 Image showing toilet locations across all three floors.

8.4.3   *Developing a book location system*

Once a sustainable set of floor plans in which each individual shelving unit could be uniquely identified and modified was produced, the web developer realised that these could be used as the basis for a system to help users locate books.

The Library website is built on a content management system developed in-house using PHP and a MySQL database, which allowed a custom application to be built that would return an image of the relevant floor section, with the shelving unit holding the classmark of the book highlighted in response to a user entering the classmark of a book. The system assigns a classmark number range to each shelving unit and then displays the requested shelves as a watermark overlaid on top of the original floor plan. This gives the impression that the shelving block where the requested book should be shelved has been highlighted in a contrasting colour.

The system was built by first rendering each shelving unit layer as a separate file. Transparent copies of each floor were then made, each with a different shelving unit highlighted in a contrasting colour to shelving units on the floor plan and a unique identifier. This method ensured precise alignment of the overlays with the underlying floor plan, such that when one or more transparent overlays are overlaid onto a floor plan to form a composite image in response to a user query, the shelving block(s) containing the desired classmark (range) appear to be highlighted.

A database was created comprising all the shelving unit overlays, together with the classmark ranges found on each shelving unit. When a query is entered, the database is queried and returns which shelving unit(s) correspond to that classmark number. Some simple mathematical operations are performed on the query, with each classmark entered being broken down into a start and finish range corresponding to a range of classmarks related to the level of granularity suggested by the initial query. For example, a query for classmark '600' would return all shelving units holding items with classmarks in the 600s, a more specific search for classmark '620' would return all shelving units holding books in the 620s, whilst a search for '620.157' would return the single shelving unit in the library holding items with classmarks between 620.11 and 620.12.

A subject/classmark table was later added to the database, allowing users to search for classmark ranges by entering a subject name and returning an image with all the shelving units highlighted that corresponded to classmarks associated with that subject in the database. A search for 'Technology' for instance would highlight all the shelving units holding books with classmarks in the 600s.

Recording possible book locations rather than individual books meant that searching for individual books by classmark almost always highlights only a single shelving unit, yet it is also possible for the system to answer broad enquiries by classmark or subject name. This gives users the impression that the system 'knows' where each book and subject is shelved.

With the database and image library in place, the actual PHP code to make the system work was relatively simple, comprising a URL that calls the script with a search parameter: either a classmark or a subject term. The script parses the query in the case of a classmark to find a start and finish range and extracts the relevant location details from the database. The script then selects the relevant base floor plan from the image library, along with the relevant shelving unit watermarks, and creates a composited image. In Fig. 8.3, the arrow and the shelving unit highlighted by the arrow are the 'watermark' composited onto the base floor plan.

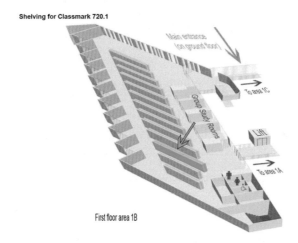

Figure 8.3 Composited floor plan image showing the location of a shelving unit corresponding to a search query.

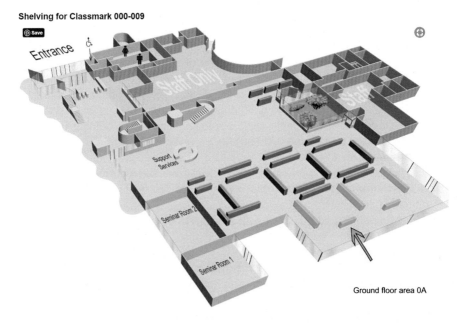

Figure 8.4 Actual mobile phone display on a Galaxy S5 smartphone.

The book finder tool was implemented as a self-contained application within the Library's website.[1] It was designed to be 'responsive', using CSS to dynamically resize the images to fit the screen size of the user's device. This made the images useable even on the comparatively small screens of smartphones, as shown in Fig. 8.4.

As all that is needed to generate a location map is a URL with a parameter,[2] we realised that it would be a relatively simple task for our library management system supplier to include a location map link in library catalogue records, which they have done by adding a 'Locate on shelf' button. Clicking this button summons the composite floor plan with the corresponding shelving block highlighted if the book is a printed resource (and therefore has a classmark associated with it) and the item is currently available. If all copies of an item are on loan, a 'Reserve this item' button is highlighted instead, so that users are not directed to an empty bookshelf.

The addition of a black-bordered arrow (see Figs 8.3 and 8.4) improved accessibility by supporting colour-blind users (Arnheim, 1974, p. 332; Bloomer, 1990, pp. 95–97). The personalised floor plan is available to download at a higher resolution for those with lower visual acuity. Although not shown in the figures above, the library floor and classmark number searched for are also shown beside the floor plan image.

8.5 Uptake and impact

Snap focus groups comprising an opportunity sample of 52 users were surveyed in the mixed learning style zones of the University Library in October 2019, approximately one year after the tool was launched. Within 6 weeks of the start of term, over a third (36%) of first-year users and over half of the second- and third-year users (57% and 58%, respectively) reported having used the tool. Whilst most respondents felt that a GPS style positioning system would be the ideal solution, Fig. 8.5 shows the tool was well received with 71% of all respondents reporting that they intended to use the tool in the future, after they had seen the tool being demonstrated.

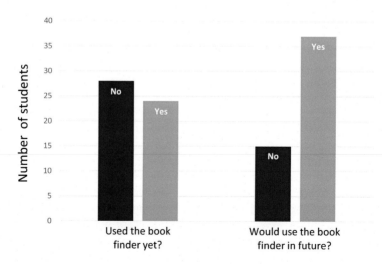

Figure 8.5 Comparative bar chart showing proportions of users who had used the book finder tool before the survey and who intended to use it in the future.

Moreover, 56% of respondents volunteered that they found the tool very clear and easy to use. 35% of respondents reported difficulties orienting the floor plan with respect to landmarks such as stairwells, and working out which shelving block in the library corresponded to the highlighted block on the 3D floor plan. Most of these respondents suggested shelving blocks should be numbered and matching block numbers be included on the floor plans. A few expressed frustration that the floor plans did not highlight a more precise location, such as the side of a shelving block or even the shelving bay on which a classmark was located.

8.6   Critical reflection

The project was successful thanks to lean project management, efficient software development and testing. A major contributing factor to the success of the project was the segmented development process with each stage carried out as a separate, self-contained smaller project, each considered an end in itself. After each stage of the project was completed, we considered if and how the product might be developed further. For the most part, this helped manage staff stress levels and packaged the work into manageable short-term sprints with clear deliverables, each building on the one before to deliver an increasingly sophisticated product.

This incremental approach had its own limitations, however. Without an overarching project brief approved by senior management, the web developer found himself isolated and unable to delegate work to colleagues because they were all facing competing priorities within their own teams. As is frequently the case for staff with unique skillsets in a department undertaking project work, the web developer found the work required difficult to predict in advance and complete in a reasonable timescale. Work that could have been carried out by others could not be scheduled into their duties without severely extending the elapsed time of the project.

As a result of time constraints, the subject keyword search was initially limited to broad subject categories. This disappointed some users, who expected to be able to carry out a Google style search and find the locations of very narrow topics. The Promotions Team attempted to remedy this by showing the subject search used for broad subject searches in advertisements for the service, but the tool only became popular amongst library users some months later after it was integrated with the library catalogue. 'Failed' searches for terms not included in the database are collected and inform refinements to the subject database that are made as time allows.

The tool is restricted to showing a single shelving unit or continuous run of shelving units for each classmark or subject. The system was developed to accommodate the possibility of the same classmark spanning two shelving units or even two floors of the library. With subject keyword database searches for subjects such as Geography and Sports Science that are spread widely across the collection, the subject database offers options to specify the major divisions of each subject, for example Human or Physical Geography, for which there are well-defined classmark/shelving block ranges.

It is also not possible to divide the floor plans more finely than by shelving block because updating the classmark database to reflect accurately classmarks on the shelves would then become a disproportionate burden. In a library such as Portsmouth, classmarks and subjects ebb and flow along the shelves as books in different subject areas are borrowed and returned. Changes happen rarely and predictably at the shelving block level; in contrast, tracking classmarks as they move between bays would require continual updates.

The tool is effective because it generates images instantaneously that display clearly even after being adjusted to fit onto a smartphone screen, but only the section of the floor where a book is shelved is shown in the compiled image. It is possible to change to a general 3D plan of the entire floor and back again but this still confused some users. It is not possible to include block numbers that would be clear and legible when displayed on smaller mobile devices. It has been argued that some users will be unable to recognise the area of the floor from its shape and layout before they can look for the shelves highlighted on the floor plan. This display limitation also makes it difficult to combine this tool with other indoor positioning and navigation technologies.

8.7 Directions for future development

8.7.1 Locating unshelved and misshelved books

Users have expressed frustration that books shown as available in the library catalogue are not always on the shelf where they are expected. Adding additional overlays and locations would allow areas of the library other than shelves to be identified as more possible locations for books. A library-wide sensor network capable of detecting RFID or other tags in books could allow copies of a book to be accurately located wherever they are in the library, including on bookshelves, shelving trolleys, in staff areas or in use in a study space, and from its location infer how likely that copy is to be currently available.

8.7.2 Using information kiosks to give directional information

Touchscreen information kiosks are a popular way of accessing the library catalogue. If the fixed location of a particular information kiosk was added to the database, it might be possible to display the mathematically shortest path from the kiosk to a shelving unit, at least in the same library area, using a method similar to that described by Pearson et al. (2017). This could even be sent to the requesting user's smartphone via Bluetooth so they could carry the directions with them.

Once an accurate, standardised indoor positioning has been developed, an augmented reality interface could be added, such that the smartphone camera view of the library walkways appears overlaid with wayfinding arrows showing the direction of the mathematically calculated shortest route to the destination shelf stack. The addition of a 'path obstructed' user feedback button and programmed, time-limited planned route closures for building work would trigger the system to suggest alternative routes.

Conclusion

Indoor positioning and navigation systems are being developed that show great promise for helping library users find particular books and subjects, but a standardised method of sufficient accuracy has yet to be developed. We have presented a practical web-based method of offering instantaneous visual guides to the location of library books that can be easily incorporated into a library resource discovery system by means of custom URLs. A small survey confirmed that the majority of users like the book finding tool and that most find it intuitive and useful, although it appeared that some very basic familiarity with the use of floor plans or maps was still required to use the tool effectively.

Endnotes

1. University of Portsmouth Library website, 'Where can I find my subject': https://library.port.ac.uk/classmark/
2. University of Portsmouth Library website, 'Shelving for classmark 123': https://library.port.ac.uk/classmark/classfind.php?cm = 123

References

Arnheim, R. (1974). *Art and visual perception: A psychology of the creative eye* (Revised ed.). Berkeley, CA: University of California Press.

Bloomer, C. M. (1990). *Principles of visual perception* (2nd ed.). London: Herbert Press.

Bowman, S. A. (2013). BYOD! We don't think so. In M. Ally, & G. Needham (Eds.), *M-libraries 4: From margin to mainstream — mobile technologies transforming lives and libraries* (pp. 47–52). London: Facet Publishing.

Fitzmaurice, G. W. (1993). Situated information spaces and spatially aware palmtop computers. *Communications of the ACM, 36*(7), 39–49. Available from https://dl.acm.org/citation.cfm?doid = 159544.159566.

Hashish, I.A., Motta, G., Meazza, M., Bu, G., Liu, K., Duico, L., & Longo, A. (2017). *NavApp: An indoor navigation application: A smartphone application for libraries*. Paper presented at the 14th Workshop on Positioning, Navigation and Communications (WPNC), Bremen. https://doi.org/10.1109/WPNC.2017.8250047.

Huang, T.-C., Shu, Y., Yeh, T.-C., & Zeng, P.-Y. (2016). Get lost in the library? *The Electronic Library, 34*(1), 99–115. Available from https://doi.org/10.1108/EL-08-2014-0148.

Ma, Z., Poslad, S., Bigham, J., Zhang, X., & Men, I. (2017). *A BLE RSSI ranking based indoor positioning system for generic smartphones*. Paper presented at the 2017 Wireless Telecommunications Symposium (WTS), Chicago. https://doi.org/10.1109/WTS.2017.7943542.

Mansouri, A., & Soleymani Asl, N. (2019). Assessing mobile application components in providing library services. *The Electronic Library*, *37*(1), 49−66. Available from https://doi.org/10.1108/EL-10-2018-0204.

National Autistic Society. (2017). *Communicating*. Retrieved from: https://www.autism.org.uk/about/communication/communicating.aspx.

National Union of Students. (2011). *Race for equality: A report on the experiences of black students in further and higher education*. London: National Union of Students. Retrieved from: https://www.nus.org.uk/PageFiles/12238/NUS_Race_for_Equality_web.pdf.

Pearson, J., Robinson, S., & Jones, M. (2017). BookMark: Appropriating existing infrastructure to facilitate scalable indoor navigation. *International Journal of Human-Computer Studies*, *103*, 22−34. Available from https://doi.org/10.1016/j.ijhcs.2017.02.001.

Pope, H. (2018). Virtual and augmented reality in libraries. *Library Technology Reports*, *54*(6), 1−25.

Stevenson, J. (2012). *Black and minority ethnic student degree retention and attainment*. York: Higher Education Academy. Retrieved from: https://www.heacademy.ac.uk/system/files/bme_summit_final_report.pdf.

Wilders, C. (2017). Predicting the role of library bookshelves in 2025. *Journal of Academic Librarianship*, *43*(5), 384−391. Available from https://doi.org/10.1016/j.acalib.2017.06.019.

Wong, B., & Chiu, Y.-L. T. (2019). Swallow your pride and fear': The educational strategies of high-achieving non-traditional university students. *British Journal of Sociology of Education*, *40*(7), 868−882. Available from https://doi.org/10.1080/01425692.2019.1604209.

Xiao, A., Chen, R., Li, D., Chen, Y., & Wu, D. (2018). An indoor positioning system based on static objects in large indoor scenes by using smartphone cameras. *Sensors*, *18*(7), 2229−2246. Available from https://doi.org/10.3390/s18072229.

The White Rose University Press: an academic-led open access publisher

9

Tracey Clarke
Tracey Clarke Consulting, Sheffield, United Kingdom

9.1 Background

White Rose University Press was formed in 2015–16 by the universities of Leeds, Sheffield and York representing the latest initiative in a long-standing regional collaboration dating back to 1997. Collaboration at institutional level has subsequently evolved resulting in numerous shared ventures including discipline-specific doctoral partnerships, a studentship network, a collaboration fund and most recently the White Rose Office in Brussels. Alongside this shared institutional endeavour, the library collaboration has also flourished.

The White Rose Libraries (WRL) cemented their collaboration after several years of informal joint working, when in July 2004 the shared institutional repository — White Rose Research Online — was established in response to the 2002 Jisc FAIR programme and the SHERPA strand in particular. This is still the only such shared repository service in the United Kingdom (Petherbridge, 2018) and was in part a strategic response to the prevalent dysfunctional academic publishing paradigm, with WRL seeking to act as an agent of a broader network of what became 'green' open access repositories. The aim at that time was to deliver high-quality research outputs outside of paywalls to a broader audience much faster than the processes of traditional publishers would support. This was followed in 2007 by another shared repository — White Rose eTheses Online (WREO) — again a response to a national concern. Both shared repositories were built on the EPrints platform and subsequently integrated into research systems at all three universities. In this way, the WRL established a shared technology framework that was flexible enough to allow site level integration whilst maintaining the cost efficiencies of the shared central service.

It seems entirely logical therefore that 11 years later the same consortium sought to revisit its original aims with the creation of an open access press operated on a shared service model. This open access press initiative, although originally nurtured by the relevant libraries, has transitioned to become an academic-led enterprise with a robust quality model and transparent governance alongside innovative production and cost models.

Technology, Change and the Academic Library. DOI: https://doi.org/10.1016/B978-0-12-822807-4.00009-9

9.2   Why an open access press?

Although White Rose's original aim when creating its shared repository infrastructure — to influence the publishing paradigm — could be considered understated, there is little doubt that this latest open access press publishing venture is overtly looking to offer an alternative route to that of traditional publishing houses and to disrupt the existing market. The same can, of course, be said of the other recent institutional incursions into the open access publishing space, most notably UCL Press, Helsinki University Press (HUP), the LSE Press, MAP (Universities of Cologne and Munich), the University of California Press and many others.

The possibility of a press offered other benefits aside from delivering high-quality research to a broader audience with a free dissemination model. It was an opportunity to address rights management and licensing, offering a model whereby researchers are not compelled to sign away rights to their works. At a strategic level, it was also an opportunity to work with researchers in regaining control of some key outputs eligible for the REF and to capitalise on conversations about open access between researchers and librarians. Many academics, although sometimes expressing frustration about fluctuating open access policy and its attendant bureaucracy, had come to be ardent supporters of its high-level aims. The press provided the opportunity to reach beyond those supporters to researchers across the discipline spectrum and to engage in a meaningful and practical way. It was also felt, given the high level of trust that already existed within the WRL consortium and the pooling of existing abilities that had already been demonstrated, that the libraries did possess many of the key skills needed to establish a press and the governance framework needed for its operation.

9.3   Planning

Initially, the new press was planned and negotiated by staff within WRL having successfully floated the idea to key influencers and senior staff at the three universities. At this point, it is likely that the trust built up within their respective institutions made it easier to proceed at risk with the project. The WRL consortium was sufficiently mature to have recruited to a White Rose Executive Manager role just before the launch of the press planning process. It was on the second day in the new role that 'project press' was started. With hindsight, this may have represented a considerable ask of the new manager, but the challenge was accepted with aplomb and provided the opportunity for the new recruit to make a mark within the consortium. In fact, recruiting a high-quality, skilled and motivated staff resource not only proved to be vital to the success of the planning process but also to the transition from theoretical to operational. Appointment to a press-related Administrative Officer role followed shortly and a new White Rose Executive Manager was appointed almost directly before the press switched to operation in 2016.

The planning was not confined to technology solutions as this was to be an academic-led endeavour − any platform would need to fit in with the quality model, governance and legal framework. It was important to signal quality and a rigorous peer review model at an early stage to avoid any taint of vanity publishing (Speicher, 2018). This was done by committing to a two-tier governance structure with senior university staff and high profile researchers being recruited to the editorial board. This was chaired at Vice President level and every effort was made to ensure coverage of the full discipline spectrum to demonstrate the scope of the press and to increase engagement at all three universities. Alongside this, a management board was created which comprised senior library staff from each university, academic representation at Pro Vice Chancellor level plus press staff. This second board was chaired at University Librarian/Director level with this incumbent also sitting on the editorial board to establish a solid communication channel between the two boards. It was this detailed governance plus regular planning meetings within the WRL consortium at Director and Associate Director level that paved the way for key technology and business decisions.

9.4 Technology and platforms

In order to implement an open access press, WRL undertook a review of the technologies available to support key press functionality. In the past, the possibility of running a publishing platform on the existing EPrints infrastructure was considered but swiftly dismissed given the shared ambitions around production values, quality and scope of the content. In previous years, the consortium had only considered hosting journals, something that has been successfully done elsewhere utilising EPrints, but as the scale of the new project expanded to include monographs an alternative solution was sought. It was also vital that any technology solution selected should support researchers and enable an academic-led enterprise to emerge. In short, any solution had to provide editorial and peer review functionality supporting the back of house publishing processes in addition to an attractive 'shop front' that supported discoverability, dissemination, appropriate metadata standards, indexing and print on demand transactions.

There is no blueprint for setting up an open access press and technology and platform choices will be driven by attitudes to risk, appetite for change, and the inherent strength of any collaboration including levels of trust between stakeholders plus the prevailing resource envelope. The White Rose Libraries actively considered three alternative technology solutions as part of an options appraisal of functional press models:

- The first model centred on an in house solution based exclusively on open source systems for both monographs and journals, the latter supported by the OJS (Open Journal Systems) software created originally by the Public Knowledge Project and implemented by many UK and international universities.

- The second option centred on the partner press model necessitating a negotiated agreement with a platform provider to provide back-office publishing systems and to host and disseminate published content. In the case of White Rose, the partner press explored was Ubiquity Press based in London and subsequently California.
- Finally, White Rose considered a full university press model such as that in place at University College London (Ayris & Speicher, 2015) and the University of Liverpool. This latter model would involve investing in end-to-end infrastructure with all the associated costs and processes.

The contract with Ubiquity Press was signed in late November 2015 with the decision largely based on a pragmatic mixture of limiting risk as far as the initial layout was concerned, a realistic view of the resources likely to be made available to subsidise staff costs and the potential impetus delivered to the project by using preexisting infrastructure already in use by other small presses within the Ubiquity Partner Network. Looking at the project holistically this halfway house approach seemed affordable. White Rose felt it had the necessary relationship management and negotiating skills in house to succeed with a partner press, and it left press staff more time to devote to setting up the governance and quality frameworks plus the marketing and communications strategies necessary to supplement any of the three functional models considered.

9.5 Challenges

Publishing can be a complicated endeavour and its challenges are routinely underestimated. Some of those challenges do relate to technology and the publishing platform or platforms selected. However, in the case of the White Rose University Press, the main challenges related to embedding the chosen technology solution into the press as a whole. Any open access press must have certain essential elements ranging from staffing, editorial, legal and governance strands to advocacy, support for authors, commissioning, marketing, brand development and business planning. Technology is consequently only part of the overall enterprise albeit a fundamental and enabling layer.

Once the partner press model was selected as the overarching technology solution, significant emphasis shifted to building a constructive relationship with Ubiquity Press. Contractual safeguards and levers were, of course, in place, but it became clear early on that innovations were needed to meet the press's ambitions and to solve operational problems. In particular, existing open access journals moving to the press had been accustomed to certain production values and editorial functionality and the latter was partially absent from the original offer. In fact, this service was available from the platform partner but had not been specified in exact detail during the original contract negotiations. This highlights the need to fully establish shared definitions of the specialist terms used and not rely on 'common usage' understandings during the setup phase. Fortunately, press staff, having built a robust but constructive working relationship with the partner, were able to introduce relevant functionality and more rigorous methods, resulting in more than satisfied editorial boards and an improved offer all round.

Perhaps surprisingly, the other main challenge came in the form of print on demand (PoD). Feedback from researchers in many disciplines indicated that delivering print versions to the market would be important and this has subsequently proved to be the case with significant download figures for several monographs. The initial PoD mechanism was felt to be inappropriate as it linked through to a large internet vendor based on a commercial/wholesaler retail model. This resulted not only in a commercial association that was unpalatable in an open access context but also in fluctuating market prices being applied to PoD transactions. The press was committed to enabling high impact and maximum access to content. Therefore a new PoD solution was negotiated and implemented which more accurately reflected the free dissemination model. This subsequently exerted maximum control on how the print was offered for purchase.

9.6   What would have been done differently?

It is fair to say that not all elements of the press project went as smoothly as others. Advocacy within the three collaborating universities was handled differently at each site mirroring the different organisation structures in place at the three libraries. On reflection, it would have been more productive to have started advocacy right at the beginning of the press project and to have approached it slightly more consistently. This would have saved time later on in the planning process, as all three sets of senior management would have been on the same page at the same time.

From a change management perspective, it would also have served the press better to have engaged directly with library colleagues not working in the open access area far sooner in the project. With hindsight, certain assumptions were made about the level of awareness across the three separate library organisations, with regard to open access and its strategic goals. In fact, subsequent deeper engagement with a broader, more diverse library staff group by core press staff has done much to counter this shortfall raising the press profile but also surfacing and addressing many of the nuances and complexities inherent to open access policy. The press and the three universities have benefitted from the leadership shown by press staff as they grow in experience and establish their own profiles alongside that of the press.

Reflecting more closely on the technology choices that could have been made had the libraries been more experienced with open access publishing platforms, they may well have elected to differentiate between monograph and journal publishing streams by selecting a hybrid solution of two systems. There is no doubt that the Ubiquity Press solution for monographs has been successful in many regards. It may however have been prudent to spread the business across another platform for journals in addition to the existing partner choice. This would have permitted more control over APC rates and mitigated the risk of relying on one partner and their capacity to deliver as their business grows. Additionally, a more flexible brand framework would have been possible allowing different strands for undergraduate content and textbooks, possibly also utilising open source journal software for text-book production. On the other hand, this dual approach would have attracted extra relationship management overheads and hitherto there is no evidence of the press's existing journals being dissatisfied with the current commercial arrangement.

9.7 Next steps

As the press grows and continues to build its reputation and prestige it can start to scale up in terms of published outputs, infrastructure and legal standing. It has demonstrated success not just in terms of the number of monographs published[1] and journals hosted,[2] but also with regard to quality, reach and impact.

Star Carr Volumes 1 and 2 from York, about the very significant Mesolithic site at Star Carr, were critically very well received with distinctive high-quality production values. The press was also able to be flexible around the publication timeline for these volumes, dovetailing with related journal articles and requests from the relevant research project funder. Since April 2018 these two monographs have been downloaded more than ten thousand times.

With regard to impact within the curriculum, press outputs have also been embedded in university teaching, the most notable examples of this being *320 Rue St Jacques: The Diary of Madeleine Blaess* at Sheffield and the *Undergraduate Journal of Politics and International Relations (UJPIR)* at Leeds.

The press also hosts four journals on subjects as diverse as orthoptics and African cultural heritage as well as the *Journal of the European Second Language Association (JESLA)*.

Looking forward, in addition to the three monographs already published there are eight more commissioned and currently in the publication progress. With increased interest, it remains to be seen, given the extent of its ambitions, if the press opts to retain its original functional model or decides that in scaling up other technological solutions can be incorporated into a more flexible framework. In the meantime, it is taking steps to maximise discoverability and to secure its content for the future with monographs being deposited with the JSTOR platform. The press is also looking at dark archive and preservation strategies.

9.8 Conclusions

Even though the White Rose University Press goes from strength to strength, expanding its monograph and journal portfolio and starting to attract repeat business, it is not remotely realistic to imagine that it will change the prevalent publishing paradigm by itself. It is still a small press albeit one with a rigorous quality model and high production values. It is, however, encouraging that other open access presses were established in advance of the White Rose endeavour and yet more have launched subsequently.

Furthermore, many universities are exploring the concepts involved in an academic press and having the conversations with their researchers about what they want from publishing. These conversations are often happening with library input and making use of many of the skills core to librarianship. It is in this space where technology offers only part of the solution, with libraries being well placed to listen to stakeholders and to mine a wealth of experience relating to service development and delivery. Libraries can deploy not only strategic and operational planning competences but also the softer skills necessary to define and run an enterprise where the requirements of the academy should be paramount.

It is the emergence of these university open access presses set in the context of open access policy developments such as Plan S, more sophisticated, granular and permissive licensing initiatives plus widespread disenchantment within academia at all levels about the ruinously expensive and often slow commercial publishing environment, that is truly significant. Publishing is a complex business, but it is made more complex by the need for traditional houses to service shareholders by constantly increasing revenue and profits. Open access presses are not encumbered in the same way and their mission is to directly support the academy by disseminating research outputs as broadly as possible. Establishing an open access press is attainable with appropriate motivation, commitment, resources, leadership and planning. Could this be the start of the academy taking back control of scholarly publishing to deliver the societal impact and reach agenda, which hitherto has been downplayed in deference to profits?

Endnotes

1. White Rose University Press Publications: Monographs. Corbière (2018), Michallat (2018), and Milner, Conneller & Taylor (2018a,b).
2. White Rose University Press Publications: Journals
   British and Irish Orthoptic Journal: https://www.bioj-online.com.
   Journal of African Cultural Heritage Studies: https://www.jachs.org.
   Journal of the European Second Language Association (JESLA): https://www.euroslajournal.org.
   Undergraduate Journal of Politics and International Relations (UJPIR): https://www.ujpir-journal.com.

References

Ayris, P., & Speicher, L. (2015). UCL Press: The UK's 'first fully open access' university press. *Insights, 28*(3), 44−50. Available from https://doi.org/10.1629/uksg.257.

Corbière, T. (2018). *Oysters, nightingales and cooking pots: Selected poetry and prose in translation.* York: White Rose University Press. Available from https://doi.org/ 10.22599/Corbiere.

Michallat, W. (2018). *320 rue St Jacques: The diary of Madeleine Blaess.* York: White Rose University Press. Available from https://doi.org/10.22599/Blaess.

Milner, N., Conneller, C., & Taylor, B. (Eds.), (2018a). *Starr Carr volume 1: A persistent place in a changing world.* York: White Rose University Press. Available from https://doi.org/10.22599/book1.

Milner, N., Conneller, C., & Taylor, B. (Eds.), (2018b). *Starr Carr volume 2: Studies in technology, subsistence and environment.* York: White Rose University Press. Available from https://doi.org/10.22599/book2.

Petherbridge, K. (2018). *White Rose University Press: Open access setting scholarship free.* Paper presented at the RLUK Conference 2018, London, UK. Retrieved from: <https://www.youtube.com/watch?v = bqwabTXq5zg>.

Speicher, L. (2018). *A new approach to open access monograph publishing.* Retrieved from: <http://choice360.org/blog/university-press-forum-a-new-approach-to-open-access-monograph-publishing>.

Mutual benefit from library collaboration with computational biologists: the cropPAL project at the University of Western Australia

10

Kylie Black
University Library, University of Western Australia, Perth, WA, Australia

10.1 Introduction

The University of Western Australia (UWA) Library partnered with researchers in the Australian Research Council's Centre of Excellence in Plant Energy Biology in 2016−17 to produce cropPAL2,[1] a database providing the subcellular locations for proteins in crops significant for food production. The project was funded by the Australian National Data Service (now the Australian Research Data Commons, ARDC) as part of its High Value Collections program, with the team consisting of computational biologists, software engineers and a librarian.

The original cropPAL1 database was developed to index and link the rapidly growing collection of data in plant genomics and breeding methodologies that were difficult to discover and therefore underutilised. The database provides open access to protein subcellular locations and interaction data for wheat, barley, rice and maize. cropPAL indexes data generated over 10 years by over 300 institutions as reported in the published literature, and linked to global plant catalogues such as EnsemblPlants.[2]

Improving the discoverability of this data can have a profound impact as it has the potential to be used in innovative crop development to increase global food production. In cropPAL1, the project team had problems sourcing the literature containing the protein interactions and subcellular locations to be indexed in the database. This is a notoriously difficult type of information to find as it is rarely mentioned in the title or abstract, and the relevant data are typically found in the materials and methods sections of reports and articles. The Library was not involved in this project and a great deal of staff time and energy was spent sifting through large numbers of search results. For wheat, only 10% of the articles retrieved were found to contain relevant data.

The cropPAL2 project ran from January 2016 to June 2017 and it added protein data for the crops of banana, canola, grapevine, potato, sorghum (used to feed cattle), soybean and tomato to the existing cropPAL1 database. The ARDC funded the

Technology, Change and the Academic Library. DOI: https://doi.org/10.1016/B978-0-12-822807-4.00010-5

project and, as with many of their projects, encouraged collaboration between the scientists and the Library. In this case, the partnership was especially logical given the history of problems with searching, and that the relevant subject library was physically located next to the Centre for Plant Energy Biology.

This was the first time that the UWA Library has been a formal partner in a research project, and with the Library's values of collaboration, efficiency, responsiveness and innovation (University of Western Australia, 2014, p. 2), it was a good fit. Involvement in cropPAL2 provided an opportunity for librarians to contribute directly to a research project that has economic, social, health, environmental and academic impact. It also allowed the Library to assist the University in meeting a number of objectives in its strategic plan relating to internationally renowned research, including undertaking 'research across all our disciplines, focused on issues of relevance to our communities and industries, while generating understanding and solutions of global value' and building 'problem-oriented multidisciplinary teams' (University of Western Australia, 2013, p. 7).

Traditionally, for a project gathering a large amount of literature such as this, the Library involvement might have been limited to a couple of appointments with researchers to develop the search strategy, then possibly involvement with managing data and minting a DOI at the end of the project. With the Library as a partner in the project, there was involvement throughout the entire cycle to mutual benefit, as shown in Fig. 10.1.

The Library contributed to cropPAL2 through librarian expertise in searching and retrieving scholarly literature, formulating and executing complex search strategies, bibliographic database tools, metadata and research data management. These skills were critical to the success of the project in terms of increasing the efficiency

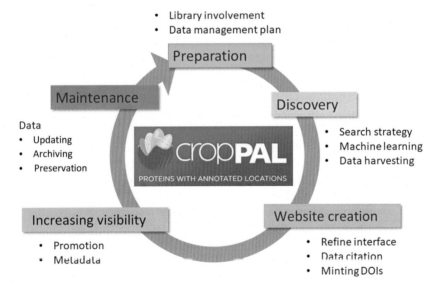

Figure 10.1 Library involvement in cropPAL2.

of the cropPAL2 data collation process and ensuring that the dataset was described, stored, and made available in an open access format. There is now an opportunity to further promote these skills and expertise to other parts of the UWA research community.

Additionally, the project provided a valuable and rare opportunity for a librarian to be fully embedded within a research team and within the research process. This resulted in an increased confidence in the librarian to be able to directly and positively contribute to the research process.

Two sections of the UWA Library were involved: Library Engagement; and Research Publication and Data Services. Both were involved throughout the 18 months of the cropPAL2 project and Library Engagement has ongoing involvement in updating the database and studying its impact as well as commercialisation.

10.2 Benefits for Library Engagement

The cropPAL2 project demonstrated that for searching, capturing and dealing with permissions around the literature, the collaboration between scientists and librarians was highly beneficial. Being embedded in a research team led to insights into how research projects are conducted and especially the need to balance time spent doing research with other tasks, for example the reporting required, attending project meetings, conferences and writing papers. At a more detailed level, it was very informative to see how computational biologists search for and manage biological information. Insights were also gained in relation to how coauthorship may be used as currency, to acknowledge the contributions of other researchers to the project. It is an especially valuable currency when the researcher has a high H-index and track record of being highly cited.

The project was managed very closely, with a core team of three people (the project leader, ARDC representative and librarian) having weekly meetings to keep each other updated on progress. This maintained momentum and the project timeline was monitored to keep the project running to schedule, with the project completed on time and on budget. Having a very open and collaborative management style enabled the librarian to feel a highly valued member of the team, making contributions and being consulted on issues outside of the traditional library purview. Indeed, a strength of the project team throughout cropPAL was that a good idea is a good idea, no matter who suggests it, and that all members of the team are treated as equals despite coming from diverse backgrounds with different levels of qualifications.

Another strength of the team was acknowledging when experts needed to become involved, and this mindset was a factor in the Library becoming involved in the project. The team's network was able to be drawn upon to assist with the project, in areas ranging from subject expertise in particular crops, through to IT skills in building databases and machine learning. This approach then led to the team participating in the ON Prime program to learn, from experts, how to begin the process of commercialising the software and, during ON Prime, how to make the most of the mentors' expertise and experience with start-up companies in IT.

Forming a close working relationship with the scientists in the Centre of Excellence in Plant Energy Biology has led to assistance in other areas, such as librarians providing data for grant applications and regular consultation with the Library for all projects involving large datasets. In addition, the librarian involved in cropPAL has been invited to speak at a local data bazaar for these researchers, such has been the value of the Library contribution to cropPAL. It is also very useful to have Library champions who are always willing to assist with any queries that the Library needs to ask research staff.

10.3   Benefits for Research Publication and Data Services

In research data management, there were benefits for the Library in working closely with real researchers with real data, addressing issues such as versioning, allocating DOIs, and the differences between new versions and updates. Scientists involved in cropPAL represented the senior user group for a Library data repository project reviewing dataset maintenance and advising in a repository platform migration project aimed at improving the hosting of research datasets.

The scientists in the Centre of Excellence in Plant Energy Biology were keen to maximise the discoverability of cropPAL, and with this in mind library staff worked on the metadata and online discoverability, both through Google and subject-specific resources. This increased awareness of research data management within the Centre of Excellence has led to their use of better systems for storing research data and making their dataset readily available through Research Data Australia.

10.4   Benefits for the researchers

Librarian expertise in search strategy and data management was part of the original project proposal and resulted in a number of contributions. In the area of literature searching, the librarian was able to identify functionality within the Europe PubMed Central (Europe PMC) database,[3] which facilitated specific section searching techniques to improve the relevancy of overall search results. The cropPAL database relies on extracting relevant data from the published literature, so efficient searching is critical. Whilst the researchers were already aware of the existence of Europe PMC, librarians were able to develop search strings that bypassed the functional limits of the interface. Library staff analysed how the section search could be developed further by referring to the literature (Kafkas et al., 2015) and then applying these learnings to the problem of finding protein data for the selected crop species. Librarians were also able to leverage off the results of the literature searches that were carried out by researchers in the creation of the original cropPAL1. The scientists had retained records of all the literature that had been manually assessed for cropPAL1, which made it an excellent database to test the effectiveness of search strategies.

The collaboration between researchers and librarians was more complex in relation to research data management, as the cropPAL2 dataset was used as an example in relation to data promotion, storage, versioning and management. This was part of a Library project to decommission the internal system and migrate the data to the UWA Research Repository. In particular, discussion of the issue of data inheritance led to new approaches towards how data are submitted and linked to UWA staff to ensure ongoing data maintenance and accountability. Further discussions around the data archiving and security influenced the organisation of server and back-up server infrastructure within the wider University system. The benefit for the researchers was in understanding more about these issues and being able to apply them to the cropPAL2 dataset as it was being developed. The project's final report best summarises the benefits to the researchers: 'the positive change in attitude towards the value of a tight collaboration between the local institutional library services and lab-based scientists' (Hooper, 2017, p. 3).

Both cropPAL projects involved many hours of manual article evaluation and data extraction, and the team decided that developing in-house software could make managing the process of article evaluation by multiple people much easier. Key characteristics of the software are as follows:

- Not assessing the same article twice
- Easy to find new articles through saved searches in PubMed and Europe PMC
- Simplifies adding new articles to cropPAL
- Provides real-time access by group members to the database
- Useful links to access the information regarding a paper such as full text, the journal and number of citations
- Cut and drop function to save images and notes
- All information is tabulated so easy to import/export data or run queries

Significantly, the cropPAL database was developed in a fraction of the cost for manual curation, representing a 90% saving in time and personnel salaries. The team realised the in-house software was highly innovative and could be applied across many areas of research, and may be worth commercialising.

10.5 ON Prime: first steps to commercialise the cropPAL in-house software

A group of scientists, a software engineer and the Engagement Librarian involved in cropPAL formed a four-person team to commercialise the software, known as DeweyFish. The group successfully applied for the CSIRO's (Commonwealth Scientific and Industrial Research Organisation) ON Prime program for late 2018, to begin the process of market research, making industry contacts and learning more about potential sources of funding and issues around intellectual property. Each team is assigned a mentor who has experience with start-up companies, and throughout ON Prime the participants regularly share their work with the other teams and provide feedback. The role of the librarian was twofold: to bring technical knowledge of literature searching; and to bring the perspective of researchers in fields of study outside of plant biology.

Once accepted, there was no financial cost to participants and the organisers facilitated team work by flying in one of the team members from Adelaide, a three-hour flight each way. However, ON Prime is a significant time commitment, with five face-to-face sessions run over six full days, spanning eight weeks. There is a large time commitment between sessions with further work as a team and a target of 100 interviews with potential customers or users to be conducted within this eight-week period. These data are invaluable for researching customer pain points and market validation. For every team in the DeweyFish cohort, the insights gained from the interviews resulted in a pivot point, where the direction of the project changed significantly.

10.6   Interviews

The backbone of the ON Prime program is each team developing several hypotheses to test by conducting a large number of interviews with a range of potential customers or stakeholders. Team DeweyFish had 15 hypotheses and these evolved as the interviews progressed. Early in the program, the participants learned about interview technique and formulated interview questions. Some of the Team DeweyFish's hypotheses were as follows:

- Advanced search techniques (going beyond keywords in title and abstract) are needed for precise searching.
- Researchers waste time looking at studies more than once.
- Scientists do not like to take notes and collect data out of individual studies into spreadsheets.
- If it was easier to find and parse, scientists would reuse more of the existing data.
- Data are not shared or retained after the research is completed.

As a result of the 66 interviews conducted across a range of fields of research, Team DeweyFish had one pivot, realising the software would have limited applicability in the humanities due to the need to refer to historical documents and different formats of material. The interviews led to other significant insights, such as the following:

- Managing the literature is more difficult than initially finding it.
- Lack of awareness of scholarly databases, with researchers using Google or Google Scholar instead.
- Research data are not widely shared, or data sharing is perceived to be a practice for senior researchers.

From the library perspective, accessing the notes from interviews conducted by nonlibrarians is valuable in determining how researchers find, use and manage information when they have not sought assistance from librarians.

The Team has decided to focus its prototyping efforts in the area of medical research where the technology could greatly assist with systematic reviews, both in the original review and particularly in updating existing reviews. The team members with expertise in software development are working on the functional requirements as a result of the interviews conducted in ON Prime and by closely examining other products that do part or all of what DeweyFish does. Other team members are investigating sources of funding and will be conducting more specific interviews within the chosen market segment.

10.7 Reflections on cropPAL2 and DeweyFish

Library Engagement has been involved throughout the cropPAL2 process, which started with a request for assistance with literature searching but the librarian became a key team member, drawing upon a wide range of skills, knowledge and abilities. The initial request was for librarian expertise for literature searching, in a similar way to librarian involvement in systematic reviews in the health sciences. Later, in Team DeweyFish, a key part of the librarian role was knowledge of information sources and research practices in subjects other than biology and being able to apply this knowledge to the commercialisation of the cropPAL software. The librarian was soon part of the core team working on the cropPAL2 and DeweyFish projects and contributing ideas that are outside a traditional librarian role. For example, with DeweyFish, the librarian was working with the team to decide the best route to commercialisation, including exploring potential sources of funding and which part of the software to develop first. Rather than traditional librarian skills, this drew on the ability to think creatively and analytical and problem-solving skills. It certainly helped both the librarian and the project team begin to appreciate the transferability of librarian skills, as professional information seeking, evaluation, critical thinking, analytical and communication skills — which librarians use every day — were a key part of the role. The librarian became not just a member of the project team, but a trusted source of information in a truly reciprocal partnership. The scientists and software engineers were largely outside their areas of expertise during DeweyFish too, but with assistance from the mentor and participating in the program the team successfully combined different skill sets in a productive experience, resulting in a blueprint for the way forward.

This kind of intensive collaborative partnership, whilst hugely beneficial, does raise questions of resourcing. There is a large time commitment, and depending on which stage the project is at, it could vary from an hour to a large proportion of the working week. For managing workload, it was therefore important to have an idea of the times where a large commitment would be needed. At the end of ON Prime, the participants were asked to provide feedback and whilst all the teams found the program highly beneficial, none had expected the large time commitment, largely for conducting the interviews and for working as a team between face-to-face workshops. As the librarian still works closely with the cropPAL and DeweyFish scientists, this time commitment is ongoing, particularly in supporting grant applications when analytics and metrics are needed to evaluate engagement and impact. As this is the first such collaboration for the UWA Library, the librarian has been encouraged to contribute as much as possible as this partnership is an ongoing priority. However, other such partnerships would need to be considered strategically and balanced against other priorities.

Overall, the librarian's experience in cropPAL2 and DeweyFish has been highly successful and the benefits of this collaboration are regularly in evidence. The most valuable lessons came out of the unexpected depth of involvement in the project. This commenced with professional expertise and technical ability in developing complex search strategies, but the librarian's role soon grew to understand the larger project and use analytical and critical thinking skills to solve much bigger problems. For the librarian, there were multiple lessons in this: the realisation that librarians do have a key role to play in research projects; and that role is significant and can be key to the success of the project. Having the confidence and self-belief that librarians can move from a peripheral role to a central role in research projects can change the way librarians perceive and communicate research and education support services.

10.8   Impact of cropPAL2

This collaborative project has had an impact in two broad areas: metrics, as citations and altmetrics to the article describing the database and web traffic to the cropPAL2 website; and in mutual benefit to the Library and researchers from working in close collaboration as described earlier.

cropPAL2 is described in an article by Hooper, Castleden, Aryamanesh, Jacoby, and Millar (2016), which users of the cropPAL database are encouraged to cite in their publications. To date, Scopus shows that the article has been cited by researchers affiliated with 15 countries spread evenly around the world, from 41 different institutions (see Fig. 10.2).

The Altmetric score is 21, placing it in the top 25% of all research outputs scored by Altmetric, which includes social media, news items, saves to Mendeley and downloads from the University of Western Australia Research Repository, full text and abstract views in the EBSCO database. The subject areas of the citing publications show that it is having an impact outside of its areas of Biochemistry, genetics and molecular biology and Agricultural and biological sciences (the subjects assigned to *Plant and Cell Physiology*), with citations appearing in journals with subject categories of Multidisciplinary, Engineering and Medicine.

From the Library perspective, the cropPAL collaboration is also showing some impact within libraries. As a result of a paper at the International Association of University Libraries (IATUL) conference in 2019 (Black, Hooper, Castleden, Aryamanesh, & Millar, 2019), there was a fourfold increase in the number of cropPAL website views on the next working day.

Figure 10.2 Global distributions of citations to Hooper et al (2016). Citation data from Scopus.

Throughout the cropPAL2 process and now commercialising the software as part of Team DeweyFish, the Library has played a key role in providing expert knowledge of literature searching and management, and research data management. Being an equal member of the research team also led to benefits in learning how scientists conduct their research and in building relationships with Faculty to mutual and ongoing benefit.

Endnotes

1. cropPAL2: http://crop-pal.org/.
2. EnsemblPlants: https://plants.ensembl.org/index.html.
3. Europe PubMed Central: https://europepmc.org/.

References

Black, K., Hooper, C., Castleden, I., Aryamanesh, N., & Millar, H. (2019). *Going to market with DeweyFish: The journey from partnership to commercialisation. Shifting sands and rising tides: Leading libraries through innovation; The 40th International Association of University Libraries Conference, Perth, Western Australia.* West Lafayette, IN: Purdue University Press. Available from https://docs.lib.purdue.edu/iatul/2019/value/4/.

Hooper, C.M. (2017). *Final report: High Value Collections program.* The University of Western Australia ARC Centre of Excellence in Plant Energy Biology: The compendium of cropPAL2 [unpublished].

Hooper, C. M., Castleden, I. R., Aryamanesh, N., Jacoby, R. P., & Millar, A. H. (2016). Finding the subcellular location of barley, wheat, rice and maize proteins: The compendium of crop proteins with annotated locations (cropPAL). *Plant and Cell Physiology,* *57*(1), e9. Available from https://doi.org/10.1093/pcp/pcv170.

Kafkas, S., Pi, X., Marinos, N., Talo, F., Morrison, A., & McEntyre, J. R. (2015). Section level search functionality in Europe PMC. *Journal of Biomedical Semantics*, *6*(7). Available from https://doi.org/10.1186/s13326-015-0003-7.

University of Western Australia. (2014). *University Library strategic directions*. Perth, WA: University of Western Australia. Available from http://www.library.uwa.edu.au/__data/assets/pdf_file/0003/2778114/University-Library-Strategic-Directions-2015-2020.pdf.

University of Western Australia. (2013). *UWA 2020 vision: Strategic plan 2014-2020*. Perth, WA: University of Western Australia. Available from http://www.web.uwa.edu.au/__data/assets/pdf_file/0010/2538343/114085-VICCHA-StrategicPlan-v3.pdf.

Brave new world?: Cardiff Metropolitan University Library Service's implementation of a next-generation library management system

Mark Hughes
Library Services, Cardiff Metropolitan University, Cardiff, Wales, United Kingdom

11.1 Introduction

In 2013, the Wales Higher Education Libraries Forum (WHELF) took the decision to procure and implement a shared 'next-generation' library management system (LMS) across its member organisations. That project was the largest scale implementation of its kind in the United Kingdom to date, covering in scope 11 organisations, 88 library sites, over 600 library staff, over 10 million bibliographic records, and migration from 6 different legacy library management systems. The implementation completed with the final site going live on 25 August 2016, and the collaboration has continued to build on that since.

Much has already been written[1] and a number of conference papers presented on the overall project so the intent of this case study is not to repeat that work. Instead, this study will focus on the project from the perspective of the Library Service at Cardiff Metropolitan University (Cardiff Met). The case study will cover Cardiff Met's role and input during the project, the impact on services provided, the impact on library staff, and finally some reflections as to where the project may lead in the future.

11.2 Cardiff Metropolitan University shared LMS implementation

For background context, Cardiff Metropolitan is a dual campus teaching-focused university with around 10,000 FTE students and 700 staff. At the time of writing in 2019, the library service has a staffing establishment of 31 posts, an annual resources budget of a little over £1.2 million, and provides access to around 170,000 printed volumes, around the same number of e-books, and over 60,000 serial titles.

In 2013, Cardiff Met Library Service was in a position similar to that of a number of other Welsh university libraries in terms of its technology. A legacy library

Technology, Change and the Academic Library. DOI: https://doi.org/10.1016/B978-0-12-822807-4.00011-7

management system (in Cardiff Met's case, Talis Alto with Serials Solutions Summon used as the discovery product) had been in place for an extended period, and a review of the provision was due within 2 years. There was an ambition to develop and improve services, with a sense that the underpinning library system technology held much of the key to delivering that. The service was also keenly aware that undertaking a library system procurement and implementation independently would be a complex and resource intensive activity, which would be a challenge to meet under its existing staff and resource base. Given this background, and a recognition of the potential opportunities a shared Welsh approach to implementing a library management system would bring, the library service was an early and enthusiastic sign up to the WHELF shared library system idea.

Once the WHELF decision to move forward collaboratively had been made, and each institution had confirmed its participation, Cardiff Met formed a project team to engage fully with the process from the earliest stage. The initial, small project team took part in all of the initial LMS tender preparatory work. This included a review of Cardiff Met's expectations for what it hoped to achieve with a 'next-generation' LMS, an overview of the scope of existing systems and data which would require migration, and an overall high level timeline of when any new system would need to be in place. All of this information was fed into the wider project through the work on creating a shared WHELF 'functional requirements' specification for the shared system.

That initial engagement and involvement with the wider WHELF group gave an indication of how the 'soft benefits' of working collaboratively on the project would impact on Cardiff Met's staff and service. The exposure of staff to the wider pool of ideas, knowledge, expertise and ambitions of colleagues from across such a range of institutions kick-started a change of mindset and approach that has arguably had as great an impact as the actual implementation of the system itself. This will be discussed in more detail in the later section.

Moving back to the timeline of events, work progressed through issuing a full tender for the shared LMS under European procurement regulations in January 2014, and an extensive period of evaluating responses took the partnership through the bulk of that year. On 18 December 2014, WHELF announced it had selected Ex Libris, with their Alma system and Primo discovery product, as the chosen supplier. Work on an implementation plan started immediately, with a 'tranched' approach of three implementation groups at its core.

From a purely financial point of view, taking part in the shared LMS procurement enabled Cardiff Met to make a substantial saving on the cost of a 'next-generation' LMS in terms of both implementation and the ongoing maintenance costs across the lifetime of the contract. This was a key benefit to the service, as, if procuring independently, it is unlikely that a level of pricing would have been available to make such a change financially viable for the service. More detailed information on the cost benefits across the partnership is available in the Cambridge Econometrics report on the project (Cambridge Econometrics, 2017).

Cardiff Met opted to be a part of tranche 2 for implementation, alongside University of Wales Trinity Saint David. This group would undertake implementation between August 2015 and March 2016. At a Cardiff Met level, a project team led from the Library under the institution's recommended project framework, a modified Prince2 approach, ran the implementation. At WHELF level, the overall project was coordinated by a Programme Manager and a 'WHELF LMS Management Board' on which each institution had representatives. That engagement at the higher WHELF level both maintained the exposure of Cardiff Met to the wider pool of ideas and knowledge, and also, at a more immediate level, enabled knowledge sharing from the earlier tranche institutions that significantly aided those implementing as part of tranches 2 and 3. Cardiff Met was a direct beneficiary of this and arguably experienced a smoother transition to the new system because of it.

Throughout this, from a local management point of view there were very straightforward challenges to deal with in terms of aligning local implementation work and decisions back to the wider project and juggling project timelines. On the leadership side, the shared approach opened up unique opportunities to lift people's gaze out of the day-to-day work and engage with the Wales-wide vision for developing services.

Cardiff Met went 'live' with the Alma and Primo systems in March 2016, on time, on budget, and as per the implementation plan. Engagement with the rest of the institutions continued at the WHELF Management Board level moving through 'post implementation' to 'business-as-usual'. Cardiff Met staff now found themselves as the sharers of information and experience gained through having completed implementation, and continued to pay that forward to the tranche 3 institutions. Ultimately, the final WHELF implementation went live on 25 August 2016, completing the initial cycle of collaboration. Since that date, WHELF partners have continued working together on the shared LMS, covering business-as-usual activities, collaborative service developments, and sharing knowledge of best practice in making the most of the system. As this case study is being written, the initial contract with Ex Libris has passed the mid-point, and the WHELF LMS partners are undertaking a review of what has been achieved, where further collaborative opportunities may lie, and starting to map out its ambitions for the future in terms of the shared LMS.

Having given the timeline of key events, there is now a context in which to place some discussion of the impacts of the project on Cardiff Met. These seem to logically fall into two interlinked but distinct areas: the impact on library services; and the impact on library staff. Both of these are key to understanding what involvement in the WHELF Shared LMS has meant to Cardiff Met, but also how that has spun out from that project and made some deeper changes to the service than a relatively straightforward change of system platform.

11.3   Impact on library services

The implementation of the WHELF Shared LMS has had a twofold effect on library services. Firstly, through the shift to a true 'next-generation platform', and some of the advantages that brings (e.g. cloud based, scalable, improved 'uptime' availability), and, secondly, through the opportunities that being able to build consortia level services offers. Both are areas where the library service has made significant progress since going live.

For Cardiff Met users, perhaps the biggest and most noticeable change that came with the new system was in the discovery interface. There had been a mature and well customised situation of Serials Solutions Summon in place for users to discover and access library collections, but with the new system came Ex Libris Primo (locally branded and presented as 'MetSearch' to users). There was a very different look and feel to the new system from what had gone before, and, in addition, it was initially in quite an 'out of the box' configuration with only very basic customisation in place.

Whilst change was generally well received by users, there were areas of negativity, especially around the perception of increased visibility of articles in search results that users were then struggling to access. A substantial effort has been put into improving MetSearch since 'go live', and, in particular, the launch of a revised User Interface (UI) for Primo made a significant difference. The new UI created a positive impact on the perceived issues, with more full text links visible in search results, a cleaner view for item details, and full text options available in a single click from search results. A welcome additional feature of the new UI has been a hugely improved experience for users on mobile devices, including availability on the corporate student app, which was one of the priorities for the Library Service. Recent comments, in particular, those received via the annual National Student Survey, indicate significantly more positive overall views now, and usage statistics of digital material made discoverable through MetSearch have shown a consistent increase since its introduction.

Underlying much of the functionality of MetSearch is the metadata about Cardiff Met's collections which both enables discovery and aids in managing those resources. Metadata management was an area where expectations had been high due to the availability of the 'Community Zone' data within the Ex Libris Platform and a priority for Cardiff Met was to look at ways to enhance the discoverability and usability of collections, in particular the digital collections, through better collaborative metadata management. That aim has seen slower progress as the ambitions, in particular around digital collections, exposed some issues with the Community Zone functionality and, more widely, issues around data quality, timeliness of updates, and ability to share records between institutions under licence. Nevertheless, there is a longer term positive outcome here, as what WHELF's experience has enabled is a set of constructive conversations around the metadata ecosystem not just with Ex Libris, but also across the wider supply chain. That work and those conversations have aligned with work by Jisc underpinning the National Bibliographic Knowledgebase[2] and have been taken up at national level through that, with Cardiff Met and WHELF staff members remaining heavily involved in driving things forward.

From discoverability of resources, the next collaborative opportunity lay in users obtaining access to material. In this arena, Cardiff Met and WHELF have made advances. The WHELF partners have created a pan Wales 'Resource Sharing

Network'. Underpinned by functionality within the Alma system, this has enabled all the WHELF LMS institutions to manage requests for items not stocked, which would traditionally be interlibrary loans from within the partnership. This route obviates the need for a significant proportion of what would normally be requests to supply to the British Library under traditional UK interlending models. A full year's pilot of this scheme resulted in small but appreciable financial savings across institutions and a reduction overall in supply times for both print and digital material, both factors being very positive for Cardiff Met. This scheme is well used and has been adopted fully as a mainstream service by all the partner institutions. It represents an ongoing benefit.

The next-generation platform of Alma has offered up a collaborative opportunity to Cardiff Met for improving the processes of acquiring material. A lot of work has gone into acquisition workflows to make them as efficient as possible, and there has been ongoing WHELF work looking at API integrations to suppliers to hone those processes even further. This has been a critically impactful piece of work for Cardiff Met as, due to institutional level change, the Library Service has seen a growth in resource spend of approximately 10% set against a reduction in staffing by nearly 13% in the period since the Alma implementation.

The final part of the resources and services puzzle lies with collections. They need to be understood to be managed well, and that has been another area where the move to Alma impacted. The analytics and management information available in the system have enabled a far better, more granular, and more accessible view into what is happening with collections, both physical and digital—for example what is being used, what is not, what has long waiting lists, what has newer editions available, what titles overlap in content packages, etc. This has engendered a more proactive approach and tighter focus to collection management, with clear evidence-based decisions made on content acquired, renewed or discarded.

To sum up, the big impact on services has been around content for Cardiff Met. System-related improvements to discovery, access, and the management of collections made available to users has enabled more material to be acquired, managed and delivered to users more efficiently than had previously been possible. The payback is clear. Since implementation, per student e-journal downloads have increased by over 10%, and e-book accesses have almost doubled. Print material loans have continued to fall, in line with wider sector trends, but the rate has slowed significantly for Cardiff Met.

11.4 Impact on library staff

Work during the project itself required a predictable mix of skills from staff — around project management, around technical issues and around interteam communication. Anyone who has dealt with a system migration would be able to identify with these. The link to the wider WHELF group added the need for people to be behaving in a much more outwardly focused way, for example to be aware of how local configuration decisions might impact on wider collaborative opportunities, who to talk to about such issues and how to negotiate to mutually agreed solutions where there may be conflicting views. So, at a micro level, there were clear opportunities for people to refine their core skillsets through the project.

Stepping back to a more macro view, the impact on Cardiff Met staff from the involvement in the shared LMS project has been interesting, in some ways unforeseen, and certainly of significance to the service. Alongside the changes to workflows and processes that would come with any change of library system, the shared LMS project has opened up, perhaps even mandated, different approaches to work. What lies behind this has been the collaborative nature of the project. From the outset of discussions, library staff have been involved in groups, working with colleagues from other institutions towards commonly identified goals. This peer group working with other institutions has meant all the staff involved have been exposed to a far wider pool of knowledge, expertise, ideas and experiences than would otherwise have been the case in their day-to-day institutional roles.

As the WHELF project progressed, these groups became formal 'working group' teams, continuing these peer relationships and normalising the emerging practice of pooling knowledge more effectively to address issues. Staff involved clearly saw the benefit to this approach and advocated it to others. The impact has been that in the latter project stages and post go-live there has been huge growth activity from communities of practice springing up across the WHELF partners surrounding the core LMS work. A quick review of the shared WHELF LMS Yammer platform shows over 20 active groups covering everything from analytics to Alma technical groups, from scholarly communications through to learning and teaching support. Cardiff Met have members right across, contributing to, and benefitting from that shared community knowledge.

How staff work together within Cardiff Met teams has also seen change, partially driven by the collaborative work approach. With WHELF, working in a mix of formal team and informal group structures across a distributed geographic area, a need was identified for mechanisms to enable that, and use of tools like Skype, Google Drive, Basecamp and Yammer became common. At Cardiff Met, institutionally there was already a drive towards using some of these tools to underpin a more digitally enabled work environment. The WHELF experience gave the library staff added familiarity and confidence that drove a fast and widespread adoption locally and it is now common to find all Cardiff Met library staff undertaking cross team meetings using Skype or Microsoft Teams, collaboratively editing documents on Microsoft Teams, and working across Yammer channels to support information sharing. What this has meant is that work is done faster, better, and with a wider pool of staff engagement than had been the case before.

Stepping back from the detail to a high level view, and there is still a palpable impact to be seen. It is not something that can solely be attributable to the LMS work, or shown in graphs and hard data, but from a manager's perspective, there is a noticeable sense of confidence across the library staff, having been part of such a successful big project. That confidence plays out in proactive and engaged attitudes to service development that has helped drive other areas of work, and in staff's ability and willingness to engage externally, for example with Jisc working groups, and advocate and contribute to ideas and changes that benefit the wider library community.

11.5   Where next for Cardiff Met and the shared LMS?

With three years since Cardiff Met's implementation completed, it is a useful point for reflection and to map the ambition going forward. From a Cardiff Met perspective, the experience to date has been very positive, and there has been clear benefit to both library users and library staff, some of which has been unpicked in this study. There is very much an enthusiasm to keep going and do more with the WHELF consortium and the shared LMS in recognition of both the value of the collaboration and quality of the end product.

Local priorities are for continued progress on improving the metadata management landscape, doing more work with analytics to underpin evidence-based service decisions, further improving automation in some of the acquisition processes, and to continue evolving and improving the discovery interface.

These priorities also open up collaborative potential for a 'Shared Collection Management' theme for WHELF to explore at consortia level, and these conversations will surely take place as WHELF too maps out its wider future ambition at this mid-point in the shared LMS contract.

Whatever the shared future ambitions turn out to be, the journey that started for WHELF and Cardiff Met back in 2013, definitely has some distance to travel yet, and there is a genuine sense that it is taking everyone to the places we want to go.

Endnotes

1. WHELF blog. Posts tagged 'LMS': http://whelf.ac.uk/?s = LMS&submit = Go.
2. Jisc Library Services web page. Posts tagged 'NBK': https://libraryservices.jiscinvolve.org/wp/category/nbk/.

Reference

Cambridge Econometrics. (2017). Evaluating the benefits of the WHELF consortial approach to a library management system (LMS): Report prepared for Jisc and WHELF. Retrieved from: http://whelf.ac.uk/sharedlms/benefits-report.

Scottish Higher Education Digital Library: the e-book journey

Wendy Walker
University of Glasgow Library, Glasgow, Scotland, United Kingdom

12.1 Scottish Higher Education Digital Library

Led by the Scottish Confederation of University and Research Libraries (SCURL),[1] the Scottish Higher Education Digital Library (SHEDL) has collaborated successfully since 2009 to procure access to almost 3500 electronic journals for the 18 Scottish higher education institutions (HEIs), the National Library of Scotland and National Museums Scotland (Stevenson, Ashworth & Evans, 2018). Scottish HEIs are committed to SHEDL, particularly in the context of the Scottish Government's commitment to shared services, and the SHEDL brand is well recognised in the publishing landscape. The principles underpinning SHEDL are transparent: fair proportional contributions from all institutions; equity of access for all higher education staff and students; openness with publishers about affordability and expectations; financial commitment up front and for contract periods; and legal compliance within EU tender limits.

12.2 Scottish Working Group for Electronic Books

Scottish institutions have a long history of working together to procure electronic book (e-book) content. In 2008, a Scottish Electronic Books Working Group was formed, and the group began working together to procure e-books with the support of Advanced Procurement for Universities and Colleges (APUC),[2] the procurement centre of expertise for all Scotland universities and colleges.

SCURL decided in 2017 that all joint content procurement undertaken by SCURL members would come under the SHEDL brand and the Scottish Electronic Books Working Group now operates as a separate SHEDL E-Books Working Group, reporting to the SHEDL Steering Group along with groups for Journals, Subscription Management, Print Books and Learning Content. The group includes a Chair, Vice Chair and representation from all other institutions. The Chair and Vice Chair work closely with the APUC Library Category Lead and hold regular calls and meetings to discuss strategic and operational matters. APUC provides expertise and guidance on EU procurement regulations and has been very supportive to Scottish institutions as they have explored new strategies to procure e-books. The relationship has developed over the years as the e-book market in higher education

Technology, Change and the Academic Library. DOI: https://doi.org/10.1016/B978-0-12-822807-4.00012-9

is very fluid and strategies around provision of e-books must be both robust and flexible. As time has progressed, traditional face-to-face/boardroom group meetings are less frequent, making way for interactive group workshops, led by the Chair and APUC. All group members are invited to attend and participate. This is proving to be a successful format, at a time when it can be challenging to find a suitable non-email communication channel for all 19 institutions and the Library Category Lead.

12.3   Early days for e-books

E-book aggregated content was the focus of the Scottish E-Books Working Group for the first few years and frameworks were created and put in place for the purchase of individual e-books on a title-by-title basis via aggregators. However, as time progressed, there was general frustration at the lack of content, consistency and models available via this method of purchasing. In 2013, a small group of interested SHEDL members investigated the possibility of expanding the SHEDL journal portfolio to include collaborating with publishers to procure access to digital rights management (DRM)-free electronic books. Existing aggregator models were not wholly satisfying the noticeable desire for increased access to e-books for teaching and research. Demand was increasing across Scotland for an improved student experience, with more user-friendly, high quality, relevant and front list texts. Additionally, some institutions were moving their collection policies towards electronic purchasing, either to suit user needs or as drivers to save space in overcrowded library buildings. The existing Scottish e-book framework agreement was due to expire in 2014 and the group decided this was an opportune time to challenge the normal boundaries of consortia e-book purchasing with the strong SHEDL brand. The institutions were keen to continue working with aggregators but the opportunity to work with directly with publishers to acquire DRM-free e-book content was an exciting development.

A consultation exercise took place across all SHEDL institutions to discuss extending collaboration to include partnering directly with publishers to procure DRM-free e-books. The response was overwhelmingly positive and the desire for more flexible access to e-book content was strong. The group began market investigation with academic publishers to ensure there was willingness to partner. This process involved compiling a targeted list of preferred publishers based on existing e-book spend across Scotland, and consulting with those publishers. The response was variable, but mainly positive. Importantly, institutional library directors were consulted to guarantee collective institutional financial commitment. The group's strategy was to include a separate lot for DRM-free e-book packages purchased directly from publishers in the next Scottish framework agreement and the plan was to ask publishers to bid for a pot of money. The Directors realised this was a new and innovative approach and were very supportive. A decision was made to proceed.

Compiling the statement of requirements for the tender process was challenging. Criteria to be measured in the statement of requirements would include quality of content, title inclusions and exclusions, platform functionality and metadata. Business models provoked the most discussion, as it was critical that value for money be achieved. Perpetual access to content was deemed to be the preferred model with low risk on losing access to content. However, the group realised any perpetual consortia-wide deal could be prohibitively expensive. Subscription would most likely be the most affordable model, but this made some institutions uncomfortable with the lack of perpetual access to content. After much discussion and analysis of existing institutional data, the preferred SHEDL model was listed in the statement of requirements as evidence-based purchase, although potential bidders were not restricted to submitting responses based on this model alone.

12.4 Evidence-based model

SHEDL members with experience of this model at an institutional level reported paying an annual subscription fee for a collection of content with a proportion of the lease fee allocated to acquire heavily used titles in perpetuity at the end of the subscription period. SHEDL members believed this model could offer the best mix of affordability and ownership of content but were aware there could be challenging aspects of managing this kind of model at consortia level. Careful consideration was given as to how the consortium would manage the selection process. The group agreed it was vital that all SHEDL members benefit from the selection process, but certain factors had to be considered such as larger institutions were making a larger financial contribution to the deals (the SHEDL model considers the size of institutional budget and costs are apportioned accordingly) and the benefits of the selection process may not be obvious to smaller, specialist libraries. Overall, the group strove to reach a balance, and believed they could ensure all contributing libraries saw a material benefit and could point to successful perpetual ownership of content for their own institution.

12.5 Outcome

The tender was issued, attracting a great deal of interest from publishers for the DRM-free e-book lot. Submissions were evaluated on quality and cost and ten publishers were awarded a place on the framework agreement. A further competition process narrowed that to six affordable SHEDL deals with key academic publishers: Palgrave, Springer, Elsevier, Wiley, Sage and Oxford University Press. Initially, these deals offered SHEDL institutions access to over 35,000 DRM-free e-books. The evidence-based model was offered by four publishers at that time. A key point is that most publishers did not have existing evidence-based models but were willing to work with SHEDL to trial them. Two publishers were not able to offer this model and traditional subscription or outright purchase were offered instead.

The value of the evidence-based selection varied between publishers. One of the key variables between the publisher bids was the 'multiplier' applied to the value of the selected work to allow access for all institutions. Another was the amount of lease fee permitted to acquire content in perpetuity at the end of the contract period.

12.6 Successes

There have been many benefits and successes to procuring the SHEDL DRM-free e-book collections. Foremost, SHEDL has consistent access to DRM-free e-book content from quality academic publishers, supporting teaching and research. Students in some institutions are exposed to content their institution may have been unable to afford individually. There is a heavily discounted average cost per title and cost reductions and efficiency gains for processing orders as everything is achieved at consortia level. Importantly, the usage of these deals is very encouraging, both in teaching and research and the group has been encouraged by the breadth of the collections which have been accessed. The evidence-based approach has delivered content the group has confidence is of value to users and the SHEDL group works closely to achieve this. Finally, from a collection management point of view, the number of titles owned in perpetuity is now in the tens of thousands and could be argued is a much more efficient way of growing collections rather than traditional 'title-by-title' selection.

12.7 Challenges

Partnering with publishers was a steep learning curve and the successes far outweighed the challenges. However, the challenges were not insignificant. Firstly, not all key academic publishers bid in the tender process. Despite many positive conversations, certain publishers decided against bidding at the time of tender. This was disappointing for institutions and those publishers missed out on business they would not have otherwise received. From a technical point of view one of the biggest challenges was with metadata. Publishers struggled to provide bespoke metadata for a consortium and the support with this challenge varied between publishers. It is crucial to receive timely and accurate metadata for users to discover and access content and the group experienced low usage on one deal, partly due to insufficient metadata. Additional barriers to success included content coverage and numbers of title exclusions, including textbooks. Publishers were not good at explaining title exclusions and the group struggled with user expectations of what should and should not be included in a deal. During the first couple of years of the agreements, there was a shifting publisher landscape and two publishers merged during the framework agreement, causing a great deal of uncertainty over ongoing arrangements and limiting future agreements.

12.8 SHEDL management of evidence-based model

To achieve the goals set out for the consortia management of this model, a combination of approaches has been used with all relevant deals. These approaches are reviewed each year. Usage is monitored throughout each year of the deal and collated by the publisher. In deciding which titles to retain each year, representatives of the SHEDL group look at multilibrary use (i.e. usage across a high number of libraries pushes items further up the selection list) and cost (very high cost items, unless used by all SHEDL members, tend not to make the selection). Additionally, individual libraries are asked to submit their own institutional title selections according to their own criteria (e.g. presence on reading lists, local usage or subject interest) and these selections are cross-checked with the wider data to reach a final title selection which is submitted to the whole SHEDL group for approval each year. The usage data continue to be very interesting with some libraries experiencing usage for titles in subject areas in which they would not normally expect to see use. Whilst it would be naïve to suggest each SHEDL institution receives maximum benefit from every evidence-based selection for each deal, there is growing confidence that each SHEDL institution is benefitting from more than one of the SHEDL deals.

12.9 Current day

The framework agreement ended in 2017. SHEDL worked with Springer (including the newly merged Palgrave), Elsevier and Oxford University Press to secure further multiyear deals for continued access to heavily used content. Only Oxford University Press exists on the evidence-based model. Deals with the other publishers had to be terminated (with SHEDL retaining permanent access to the content purchased via the evidence-based models) either due to low usage or unrealistic price increases. This was challenging for institutions to manage with a lesson learned that SHEDL must be prepared to walk away from deals not offering value for money. Affordability was, and continues to be, one of the biggest challenges SHEDL faces in an increasingly uncertain economic climate.

A new Invitation to Tender was issued in the Summer of 2017, again open to aggregators and publishers in separate lots. The statement of requirements was refined based on the lessons learned over the previous framework, partner feedback was considered and purchasing models reviewed based on a better understanding of the value of these models. SHEDL was keen to encourage participation from other key target publishers and the tender received good interest from the publishing world. A small number of publishers were awarded onto the framework agreement but, unfortunately, library budgets were not able to support any new SHEDL e-book deal. We had hoped that some deals for more niche publishers would be able to progress with smaller clusters of institutions, but potential impact of Brexit and other economic factors did not allow budgets to support this either. SHEDL is committed to the existing multiyear deals with publishers but currently cannot support anything new.

12.10   Aggregators

E-book aggregators remain a vital element of e-book procurement and title-by-title purchasing via this route remains a key lot in the SHEDL e-book framework agreements. Whilst it is true the spend via aggregators must have decreased with publishers SHEDL had partnered with directly, there is still a huge amount of business for aggregators to receive. The aggregator landscape is better now than it was in 2014 and SHEDL institutions are regaining confidence in this type of e-book purchasing. Better models, improved DRM and the 'publisher direct' ordering some now facilitate (ordering and invoicing via the aggregator, access via the publisher's native interface) are making for an improving landscape. What has become clear though is that the e-book aggregator playing field is not level. This message has been conveyed to institutions for many years and it simply is not true. Some aggregators are receiving better terms and conditions from publishers regarding models and DRM. Aggregators need to invest heavily in their publisher relation teams and seek feedback from their customers to maintain competition amongst their peers.

12.11   Textbooks

Providing electronic textbooks to students remains one of the most difficult challenges for SHEDL institutions. Textbook titles are excluded from the publisher deals and e-textbooks are not normally available to purchase on institutional models via aggregators or publishers. Existing library budgets cannot stretch to fund e-textbooks via models from e-textbook providers and, unfortunately, the library is often seen as the place to provide access to all resources. There is some evidence to suggest some publishers are reviewing their models in this area and Jisc[3] is currently reviewing a UK wide e-textbook strategy. However, it remains unclear whether Scottish HEI libraries will ever be able to provide textbooks in the electronic form our users may expect.

12.12   Reflection and future

SHEDL's e-book journey has been an eventful one and has by no means reached the end of the road. The SHEDL E-Books Working Group experiences strong leadership in respect of the Chair, Vice Chair and Category Lead from APUC, all committed to reaching the common goal of increased e-book access for users. All participants involved in the tender process for acquiring DRM-free collections were experienced in e-book procurement and strong negotiating skills were in evidence. These skills were further developed during the tender process. SHEDL has a strong, supportive community, committed to offering opportunities for institutional members to develop their skills in e-book procurement models and access.

As a consortium we have experienced success in working directly with publishers to gain access to a wealth of DRM-free content, accessible to all Scottish HE users. We challenge the boundaries of existing business models and have been innovative in our approach, learning along the way that there is an element of risk in this type of approach to e-book procurement. We endeavour to continue pursuing partnerships with publishers to gain access to DRM-free e-book collections (budgets permitting) as we are aware of the positive impact increasing access to this type of content has on our users in terms of portability and usability. We have good evidence of heavy usage in both teaching and research, with positive feedback received from academic staff, researchers and students. We recognise the importance of competing e-book aggregators and are committed to supporting them as they strive to develop new models and build new and different relationships with publishers in an increasingly complex market. We support publishers looking at a variety of models to provide textbooks to students and the work ongoing in the UK HE community around the provision of e-textbooks. We are turning our attention to the open access landscape and noting with interest the various models some publishers are introducing. Digital preservation will feature heavily in our future strategies as we accumulate more and more electronic material and we want to challenge publishers and aggregators on their strategies in this area, whilst looking at our own SHEDL strategy. Library budgets could be facing difficulties in an increasingly uncertain economic climate, but it is imperative we continue to address the continuing challenges and barriers in providing e-book content and understand the value in meeting the demands and expectations of our users.

Endnotes

1. SCURL: https://scurl.ac.uk/.
2. APUC: http://www.apuc-scot.ac.uk/mobile.php#!/welcome.
3. Jisc: https://www.jisc.ac.uk/#.

Reference

Stevenson, A., Ashworth, S., & Evans, J. (2018). The Scottish Higher Education Digital Library (SHEDL): Successes, challenges and the future. In J. Atkinson (Ed.), *Collaboration and the academic library: Internal and external, local and regional, national and international* (pp. 195−204). Oxford: Chandos Publishing. https://doi.org/10.1016/B978-0-08-102084-5.00018-3.

Engaging tertiary students with university archival collections and digitisation processes

Ann Hardy and Gionni di Gravio
University Library, University of Newcastle Australia, Newcastle, NSW, Australia

13.1   Introduction

In 2016, the University of Newcastle (UON) (Australia) Auchmuty Library embarked on a new venture to promote and augment a newly established Work Integrated Learning (WIL) course in the new BA, and to provide for placements in Cultural Collections. In 2017 the GLAM^x Living Histories Digitisation Lab was established for students in the UON's WIL programmes. The lab provides a unique opportunity in the tertiary teaching and learning sphere for students to engage in practical education and learn the technical know−how to be able to transform any physical format into a digital object, and access to the entire gamut of GLAM professions across conservation and preservation, archival science, librarianship, digitisation, metadata and data management, curatorial work, three-dimensional (3D) scanning, virtual reality (VR) technologies and digital heritage skills. Students learn practical and technical skills to transform any physical format into a digital object. This chapter discusses some of the digitisation projects undertaken by WIL students and two specific projects are discussed that use quite specialised types of digitisation. The first is the Deep Time project requiring 3D scanning technology, and the second is the audio−visual digitisation of the NBN Television archive. These two case studies are discussed further in this chapter. Digital projects are curated on social platforms and shared with a global audience on the University of Newcastle Library's Cultural Collections (UONCC) digital platform 'Livinghistories@UON'.

13.2   GLAM^x Living Histories Digitisation Lab

In 2017, the GLAM^x Lab was established for students in the UON's WIL programmes across all faculties and disciplines. It is a work space whereby students can gain important practical experience and skills that relate to the GLAM sector industries (Di Gravio & Hardy, 2018). The lab is part of Cultural Collections at the University's Library and students can learn digitisation and other cultural sector skills.

The GLAM^x Lab is a sector first initiative for the UON and provides unique opportunities in the tertiary teaching and learning sphere for students (Di Gravio,

Technology, Change and the Academic Library. DOI: https://doi.org/10.1016/B978-0-12-822807-4.00013-0

Hardy, Tredinnick, & Wood, 2017). The idea for a 'GLAM' Lab was the vision of Gionni di Gravio, University Archivist, who had been advocating to have a physical lab established at the Auchmuty Library. There was a need for training spaces because of emerging new industries associated with the GLAM sector.

A major breakthrough came in 2016, when Professor Marguerite Johnson brought her 'Sex and Scandal' class into Cultural Collections, and on this visit Gionni di Gravio spoke to the class about his vision to establish a GLAM^x Lab (i.e. Galleries, Libraries, Archives and Museums to the power of 'x') training facility. The UON's substantial archives and special collections holdings would need 'an army' of workers to properly access, digitise and make them available to the wider community. After describing his aspirations to have a training facility, Professor Johnson took the idea up directly with the UON's Vice Chancellor. An early challenge was to gain cross-unit collaboration and engagement (partnering with the Library) to establish the Lab. However, the idea was a good fit with the proposed introduction of a WIL course in the new BA at the UON. In September 2016 planning began to establish the GLAM^x Lab and by January 2017 GLAM^x was born in partnership with the Faculty of Education and Arts (FEDUA), the IT Innovation Team and the University Library, providing 10 student WIL places with the aspiration to accommodate 5 Aboriginal cadets. A key driver of the initiative was Mark Sutherland, Associate Librarian, who showed good leadership in ensuring the lab was resourced, with strategic direction led by Gionni di Gravio and his fellow stakeholders with Dr Greg Blyton from the Wollotuka Institute for Aboriginal Research.

An opportunity arose when a redundant library space, previously a student study area, was made available, large enough to accommodate 10 WIL students. Ten close to end-of-lease staff PCs were sourced and desks were located and assembled. There was some initial confusion as to whether the computers were to be reimaged as 'student' or 'staff' computers. It was later clear that as we were creating a real world working environment, they would have to be 'staff' machines, with the wider range of functionality including access to IT support and the digital storage drives available on the University's servers. Start-up funds to establish the lab and its Deep Time pilot project were modest; FEDUA financed 10 Epson V800 flatbed scanners and contributed to purchasing the 3D Artec Spider scanner used to create 3D scans of Aboriginal artefacts as part of the Deep Time project. Other costs related to IT Innovation costs in creating the 3D dig, and the day-to-day operations of the lab such as administrative support and purchase of specialised software and equipment. These latter costs primarily came out of the UON Library's budget. A lesson learnt was that the team underestimated the amount of IT resources and support required to ensure the maintenance and functionality of computers. This was essential because the core business was digitisation. The more specialised digitisation of audio–visual material and the 3D scanning were particularly challenging and required expert support.

There were very few risks in establishing the GLAM^x Lab, particularly in terms of financial risk. The lab was established on a small scale, with existing infrastructure such as computers, office equipment and existing spaces. There was some support from the UON hierarchy for the concept of the GLAM^x Lab and any risk that the initiative would fail was a risk the Library was willing to take because it was such a new concept. There were no existing 'GLAM Lab' models that could be followed, so an organic process was undertaken, learning as we went. In 2017, the GLAM^x Lab was the only one of its kind in operation at an Australian university (Photos 13.1−13.4).

There are 3 rooms in the GLAM^x Lab, the main lab containing 10 workstations each having computers and flatbed scanners. This lab also has a VR and Oculus Rift set up where VR and 3D projects can be viewed on a large screen. The screen is also useful for group learning and sharing projects that WIL students have been working on[1]. The Artefact Conservation Atelier is a smaller lab containing a 3D scanner, reflective 3D scanning lightbox and turntable, and laptop computer with Artec Studio software. Approximately 2.5 m of shelving is available in this lab, used to hold artefacts in the interim for accessioning, and ease of access for research and illustration. The digitisation of indigenous Australian artefacts for VR simulation is also done in this lab, known as the Deep Time Project[2]. The third space is the audio−visual digitisation lab housing the NBN Television archive and has specialised digitisation equipment providing for the various (at risk) film formats[3]. These projects are case studies discussed further in this chapter.

Governance of the GLAM^x Lab has been challenging due to the nature of creating a facility that is beyond established library practice. The GLAM^x Lab is supported by the Library and Academic Division at UON and operates all year round during weekdays (except the Christmas shutdown period). The manner in which the lab currently operates is adaptable and sustained by a dedicated team of full-time

Photo 13.1 GLAM^x Lab at University of Newcastle (2019). Courtesy UON.

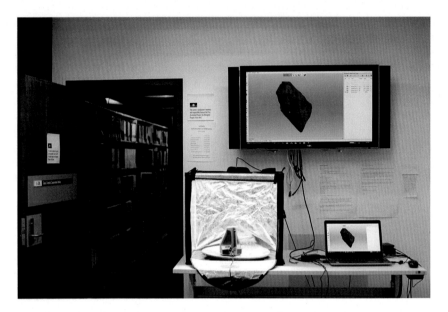

Photo 13.2 Three-dimensional scanning artefacts, GLAM^x Lab at University of Newcastle (2019). Courtesy UON.

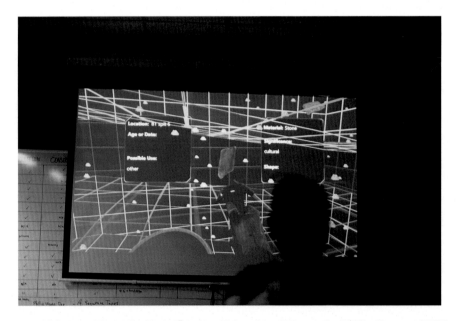

Photo 13.3 Deep Time VR, GLAM^x Lab at University of Newcastle (2019). Courtesy UON.

Photo 13.4 Audio–visual Digitisation Lab housing the NBN Television archive (2019). Courtesy UON.

casual staff and volunteers. However, for the lab to operate effectively as demands increase there will need to be a degree of formality and a staffing structure, and this will depend on the Library recognising the benefits a GLAM^x Lab can offer. In addition, because the lab was initially funded as a collaborative initiative by three distinct areas of the UON, there may be some ambiguity related to ongoing responsibilities and funding. The lab is a dynamic space whose multidisciplinary model is beneficial to all students from all disciplines[4]. Further clarity is needed around governance because this GLAM^x Lab is unique, the first of its kind at any Australian university.

In early 2017 a lab coordinator was appointed, funded by the University Library. The duties of the coordinator are to ensure whether computers and other technical devices are working and whether the administrative needs of the lab users are met. The coordinator supervises WIL students and volunteers, as well as manages the various digitisation projects. The NBN Television archive and Deep Time project have each required a high level of project management due to their complexity, something not fully realised when planning the Lab. The coordinator is part of the UON Library's Cultural Collections (UONCC) team. Other staff in this team include an archivist, conservator, rare book librarian, digital specialists and library assistants. UONCC has undertaken digitisation projects since the early 2000s, mostly two-dimensional (2D) digitisation and audio digitisation projects, whereas the GLAM^x Lab specialises in 3D scanning and audio–visual digitisation involving WIL students.

13.3   Work integrated learning student placements

The WIL programme at the GLAM^x Lab has provided work experience and career development for students interested in careers in 21st century industries, often focused 'clusters' within the creative industries and GLAM sectors. The aim is for WIL students to gain valuable practical and professional skills needed for new and emerging industries. The lab has successfully supported UON students from a range of disciplines, including the humanities, communications, education and the arts, as well as IT and the creative industries. The lab is conducive to cross-disciplinary collaborations. A report following young people's journeys over a decade (Foundation for Young Australians, 2017) has found that barriers to finding full-time work are not enough work experience, lack of career management skills and not enough jobs. WIL programmes are therefore looking at ways to enhance employability and build resilience of graduates, because a major issue for students entering the workforce after finishing university is their lack of practical skills. Many universities are revising their courses to align with 'employability' and build 'resilience' of their students.

The GLAM^x Lab addresses the issue of WIL students' lack of practical skills after finishing university and provides opportunities to work alongside professional staff to gain GLAM sector skills. They also learn about the various processes such as accessioning, conservation, digitisation, metadata and distribution.

In setting up the WIL programme it was important that students were accommodated in a safe work environment. WIL facility and training environments need to be fully compliant with the relevant legislation and regulatory standards in Australia that govern the UON's academic courses through which WIL students are placed[5]. This is to ensure that the students are properly cared for, and that the WIL programmes they are part of are regulated to provide the skills, education and experience in a safe and inclusive workplace environment, and not subject to exploitation as a source of cheap labour. Other key legislation related to the facility and its management of archival resources including the University of Newcastle Act 1989[6], the NSW State Records Act 1998[7], Work Health and Safety Act 2011[8] and Privacy Act 1988[9]. WIL students are given an induction to the library, introduced to work colleagues, invited to meetings and interact with community members and academics.

Equity and access are important in ensuring students from diverse socio-economic, cultural and disability backgrounds have opportunities and are supported. During 2017 there were 15 WIL students accommodated in the lab; and these were 80 hour placements. There was the same number of student volunteers. In 2018, there were 9 WIL students mostly from humanities and creative industries on 80 hour placements. During 2018 and 2019 a cohort of over 70 communication students also spent on average 3 hours each viewing audio—visual resources from the NBN Television archive. Students on these short placements viewed newly digitised archival footage and wrote summaries describing content, and were able to work with former television employees. There was a similar cohort of WIL students in the lab during 2019, as well as another new group from the School of Business and Law.

It has been a challenge engaging academics and WIL coordinators across the UON with the lab and we have found that the best advocates have been the students. Some have reported back to lecturers of their experience at the GLAM[x] Lab. Engaging with WIL coordinators from humanities was relatively straightforward, but gaining academics from other disciplines (such as communications, science and health) has taken some time. Further networking is necessary to introduce key UON academics to the lab so that further collaborations can be formed around WIL courses. Furthermore, because the lab is not directly associated with any particular faculty, it has been difficult to engage academics to collaborate on research projects associated with archival sources or potentially be part of Australian Research Council or other grants.

Students at the GLAM[x] Lab have the opportunity to gain paid employment. Some of the projects that employ former WIL students are funded by the Vera Deacon Regional History Fund (VDRHF)[10]. These are usually short-term employment contracts working on targeted projects. This fund was established in 2008 in honour of the generosity of Vera Deacon and provides paid employment to UON students and volunteers who work on projects digitising, researching and sharing knowledge about the history of the Hunter Region, New South Wales. Employment opportunities offered by the fund connects paid students with donors, sometimes leading to other future employment. In 2019 The Store Oral History Project employed three UON graduates to undertake 20 interviews recording stories about the Newcastle and Suburban Co-operative Society once located in Newcastle West[11]. The project was funded by a developer group donating to the VDRHF and coordinated from the GLAM[x] Lab and providing further opportunities to gain work ready skills.

Community engagement and outreach are opportunities for WIL students and a key part of work in the GLAM[x] Lab. Students are invited to share their work with meetings of the Hunter Living Histories initiative (HLH) (previously known as the Coal River Working Party) administered by UON Library (Eklund & Hardy, 2014). The HLH is an inclusive community experience, having a diversity of community and professional members and media opportunities. Some students have published their achievements on HLH social media platforms that are often further publicised by the general media, such as local newspapers and radio[12]. Students have a strong sense of accomplishment and at the heart of the WIL experience is the community.

In 2016, the UONCC launched 'Livinghistories@UON', a state-of-the-art digital online platform that brought together over 20 years of digital files. The introduction of this new platform coincided with the establishment of the GLAM[x] Lab and WIL programmes. In 2018, a new feature was added to the digital platform enabling the upload of 3D digital files where 3D models can be viewed online.

The following case studies, relating to the Deep Time project and NBN Television archive, are archival projects unique to the GLAM[x] Lab. Their success has been made possible with the availability of the Livinghistories@UON digital platform.

13.4   Case studies

13.4.1   Deep Time project

The Deep Time project is a digitisation project of Aboriginal artefacts for VR simulation (Bevan, 2017). It is a project that was undertaken in the lab with support of the IT Services' Innovation Team (ITSIT) from the UON who created the project in 12 weeks. The focus in Semester 2, 2017 was Aboriginal rock art and indigenous heritage and the University's archival holdings in Cultural Collections. One of these holdings was a collection of Aboriginal artefacts that would become part of the Deep Time project. This is a 3D digitisation project and the collection of Aboriginal artefacts was retrieved at a 6500-year-old factory site, arguably one of the country's most significant heritage sites, in Newcastle West. Over 5000 artefacts were found during the excavation and 600 of these are recorded as Aboriginal stone tools. Traditional owner groups were informed during the process and acknowledged within the VR experience to respect cultural values. The UONCC team consulted regularly with Dr Greg Blyton, Senior Lecturer of Indigenous Studies at the UON, who provided valuable indigenous knowledge. Participants were always mindful of cultural sensitivities, including touching and interacting with artefacts, particularly when there were visitors experiencing the project at the lab.

The ITSIT was responsible for the technical side of the Deep Time project. They are specialists in using new technology to enhance teaching and learning at the UON. The VR experience allows users to view digitised 3D scans of indigenous artefacts. The artefacts are digitised using a 3D scanner called the Artec Space Spider involving a process to create a realistic 3D representation. ITSIT worked with the Recollect Development team (creators of the Livinghistories@UON digital platform) to allow the platform to display 3D objects using the '3D viewer' function[13]. When the 3D scanned artefacts are uploaded to the Livinghistories@UON platform, the digitised 3D artefacts are automatically downloaded into the custom VR application created for the Deep Time project. The digital scans have associated metadata (coordinates according to the archaeologist report) embedded relating to their location in the trench so they can be viewed in a virtual archaeological trench.

Each artefact needed to be accessioned, recorded in an excel spreadsheet and given a 'call number' like any item in a library's archive or collection[14]. A favourable aspect of the project was that it had not been funded by research grants, therefore there were no restrictions in terms of a completion date. WIL students and volunteers have been able to continue 3D scanning artefacts. WIL student Emma Heath illustrated over 200 Aboriginal artefacts[15]. These were illustrated using the human hand to capture the artefacts' fine detail not always seen on a 3D scan.

Adopting multidisciplinary collaborations on any project is highly recommended. The Deep Time project is a good example of collaborations across many disciplines, and there were many benefits in this approach as it produced new knowledge about various aspects of this Aboriginal 'archive' that may not have been revealed if only one or two disciplinary approaches had been applied.

The project continues in 2020 and the VR has been revised to include filters that show the age of the artefact and the particular 'type' of stone tool. The Deep Time visualisation has also been remodelled for portable VR headsets. Considerable feedback has been received from the visitors, volunteers and students who have experienced the VR. The additional filtering function also allows the user to switch on and off fields to display particular types of tool. The Artec Studio 3D scanning software was downloaded on 10 computers in the lab to allow multiple users to create scans. The postprocessing phase is time consuming taking up to an hour to create a 3D scan. The project has also been able to be integrated in teaching and learning at the UON.

13.4.2   NBN Television archive

The lab has facilities to digitise any format of audio—visual source. As highlighted by the National Film and Sound Archive (NFSA) there is urgency that film archives be digitised, with magnetic tapes being most vulnerable and therefore a priority[16]. However, all of the audio—visual formats are considered 'at risk'. There is no funding available for digitisation and the majority of work is carried out by volunteers and students.

The NBN Television archive contains footage from Newcastle and the Hunter Region's local television station that started in 1962, the regional television station in NSW. The archive is housed across various locations and transferred in small lots at a time for digitisation at the GLAM^x Lab. There are five former NBN Television employees who regularly volunteer in the lab and are painstakingly digitising film reels, tapes and related paper sources. Other WIL students and volunteers are digitising 2D records including index cards, cue sheets and scripts. As already mentioned, WIL communication students have engaged with the NBN Television archive and viewed hours of digitised footage to identify content and write summaries. Following this, metadata is entered to audio—visual files and uploaded to the Livinghistories@UON platform. A position was funded by the VDRHF during 2018—19 to carry out this work.

As mentioned, the priority is to have vulnerable tapes (Betacam and VHS) digitised and in 2020 a total of 3100 tapes have been digitised. The target is to digitise 10 year increments so that the footage is available for commemorations and anniversaries. For example, in 2018 footage was digitised and prepared for 1979 and 1989 so that in 2019 sources were available for events, including The Star Hotel riot that occurred in September 1979 and the Newcastle earthquake in December 1989 that devastated the city and killed 13 people[17].

There were several lessons learnt from establishing an audio—visual digitisation lab. It was not initially realised how long it would take for the lab to be fully operational with all machines working that could digitise any audio—visual format. This has taken 3 years. Digitisation of audio—visual material is extremely challenging because of the various formats. Also challenging was locating original machines to run old formats, as well as having surplus machines for parts.

Another lesson learnt is the time required for project management. Digitisation projects are diverse and documenting progress of the various stages such as accessioning, conservation, digitisation, metadata and distribution is immense. The NBN Television digitisation and Deep Time visualisation have each required a high level of coordination due to their complexity, and this was not fully realised when setting up the digitisation lab. The role of the coordinator therefore is twofold. Firstly, to manage the day-to-day operations of the lab and supervision of users, and secondly, a project management role.

13.5 The future

WIL programmes are expanding at the UON and the GLAM^x Lab at the University Library is providing opportunities for students looking to enter the GLAM sector. Although no formal review of the lab has taken place, testimonials and general feedback from students, volunteers, academics and wider community has been encouraging. A survey conducted with WIL students has also shown positive results.

The WIL facility and training environment needs to be preferably of world class standard, providing a safe and stimulating environment for the students. By the end of the education and training, the student should be fully equipped, prepared, skilled and confident enough to apply for and gain any job across the GLAM sector. Best practice would be to provide suitable storage spaces to properly house archival material formats into the future, particularly film and magnetic tape formats requiring refrigerated storage areas. Conservation areas are also needed to provide adequate space for students and instructors, with designated segregated areas for decontamination. Digitisation facilities also need to house proper digitisation equipment such A4 and A3 scanners, plan and book scanners, 3D scanners and photogrammetry equipment, and workstations that can deal with the huge file formats, with sufficient processing power and network storage.

Spaces for interactions with the wider community are also important, such as areas where WIL students can showcase their work to visitors, fellow students and academics through lectures, exhibitions, 3D spaces, etc. Staffing and resourcing the WIL facility and training environment needs to be resourced with the professionals in accordance with TEQSA requirements. Staffing includes a WIL coordinator(s) and support staff to look after the WIL students' needs throughout the process of placement, and also to liaise and schedule students with the UON WIL coordinators from across faculties, schools and programmes to facilitate the smooth progress of the student through the placement to final report. Professional and assistant staff in the workplace with the professional qualifications and expertise across the GLAM sector are also needed to provide the skills, experience and supervision during the placement.

The GLAM^x Lab has provided experiential spaces for WIL students from a range of disciplines to use their own knowledge and skills in the cultural sector.

This has helped to identify different and new roles that were not there before such as data analyst, metadata entry, social media specialist, content creator, volunteer coordinator, community engagement and outreach officer. These are just a few of the roles that reflect the changing face of academic libraries.

Conclusion

This chapter has shown how the GLAM^x Lab at the UON has provided a new space and initiatives supporting WIL programmes for students and volunteers. This project is a sector leader with only two other universities in Australia (Deakin University and the University of Melbourne) having similar programmes engaging tertiary students with university archival collections.

We encourage other institutions to consider what they have in their holdings relating to their region, and where students and the wider community can engage in digitisation projects. Tapping into the rich archives and collections that are unique to a region can deliver meaningful projects. The Deep Time project and the NBN Television archive require a special type of scanning (3D scanning and audio—visual digitisation) and this is what sets the GLAM^x Lab apart from other digitisation spaces. In terms of audio—visual digitisation, the various types of format require specific equipment and machines that can 'play' formats, and successfully digitise these complex or older formats. Furthermore, having people with skills of using these older formats is also key, such as the former television employees who are passing on knowledge.

Finally, the key to the success of many of the projects in the lab has been the multidisciplinary collaborations. A real strength is the inclusion of students from particular fields and how they are matched with specific collections and projects. Students from diverse disciplines are our best advocates, often going back to their faculties and sharing with colleagues and educators the work they are doing in the GLAM^x Lab. We have found that the Library is the ideal location for a lab, as it is conducive to having students from many faculties often working collaboratively. The focus is experiences that will enhance employability and resilience.

Endnotes

1. Hunter Living Histories, University of Newcastle (Australia). CMNS2035 Media student television productions − 2019: https://hunterlivinghistories.com/2019/06/14/cmns2035-2019/
2. University of Newcastle (Australia). Deep Time explainer: https://youtu.be/ydp_RD3fKLI
3. Livinghistories@UON, University of Newcastle (Australia). The NBN Television Archive: https://livinghistories.newcastle.edu.au/nodes/view/79228
4. University of Newcastle (Australia). The GLAMX Lab − offering new skills to students from across the university: https://www.newcastle.edu.au/newsroom/research-and-innovation/the-glamx-lab-offering-new-skills-to-students-from-across-the-university

5. Tertiary Education Quality and Standards Agency Act 2011 (TEQSA Act): https://www.teqsa.gov.au/teqsa-act
6. University of Newcastle Act 1989: https://www.legislation.nsw.gov.au/#/view/act/1989/68
7. NSW State Records Act 1998: https://www.legislation.nsw.gov.au/#/view/act/1998/17
8. Work Health and Safety Act 2011: https://www.legislation.nsw.gov.au/#/view/act/2011/10
9. Privacy Act 1988: https://www.legislation.gov.au/Details/C2019C00025
10. Hunter Living Histories, University of Newcastle (Australia). Vera Deacon Regional History Fund: https://hunterlivinghistories.com/vera-deacon-fund/
11. University of Newcastle (Australia). The Store Oral History Project: https://livinghistories.newcastle.edu.au/nodes/view/89913
12. Hunter Living Histories, University of Newcastle (Australia). Emeritus Professor Ronald Godfrey Tanner & collected papers: https://hunterlivinghistories.com/2017/05/17/godfrey-tanner/
13. Livinghistories@UON, University of Newcastle (Australia). Three-dimensional scanned artefacts: https://livinghistories.newcastle.edu.au/nodes/index/q:WDXM/faceadd:4e5449443a3a3338
14. Hunter Living Histories, University of Newcastle (Australia). Rock art as a contextual archive: https://hunterlivinghistories.com/2018/10/08/rock-art-archive/
15. Hunter Living Histories, University of Newcastle (Australia). Aboriginal Artefacts Project − natural history illustration: https://hunterlivinghistories.com/2017/12/04/aboriginal-artefacts/
16. National Film and Sound Archive of Australia. Deadline 2025: https://www.nfsa.gov.au/corporate-information/publications/deadline-2025
17. NBN News. Star Hotel riot − 40 years to the day: https://www.nbnnews.com.au/2019/09/19/star-hotel-riot-40-years-to-the-day/

References

Bevan, S. (2017, November 18). University of Newcastle team time travels with virtual reality. *Newcastle Herald*. Retrieved from: <https://www.newcastleherald.com.au/story/5057677/virtual-digging-through-hunter-history/>.

Di Gravio, G., & Hardy, A. (2018). GLAM[X] Lab Living Histories Digitisation Lab: Engaging tertiary students with university archival collections. *Archives and Manuscripts*, *46*(2), 214−221. Available from 10.1080/01576895.2018.1467272.

Di Gravio, G., Hardy, A., Tredinnick, D., & Wood, K. (2017). *Engaging tertiary students with university archival collections*. Paper presented at ASA-ITIC, Australian Society of Archivists 2017 Conference, Melbourne, Australia. Retrieved from: <https://youtu.be/_FwUKTnZiPE>.

Eklund, E., & Hardy, A. (2014). Multidisciplinary approach to university-community engagement. *Australasian Journal of University-Community Engagement*, *9*(1), 77−99. Available from http://www.engagementaustralia.org.au/uploads/Vol_9_Issue_12.pdf#page = 82.

Foundation for Young Australians. (2017). *The new work mindset*. Melbourne, VIC: Foundation for Young Australians. Available from https://www.fya.org.au/wp-content/uploads/2016/11/The-New-Work-Mindset.pdf.

Planning and implementing an automated storage and retrieval system at the University of Limerick

14

Ciara McCaffrey
Glucksman Library, University of Limerick, Limerick, Ireland

14.1 Introduction

The decision to include an automated storage and retrieval system (ASRS) as part of the new library building in the University of Limerick (UL) was made to meet two seemingly irreconcilable demands — more seats for students and more storage for books. The tension between how much floor space to give to shelving and how many study seats to give to users is one that almost all academic libraries face. Libraries wishing to provide individual, collaborative, social, flexible and technology-enhanced spaces are faced with difficult decisions around what to do with their print collections. It is becoming increasingly difficult to justify large floor space devoted to storing print materials at a time when use of print collections is universally declining and use of electronic collections continues to increase. That being said, low-use print collections must still be retained, stored and managed. Libraries look to solutions like major weeding projects, off-site storage and collaborative storage agreements to cope with this major challenge. For libraries in the fortunate position of planning new buildings, as was the case at UL, the solution of an ASRS is one that merits serious consideration.

14.2 What is an automated storage and retrieval system?

The most common ways to store library print collections are via conventional open shelving or compact shelving. An ASRS presents a third option and has a much higher storage capacity, while occupying a much smaller footprint than the first two options. Instead of shelving, books are stored in large metal trays or bins. The bins are stacked vertically in a high vault and the depth of the bins varies to accommodate small, medium, large and oversized books. Material is, therefore, stored based on its size rather than a classification system and is identified by its barcode.

Technology, Change and the Academic Library. DOI: https://doi.org/10.1016/B978-0-12-822807-4.00014-2

When a user requests an item in the catalogue, a mechanical crane kicks into action, finds the right bin and brings it to the staff workstation at the base of the vault. The staff member then retrieves the correct book, sends the bin back, leaves the book at the reserve shelf and the user gets an email to say the book is ready for collection. Readers can see the system in action in the UL Library ASRS video on the Library's website[1].

ASRSs are commonly used in manufacturing; and can be easily visualised in product supply companies such as Amazon and have appeared in pioneering university libraries in North America, Australia and Asia since the 1990s. Some American and Australian literature providing individual case study experiences of ASRSs in libraries exists, for example Bullard and Wrosch (2009), Burton and Kattau (2013), Haslam, Lee Kwon, Pearson, and White (2002) and Heinrich and Willis (2014). There are a few examples of automated storage in European libraries, which are in off-site stores used for very large collections as is the case in the Boston Spa site of the British Library, the National Library in Norway (Mathisen, 2005) and, in the case of Switzerland, for collaborative storage among a number of libraries.

The system at UL, supplied by Dematic, is the first of its kind in Europe, built within a library and allowing users to directly request books stored on-site. After some deliberation about how to refer to it — automated storage and retrieval system or ASRS meaning little to anyone — we emulated Macquarie University's approach and named our system 'the ARC', short for automated reserve collection. By comparison with libraries internationally, our single crane system is small and can store up to 500,000 books. Some systems have up to 5 cranes and 10 stacks, accommodating approximately 2 million books. In UL, the ASRS is contained in a high narrow vault which runs from the basement to the second floor of the new library. Like a piece of contemporary art, a window on the ground floor gives users an opportunity to see the ARC at work, with the crane swinging high and low retrieving bins. Since the opening of the new library, the ARC has been a source of fascination for the University community and never fails to impress visitors.

14.3   The decision-making process

The new library at UL had been in the planning stages since 2006, but had been delayed by loss of funding during an international recession. The construction reemerged in 2015 and Dublin-based architects RKD won the tender to develop the design which had been approved with planning permission almost a decade earlier. It was a major extension to the original library building, doubling it in size, and was completed in 2018. The dramatic reimagining of the new library at UL, together with its many technology-infused features and spaces, are outlined by O'Riordan (2019).

UL is a 45-year-old university located in the southwest of Ireland. Library collections are still growing as new disciplines of study are added and the student population continues to grow. The original library was opened in 1997 and was built for a population of 7,000 students. In a decade that population had more than doubled, we had an overcrowded library with insufficient study seats, shelving crammed into every conceivable corner and in recent years had to move low-demand material to off-site storage at considerable cost to the University. By 2015 our collections included approximately 400,000 monograph volumes. An ASRS was not part of the original plan, which was to provide capacity for 260,000 volumes, by putting conventional and compact shelving on all five floors of the new wing.

A visit by the architects, together with senior University personnel, to US university libraries in 2015, including the award-winning Hunt Library in North Carolina State University, was the catalyst for considering an ASRS. The primary purpose of the visit, organised by the Library Director, Gobnait O'Riordan, was to look at highly innovative approaches taken to deliver a variety of innovative, flexible and technology-enhanced learning spaces. When the architects saw the ASRS they immediately understood the potential that such a high-density storage solution would have on their capacity to deliver user-centred, flexible and varied learning spaces. Following the visit they presented a proposal for an ASRS at UL which provided some compelling figures. Instead of capacity for 260,000 volumes stored on shelving across every floor, the ASRS would provide capacity for 500,000 volumes on a footprint one ninth that of conventional shelving, allowing for a 25% increase in student space. So, in essence, the ASRS would provide more storage, more seats and more space than the original plan.

The decision to include an ASRS was not one that was taken lightly. As a young Irish university, UL has a record of being pioneering and innovative, and the system certainly appealed from that perspective. On the other hand, installing the first system of its kind in Europe came with some risk to UL. There was no system like it in any European university. It would require resourcing from more than the Library, with high-level expertise and support required from Buildings & Estates engineers and maintenance crews. A further concern was the impact that the system costs might have on the overall budget. However, additional funding was identified so that the inclusion of the system was not at the cost of other aspects of the design.

From the Library's perspective, the prospect of an ASRS was initially received with some concern. There was no library in Europe that we could look to for help and advice on implementation. Integrating the library system with the ASRS system was another unknown and a critical factor to its success. If the library system could not integrate with the ASRS then the technology might work mechanically, but the system would fail as a library retrieval service. A further reservation was around our capacity to take on a major change project in addition to that of planning and preparing for the new library. The system required substantial changes in collection management, systems, services and staffing across all departments. With a library staff FTE of 46, the staff time and effort required to operationalise the system, while also managing a refurbishment and building project, was hugely concerning to library management. Finally, the staffing required to operate the system once it was implemented and where it should be positioned within our structures was very difficult to plan − who would operate it, which department, which roles and which grades?

However, the Library at UL has for many years been following a clear change agenda driven by innovation, automation and the use of technology to improve processes and services. New technologies implemented over the last decade included an array of self-service options, a book sorter, entry gates, laptop loans and a digital library. From a collection perspective, book acquisition processes were reengineered through the implementation of RFID, EDI, shelf-ready and book sorter technologies, so that the majority of books ordered by the library are received, added to stock and available on the open shelves on the day they arrive into the library. The Library's journey of both incremental and transformational change over a decade is outlined by McCaffrey (2019).

The consequence of this journey has been that librarians at UL have developed a great deal of experience in the change management required to automate processes, implement technologies, introduce new services and transform library spaces. Library leadership has a strong understanding of the change cycle, which occurs with all the predictable pain points and challenges in UL as elsewhere, but staff have developed sufficient experience to understand and navigate the process effectively. In many ways, change has been normalised for library staff over the years. One critical learning point has been that all technological changes seem daunting when first proposed, yet through careful planning, all have been successful and hugely beneficial to the improvement of library services in UL. Armed with this experience, staff had some confidence when the decision was made that an ASRS would indeed be a feature of the new library.

14.4   Preparation phase: getting ready for the ARC

The Library Director and Deputy Librarian were both on the new building design team and worked closely with the architects, the Buildings and Estates team, the contractor and a supply chain consultant to develop the specifications for the ASRS at UL, before tendering for the system. The tendering process came with its own challenges. Only two suppliers of automated storage systems made it to the final stage of the process – the more expensive option had experience of working in a library setting and integrating with a library system, while the more cost-effective option did not. The University embarked on a period of investigation and consideration, hiring a leading consultancy firm to perform in-depth assessments of both the options. After a prolonged and thorough procurement exercise, the Dematic system was selected. Dematic had 20 library customers worldwide at the time, although none in Europe. EU laws presented challenges at the final stages of agreement, as all specifications had to be adapted to comply with EU health and safety requirements around the machinery and who could interact with it.

Following the tendering decision, the Library commenced a change management programme to prepare for the ASRS. As we did for other technologies we have implemented over the years, we made contact with libraries that had ASRSs. Successful implementation at UL would not have been possible without the generous information sharing and advice from the libraries at North Carolina State University, University of Chicago, Grand Valley State University, Eastern Michigan University, Georgia Southern University and Macquarie University.

The first step was to begin the process of changing the library management system, specifying within the tender that bidders must have previous experience of integration with an ASRS. This resulted in our migration to a cloud-based library services platform provided by Ex Libris (Alma and Primo). Migrating to a new library system is a substantial undertaking for any library and required a project team and change management plan entirely separate from the ASRS project and the new building project. Migration occurred successfully at the beginning of 2017, after which the Head of Technical and Digital Services made contact with the very small number of customers of both Ex Libris and Dematic, to plan the technical integration aspects.

Within the Library, the ARC Project Team was set up in 2017, and its purpose was to plan and implement the ASRS as a library service. The Deputy Librarian, and author of this case study, led the project and the team consisted of managers, librarians and senior library assistants from technical and digital services, reader services and information services. As with the majority of UL Library projects, the team included representation from across departments, a team member was nominated as the project administrator to manage the meeting schedule and project documentation, and both staff training and communications were standing items on the agenda. The team, while still being formed, began with a visit to the Mansueto Library at the University of Chicago and then met fortnightly for the period of a year.

A project plan was put in place which outlined the main objectives of the project and worked toward a timeline based on the Dematic project plan, which set March 2018 as the date when the ARC would be handed over to UL. The main objectives were to review the Library's print collection to determine what books would be stored in the ARC, to prepare this material for loading into the ARC, to establish a service model for users, to train library staff and to communicate with the University community as required.

14.5   From planning to reality: operationalising the ARC

Some libraries use their ASRSs to store their entire print collection, which allows them to dramatically repurpose their learning spaces. UL Library made a decision early on not to take this approach. In the first instance, the new library would already double the amount of seating available so there was not an urgent need to create more space. Secondly, while the concept of the system was met with a degree of curiosity in the University, we felt that a dramatic culling of our print collections from the open shelves was not in the best interests of learning and research at the University.

A decision was made to use the ARC for low-demand material and to bring back all collections from off-site and stores so that monographs are located in one of two places — on the open shelves or in the ARC. We defined 'low demand' through collection analysis as books that had never been borrowed or been borrowed once and had been in the library for 5, 10 or 15 years. Different subjects had different criteria applied to them. In the year prior to the ARC handover, in excess of 100,000 books were prepared for loading — each book was cleaned, measured against a template of bin heights, colour coded and the last two digits of the barcode were written on the top of the book. This work was done by a team of library attendants and students, managed by the Senior Library Assistant in Reader Services who had responsibility for operations, shelving and space maintenance, and overseen by the Head of Reader Services.

In addition to extracting low-use material from the open shelves, we also prepared material that had been in store and off-site. Most libraries have one or two uncatalogued collections that are in storage awaiting a time when staff and resources will be available to work on them. For UL, it was the Hammersmith Collection, a labour history collection of 15,000 items acquired some years previously, uncatalogued and unavailable in off-site storage. A separate team of students, supervised by the Cataloguing and Metadata Librarian, worked on this collection for over a year to add it to stock with basic bibliographic records and barcodes. As books are contained in the ARC by barcode, Dewey numbers did not need to be added to this material.

The system took 9 months to build and was handed over to the Library in March 2018. There followed a period of what can be described as organised chaos! Thousands of books were loaded by students while Library, and Buildings and Estates teams familiarised themselves with the technology. In the background, systems staff worked with Dematic and Ex Libris to iron out many integration issues and at the same time the cataloguing team dealt with an unexpectedly high volume of rejections — material that the ASRS did not accept for reasons such as problem barcodes, old records and material not appearing on the system. Very quickly a 'Rejections Subteam' was created to work through this material so that it could be reloaded into the ARC. Loading took 2 months, after which all-staff training commenced, process documentation was written and a service was put in place for library users.

The ARC receives between 8 and 10 requests per day and is in operation during the serviced hours of the library, from 9 a.m. to 9 p.m. during semester. One disadvantage of the system is that it cannot operate without staff, so the service is not available late at night and at weekends when the building is open to users. However, because of the low demand nature of the collections stored in the ARC, this has not been an issue for users thus far.

The small number of daily requests also meant that the technology, though sizeable in itself, did not require additional posts or major changes to existing roles. The role most affected was that of the Senior Library Assistant (Operations) within the Reader Services Department, who now manages the ARC as part of her wider management of library storage, shelving and space. Through fortunate timing this role became vacant one year prior to the commencement of the ARC project and the new appointee brought an enthusiasm and flexibility that greatly contributed to successful implementation. The library attendant shelving team interacts most with the ARC, switching it on and off in the morning and evening, returning items to it over the course of the day and performing audits of bins on a regular basis for quality control. However, the main work of the library attendants is still stock maintenance on the open shelves, and adoption of the ARC was helped by their many years of experience working with the book sorter technology. Both library attendants and assistants bring material to the Information Desk when a request is made and the time from request to supply is between 10 and 20 minutes depending on staff availability. All staffs are trained on the basics of the ARC, so that any staff member can retrieve a book from the ARC if needed. In the event that there is a crane stoppage, the Buildings and Estates maintenance team respond within an hour and they maintain and service the machinery regularly throughout the year, with scheduled visits from Dematic twice yearly.

In communicating the ARC as a new service to library staff, we focused on the fact that it is essentially a staff-mediated shelving system, not that different from our existing theses collection, which students request and staff retrieve items from many times throughout the day. This helped staff understand the change before it became a reality. In many ways, the ARC technology was one of the most easily accepted changes by staff. This was due to a combination of things that came together – a well-managed project, an enthusiastic project team, good in-house technical knowledge, strong support from the Buildings and Estates department, a flexible staff that were well used to new technologies and the undeniable coolness of this particular technology.

Conclusion

Due to the ARC, UL Library now has all its collections on-site and available to users. It has allowed us to provide much more relevant material on the open shelves, providing users with a better browsing experience, and the process of reviewing material for the ARC allowed us to clean up thousands of records on our system. Previously unavailable collections are now available to library users. Critically, the ARC gives us a storage solution for our print collections for many years to come. Future plans to evaluate the service including reviewing what material has been requested from the ARC to ensure that it is low demand, identifying more open shelf material to be moved to the ARC and, eventually, making evidence-based decisions about material that might never be requested in the decades to come.

The greatest benefits with the ARC, however, are in what it has allowed us to deliver to library users in the new building. UL Library now has 2200 seats, 23 bookable group study rooms and a further 12 specialised spaces including a data visualisation lab, a practice presentation room, a media production room, PC training rooms and faculty meeting rooms. There are hugely popular collaborative booths, break out spaces, a new special collections and archives reading room, an exhibition space, a digital scholarship centre and a Moot Appellate Court which doubles up as a presentation space. In the first year library use increased by 31%, group rooms are in constant use and the ARC is one of the highlights of the building, in and of itself.

Overall, the project has been a remarkable success. The implementation of the ASRS, together with the opening of the new library, has been an incredible adventure for staff at UL, filled with many potential pitfalls and viewed with some trepidation during the planning phase, but has worked out more successfully than we could have ever imagined.

Endnote

1. University of Limerick Library ASRS: https://www.ul.ie/library/automated-storage-and-retrieval-system

References

Bullard, R., & Wrosch, J. (2009). Eastern Michigan University's automated storage and retrieval system: 10 years later. *Journal of Access Services*, *6*(3), 388–395. Available from http://dx.doi.org/10.1080/15367960902894187.

Burton, F., & Kattau, M. (2013). Out of sight but not lost to view: Macquarie University Library's stored print collection. *Australian Academic & Research Libraries*, *44*(2), 102–113. Available from http://dx.doi.org/10.1080/00048623.2013.795473.

Haslam, M., Lee Kwon, M., Pearson, M. M., & White, M. (2002). The automated storage and retrieval system (ASRS) in Lied Library. *Library Hi Tech*, *20*(1), 71–89. Available from http://dx.doi.org/10.1108/07378830210420708.

Heinrich, H., & Willis, E. (2014). Automated storage and retrieval system: A time-tested innovation. *Library Management*, *35*(6-7), 444–453. Available from http://dx.doi.org/10.1108/LM-09-2013-0086.

Mathisen, K. (2005). From traditional stacks to an automated storage and retrieval system. *Library Management*, *26*(1-2), 97–101. Available from http://dx.doi.org/10.1108/01435120510572923.

McCaffrey, C. (2019). Transforming the university library one step at a time: A ten year LibQUAL + review. *New Review of Academic Librarianship*, *25*(1), 59–75. Available from https://doi.org/10.1080/13614533.2018.1511438.

O'Riordan, G. (2019). Re-imagining the university library: A transformative opportunity. In D. Koen, & T. E. Lesneski (Eds.), *Library design for the 21st century: Collaborative strategies to ensure success* (pp. 221–230). Berlin: De Gruyter. Available from https://doi.org/10.1515/9783110617535-017.

Making researchers' lives easier and managing risk at the University of Adelaide: The research data project

Andrew Williams[1] and Mary O'Connor[2]
[1]University Library, University of Adelaide, Adelaide, SA, Australia, [2]Formerly University Library, University of Adelaide, Adelaide, SA, Australia

15.1 Introduction

This case study describes the research data (ReDa) project that was executed at the University of Adelaide between 2017 and 2019 to provide systems and services to support improved management of research data.

The University of Adelaide is a Group of Eight research-intensive university, and the Project was a collaboration between the University Library and Information Technology and Digital Services (ITDS) at the University, with involvement of researchers and other stakeholders. Library staff provided subject matter expertise and filled the business owner role for the systems implemented in the project.

The research for this case study comprised interviews with key players who worked on the project, and reading planning documents from the time of the project's initiation in order to understand the project's genesis.

15.2 Aims and objectives, rationale and context for the work

The ReDa project was originally intended to deliver Figshare as a research data repository following a successful proof of concept. This was seen as a response to the University's lack of an institutional repository for publishing research data, and a number of problems that flowed from that lack:

- Research publishers and funders were increasingly mandating that researchers make their data openly available. Failure of researchers to comply was perceived by University administrators as a risk to the researchers' ability to publish research papers and to attract research grants. The potential for serious cases of noncompliance was seen as a risk that research grants would have to be repaid.

Technology, Change and the Academic Library. DOI: https://doi.org/10.1016/B978-0-12-822807-4.00015-4

• The lack of a platform to make the University's research outputs citable, discoverable and accessible was seen to limit the attention and impact that the University's research could achieve, reducing citation metrics and other research performance measures, and ultimately limiting research income.

Related directly to the implementation of Figshare, the project was intended to retire the University's existing, poorly utilised and metadata-only research data repository. The repository contained and published metadata describing research data, but not the research data itself. This metadata function would be supplanted by Figshare, hence the decision to decommission the platform.

The project's next objective was to move data management planning from the existing Word template to an online tool. This was intended to reduce the effort required for researchers to complete research data management plans.

In addition, from the perspective of University administrators, tracking completion of data management plans and compliance with policy requirements was impossible prior to the project. These issues aligned with intelligence from other Australian universities about low rates of data management planning, and that planning was not necessarily delivering improvements in actual data management practice. Implementing a new planning tool was intended to add compliance monitoring functionality.

Once the project commenced, the understanding of research data management planning broadened from this compliance-oriented viewpoint to include provision of value to researchers. This was a direct effort to change researchers' perceptions that data management planning was an administrative overhead and not useful in their context. Value would be provided by various means, including:

• Integration between the research data management planning tool and other systems to reduce the effort required to complete a data management plan and push it automatically through required workflows
• Automated provisioning of data storage
• Training and support for researchers to provide guidance on good data management practices and improve awareness of data management tools and processes at the University.

The means by which the project scope changes, and the scope changes discussed immediately below, came about and were managed during the project are discussed in the next section covering planning, scope management and project management.

The decision to include electronic research notebooks in the scope of the project was also taken after the project had commenced. It was found that some research groups had already purchased subscriptions to electronic research notebook tools, or reported that they struggled with generic online collaboration tools that did not properly support researcher needs. Researchers reported poor research efficiency related to the use of paper notebooks and associated labour-intensive processes, as well as difficulties in collaboration, particularly for dispersed multidisciplinary research groups. The decision was taken to implement LabArchives as a university-wide electronic research notebook solution to improve this situation and, importantly, to recruit two staff tasked with driving its uptake among the University's research community.

Finally, the development of online research data management training was another project scope change that occurred once the project had commenced, when it became clear that researchers had a poor understanding of research data management concepts. The choice of online training was significant because this is a way to deliver training and information to a large number of people at scale. Library staff with subject matter expertise in training and the development of training courses and resources played a significant role in this part of the project.

15.3 Planning, scope management and project management

A number of factors fed into planning for the ReDa project, with strategic work at the outset and subsequent work characterised by a strong focus on researcher need and flexibility.

15.3.1 Strategic planning

At the time of writing the University of Adelaide has a *Research Data and Primary Materials Policy* (University of Adelaide, 2016), but this Policy did not exist in 2015 when University administrators started to see the need for improved research data management practice, and for University systems to support it. The work to draft the Policy was led by the Deputy Vice Chancellor (Research) and the Library, initially as a risk management response to potential loss of data when researchers left the University and lack of knowledge and documentation around where data was stored. Compliance with the Policy was simply not possible at the time it was drafted, and this was by design; systems and services would have to be built to enable compliance. For example, the Policy requires that Chief Investigators 'prepare a research data management plan for all internally and externally funded research projects' (University of Adelaide, 2016). At the time, there was no system supported or mandated by the University that researchers could use to draft such a research data management plan. This, and the intention for the Policy to drive development of such a system, is made explicit when the Policy states that Chief Investigators must 'submit the data management research plan to the University web portal (exact name to be determined once portal created)' (University of Adelaide, 2016).

Also directly relevant to the ReDa project's initial scope, the Policy requires open publication of research outcomes including data where possible. This drove the selection of Figshare for implementation in the project, following a 6-month proof of concept.

Drafting the Policy, and the work involving stakeholders across the University to get it ratified, were some of the very first tangible steps towards the ReDa project and the research data management support systems that flowed from it.

The next phase of preparation and planning for the project was drafting Infrastructure Investment Plan (IIP) documents and business cases for the systems deemed to be necessary. There were initially IIPs for Figshare and for an online research data management planning tool. There was no preferred solution for a planning tool at the time, although a Word template had been developed in the interim.

15.3.2 Scope management

In the project's early stages, team members adopted a design thinking approach, heavily focused on user need. Formal design thinking was not heavily utilised within the University at the time, and several members of the project received training to make this approach possible. The Project Manager, Business Analyst, and Change Manager in particular consulted with researchers in one-on-one interviews and in project reference group meetings about research data management problems they faced. This identified a number of issues which shaped subsequent thinking. They are presented in Table 15.1, along with the project scope changes they prompted.

Automated storage provisioning from within the data management planning tool was seen as a value that the tool would offer researchers, as opposed to a compliance overhead. Unfortunately, this was ultimately not achieved because the

Table 15.1 Issues identified during consultation and resulting project scope changes.

Issue identified during consultation	Resulting project scope change
Many researchers and higher degree research (HDR) students did not have a good understanding of research data management concepts.	Online research data management training
Research managers and supervisors of HDR students had little or no awareness of where data, for which they were ultimately responsible, was being stored and how it was being managed. They also reported difficulties with collaboration and efficiency issues.	LabArchives
Researchers did not have a good understanding of storage options and data management tools available at the University.	Automated data storage provisioning within the data management planning tool
Researchers perceived a lack of good data storage options.	Automated data storage provisioning within the data management planning tool. Also, provision of actual data storage, although this was not part of the ReDa project
Many researchers felt data management planning had little value and the Word template available at the time took significant effort to complete.	Many of the specifications for the online research data management planning tool, particularly measures to make the tool as user friendly as possible. This includes integration with Research Master to facilitate as much prepopulation as possible and prevent duplication, and with Hewlett Packard Enterprise Content Manager (HPECM) for automated record-keeping.

preferred data management planning tool solution did not become available in time, and ITDS did not have a clear future direction for data storage technology, which made the value of investing in an automated solution questionable.

The University's IIP and business case process was used to specify and win funding for these changes to the project scope.

15.3.3 Project management

Daily 15-minute stand up scrums were used for project management. This resulted in flexibility which was very effective in the changing circumstances that surrounded the project, discussed below, and the scope changes discussed above. It also resulted in close engagement between project stakeholders, particularly ITDS and the Library, who were engaged in discussion at least every day in stand up meetings and in other project meetings.

15.4 Change management

Change management, using formal change management techniques and processes, was possibly the most significant element in the project's success. In this context, 'change management' means organisational change management, the people side of change. The ReDa project took place at a time shortly following the decision from the CIO that change management was a mandatory and important element in all projects run by ITDS. The ITDS Programme Manager responsible for research-related projects had hired a Change Manager for projects prior to the ReDa project, and that initial Change Manager was the first to work on the ReDa project, including working on the IIP bids that led to it.

As the project got underway, the Change Manager worked with the Project Sponsor, the Pro Vice Chancellor (Research Operations), to ensure he understood his role in the project, and what was expected of him. This ensured that the Project Sponsor was visibly active throughout the project, and seen to be involved. The Project Sponsor led reference group meetings and made sure all contributions made in the meetings were valued and seen to be valued. The Project Sponsor's name went out on project communications, following the principle that change management staff should ideally be invisible outside the project, and that the Project Sponsor's voice should be heard.

The implication of this strong representation by and from the Project Sponsor was that he needed to be convinced of the project's value, and of the value of the systems and solutions that were intended to be shipped by the project. Maintaining the relationship with the Project Sponsor and convincing the Sponsor of this value was a change management task.

A significant outcome of change management in the project was that it brought a strong focus on the benefits for researchers − what is in it for me? The project's first Change Manager had previously worked on other research-related projects at the University. If a researcher told him about an issue, he ensured it was dealt with, pursuing it tenaciously within ITDS, Research Services and with vendors as required and representing researchers' needs. This meant he had existing relationships with and a great deal of respect from researchers at the University. He continued that approach in the ReDa project, going out into the University, consulting researchers, and bringing the resulting information back into the project and advocating for researchers. The Change Manager also used these relationships to drive researchers' engagement with the project through project Reference Groups, allowing the researchers' voices to be heard in the project's formal governance. As a result, the needs of research and researchers were very strong drivers in the project.

Another significant change management success in the project was the LabArchives support provided by two part-time Research Data Outreach Officers. They were responsible for meeting researchers in their own spaces, both 'spiritually' and physically, to drive uptake of LabArchives, and were very successful. They were both late stage PhD students, so they could speak the language of the researchers, hence meeting them in their spiritual spaces. In addition, the Outreach Officers met researchers in their own physical environments (labs, offices and scheduled meetings), which was a way to express that project team members respected and valued researchers' time. It was considered important that researchers took up and used LabArchives, particularly because this has not necessarily been the case for other products previously pushed out to the University. Change management to drive uptake is considered especially important for 'opt-in' products. There are effectively no consequences for researchers if they do not use an opt-in product (like Figshare and LabArchives), so if uptake is considered important for those systems it needs to be driven and resources applied to making it happen. Employing the Research Data Outreach Officers was innovative in the context of the University of Adelaide at the time.

The Project Managers on the ReDa project were strong advocates for change management and what it offered the project, and for the skills of the Change Managers who worked on it. This contributed significantly to the effectiveness of the change management on the project, and to the success of the project itself.

15.5   Staffing changes

It is felt that the changes to staffing on the project slowed the project down, particularly on decisions to select a data management planning tool solution. Some project funding that might have been made available was reassigned because of the resulting delays. On the other hand, the project has been very successful and the scrum project management approach, where knowledge sharing is intrinsic to project management and execution, is also considered an important part of this success. People coming onto the project learnt very quickly and came up to speed as a result of the knowledge sharing environment. If this had not been the case the staff turnover would have had a much greater effect.

A significant part of the project's success can be attributed to the willingness of the Research Technology Support Team in ITDS to learn what they needed to in order to support users with the systems flowing out of the ReDa project, thus facilitating the transition from the project phase to business as usual even as project staff changed.

15.6   Expression of values

The project can be understood as an expression and manifestation of several values held within the University. In its implementation of Figshare, the ReDa project was an expression of the value that University leadership perceives in the principles of open access and FAIR (Findable, Accessible, Interoperable and Reusable).

The project also reflected the University's organisational risk management values, in particular through the implementation of LabArchives and the development of research data management training. LabArchives offer lab managers, HDR supervisors and anyone else with research management responsibilities to have oversight of all information related to the research they oversee. Research data management training is a means to ensure all researchers at the University understand their research data management obligations and the support available to them to fulfil those obligations. This is important in an environment where research funders and publishers are increasingly insisting on good data management practice. Through its focus on training HDR students, and making this training a voluntary component of the core component of the structured programme that all PhD students must pass, the project was also an expression of a perception of HDR students as agents of change, as opposed to trying to change entrenched research data management practice among late career researchers.

The project was an expression of the perception that it is important to provide value to researchers. As discussed above, researcher need was at the heart of planning and change management in the project. Active steps were taken to understand researcher need, and significant changes in project scope were planned for and executed as a result of the information and feedback received from researchers.

Success was celebrated on the project. One person's success was celebrated by the whole group, and this engendered a strong camaraderie within the team. Real mutual respect was displayed in the project, between all staff members. The project felt like a safe space. Disagreement happened, but it was never personal. This feedback from project team members can be understood as an expression of a real desire for success of everyone involved in the project.

15.7   Impact of the project on library services and systems

15.7.1   Liaison Librarian upskilling programme

The systems flowing out of the ReDa project, and the need to promote them and support researchers in using them, have impacted on the work of the team of Liaison Librarians. The library-based members of the project team took active steps to manage this impact and mitigate the associated risk by planning and participating in a programme of training to upskill the Liaison Librarians. The programme was endorsed at the highest levels of the Library.

This programme featured 12 training sessions between December 2018 and February 2019, scheduled weekly at the same time and place for consistency and continuity. Directly relating to the ReDa project, the programme featured sessions on the University's research data management policy and the broader research data management context, and hands on training in Figshare and LabArchives. The aim was to ensure that the Liaison Librarians felt confident to respond to initial queries from researchers about the research data management systems, and knew where to direct more detailed queries. The Liaison Librarians also received training in other systems not directly related to the ReDa project.

Subject matter experts in the Library developed a research support brochure to help the Liaison Librarians understand and support all the relevant research-related systems. Liaison Librarians were listed as contacts for information about the systems and the brochure provides tangible support for Liaison Librarians in their interactions with researchers.

15.7.2   Training

The online research data management training developed in the project added an extra element to the Library's training and research support offerings. Importantly, it operates at scale and does not take up the time and resources that delivery of face-to-face training for all researchers and HDR students would require.

At the time of the project all new projects involving ITDS were required to have a training component as part of the proposal and budget submission. The form of the training was not mandated, but some training had to be developed to support new systems. As a result, the online generic research data management training discussed above was developed, as well as training for Figshare and LabArchives users.

Completion of the online research data management training is not mandatory for HDR students, but it is mandatory for HDR students to submit a data management plan in the first 6 months of their candidature.

The project engaged with the Adelaide Graduate Centre, the University department responsible for management and administration of research education. This led to a decision that the online course should include an assessment piece, and this made it possible to measure how well students had engaged with the course.

15.7.3   On the job skills development

Library staff directly involved in the project learnt a great deal. In addition to the specific research data management aspects, they learnt about project management and collaboration tools such as jira, slack, trello, wikis, scrum methodology, the concept of business owners and administrators and the concept of automated reporting out of systems. ITDS staff welcomed representation from the business on the project, reflecting previous difficulty in getting business representation and business owners. ITDS staff also appreciated the contacts with researchers and input from 'the real world' that the Library staff contributed.

15.8 Lessons learned

The work of the Research Data Outreach Officers was critical to the success of LabArchives, and could have been just as effective with the other systems implemented in the project. This approach is recommended in any situation where a newly opt-in system is implemented. In this project, related to research, the recruitment of late stage PhD students was very effective.

Engagement with Research Services is very important when implementing systems that intersect with existing processes that they manage. They are important, high interest, high influencing stakeholders and need to be engaged appropriately for best results.

15.9 What's next

In the early days following the project's completion, an important next step is to bed down support for all of the systems implemented in the project, and ensure it is ongoing and fit for purpose. This includes consideration of whether or not ongoing promotion is desirable, and for which systems.

15.9.1 Research Data Planner

One next step for Research Data Planner is to work through the small remaining development backlog. More important and significant tasks include developing closer integration with Adelaide Graduate Centre processes, and working with Research Services to start to define what quality looks like for the University's research data management plans, how to audit that and what compliance monitoring looks like.

15.9.2 Figshare

Ongoing work is needed to fully specify the University's, and particularly the Library's, institutional repository service and Figshare's place in that service. This is in a context where the University ratified an Open Access Policy in the weeks directly following the project's conclusion, and where the FAIR agenda is becoming increasingly important. Consideration also needs to be given to curation of Figshare items: is it necessary and, if so, how will it be resourced?

15.9.3 LabArchives

The Library is the business owner for LabArchives, but this is not necessarily the best fit. A decision may be required about which part of the University is best placed to support it.

15.9.4   Online training course

The course needs ongoing maintenance to ensure it stays relevant and helpful in the context of changes to the University's research data management ecosystem. It is possible that the course may be made compulsory for HDR students, and this will require careful consideration. The role of face-to-face research data management training also requires ongoing thought in order to balance the comparatively heavy consumption of time and resources in its preparation and delivery against its benefits for attendees.

15.10   Impact of the project on University research and on the University as a whole

As discussed, the University's *Research Data and Primary Materials Policy* was initially drafted as a risk management approach to potential loss of data when researchers leave the University, and lack of knowledge and documentation around where data was stored. Related to this, the systems developed in the project represent a shift toward a compliance-oriented view of research data management, where managers and administrators have visibility on research data and how it is managed. Putting the data management planning tool online, and the consequent capacity for administrators to search the content of data management plans and generate reports were seen as part of the management approach to the same risks of data loss. It did not come to fruition in the project, but automated storage provision was also seen as part of this risk management; automated provisioning would have meant that administrators knew exactly where data is stored.

The project's outputs represent moving with the times, moving into the digital world from a paper-based environment (hardcopy lab notebooks to LabArchives), and moving from a single purpose tool to a tool that offers more value (Word template to online planning tool offering reporting and a lot of precompletion as a result of integration with other systems). Figshare represents a shift toward a view that research data should be findable, accessible and reusable, or FAIR.

The project represents a significant step forward for the University, but ongoing work is required as the expectations and norms around managing research data continue to advance.

Reference

University of Adelaide. (2016). *Research Data and Primary Materials Policy.* <https://www. adelaide.edu.au/policies/4043/?dsn = policy.document;field = data;id = 7345;m = view >.

E-books and changes in collection management at Leeds University Library

16

Karen Abel, Elly Cope and Jane Saunders
University Library, University of Leeds, Leeds, United Kingdom

16.1 Introduction

Leeds University Library serves an academic community of about 45,000 staff and students. In recent years e-book downloads have far outstripped print borrowing: in 2017/18 338,124 issues of print items were recorded, compared with 11,471,200 downloads from the Library's e-books. Whilst Fry (2018) notes the difficulty in making direct comparisons between the use of print books and the use of e-books, this apparent trend to using e-resources over print correlates with the findings of Jisc's 2018 survey of the digital experience of UK students (Newman, Beetham & Knight, 2018), in which 82% of higher education students surveyed responded that they had access to e-books and e-journals whenever they needed them. That library visits have also increased at Leeds University Library by 50% over the last 5 years (outstripping the increase in student numbers) shows that the Library remains relevant to its academic community both as a study space and as an information provider. However, this shift from print to e-resources is causing the Library to change its collection management activities. Chad (2018) describes the array of purchasing and licensing models for e-books that are available. At Leeds University Library a range of purchasing channels are deployed, depending on the likely demand for the text, but this case study focuses on how practices have adapted at Leeds to improve the long-term curation and management of e-books and e-book collections.

The acquisition of e-books and their addition to the library catalogue at Leeds University Library had developed in an ad hoc way to fit in with processes originally designed to handle print. These processes were managed by two separate teams: the Resource Acquisitions Team and the Metadata Team. In 2017, these two teams were brought together under one manager as the Access and Acquisitions Team. This made it possible to review workflows across the new team. Although the purchasing of e-books was on the increase, workflows specifically to handle e-books were not in place, so the management of e-book processes was targeted as an area for review. The key challenges outlined below were identified:

- *Sourcing of MARC records*: E-books had been catalogued from scratch, a slow process involving the addition of authentication links to the 856 field. There was clearly an

Technology, Change and the Academic Library. DOI: https://doi.org/10.1016/B978-0-12-822807-4.00016-6

opportunity to speed up the processing of e-books by examining the way in which MARC records could be sourced.

- *Hybrid catalogue records*: E-books which were purchased singly (rather than as part of a package) and for which a print, or another e-book record existed, were added to the existing records. The decision to combine print and e-records was taken when e-books were in their infancy at Leeds. The aim was to improve the user experience by bringing versions of texts together in user search results on the catalogue. However, this practice not only made it difficult to identify, and therefore manage, the e-books held, but also it ran counter to emerging metadata standards designed to promote discoverability, in particular RDA and FRBR.
- *Hidden full text content*: Where the same e-book had been sourced from more than one supplier, for example where increased access is required through the purchase of additional texts, and where a different vendor offers improved terms or now has the sole rights of sale, the URL for each provider platform was located in a separate 856 field. However, it became apparent that the discovery layer only recognised the first 856 link in a record, so the additional access was not available. In some instances it was also the case that the links in the 856 fields were not to the full text, but to tables of contents or to publishers' blurb.
- *Duplication of e-book records:* Where e-books were purchased as part of a package, there were no processes for checking that titles had not already been purchased individually.
- *Management of subscriptions to e-book packages*: As the curation of these packages fell between the Resource Acquisitions Team and the Metadata Team there was no shared process for recording updates to subscriptions. Records for newly acquired content were not systematically retrieved for loading, either because the new content was not flagged with the Metadata Team, or because records that should have been available from suppliers were not chased. Records that were retrieved from the various suppliers for loading were believed to be accurate, matching the content that had been purchased. However, this was not always the case. There was therefore a mismatch between what had been purchased and the records on the library catalogue. Also, where package e-books were being added to the library catalogue there was no uniform way to indicate the package to which a particular title belonged. In many cases the shelfmark was used to indicate the origin of the text (e.g. a package or a supplier), but this was not consistently applied. There was also no list of vendors from whom content had been purchased and under what conditions. Understanding the Library's packages, and ongoing entitlements, was therefore difficult.

In order to curate e-books effectively, with accurate holdings information and easy access for users, these issues had to be addressed. A working group comprising members from the constituent areas of the Access and Acquisitions Team [Acquisitions and Reading Lists, Subscriptions and E-Resources (formed from the original Resource Acquisitions Team) and Metadata] and a member of the Library Systems Team was established and the following workstreams initiated:

- Streamlining ordering processes for single title and package e-book content
- Improving the quality of the catalogue records
- Auditing the existing content of e-book packages
- Developing approaches to usage statistics to facilitate collection management

The outcomes of each of these workstreams are summarised below.

16.2   Streamlining ordering processes for single title and package e-book content

Single title purchases, handled by the Acquisitions and Reading Lists Team, were rigorously recorded and details passed to the Metadata Team, whilst subscription and one-off 'bulk' purchases, handled by the Subscriptions and E-Resources Team, were less frequently purchased and title lists and MARC records not obtained as a matter of course. Furthermore, subscriptions to e-book content were set up by the Subscriptions and E-Resources Team but the extent of the collections and the content were not always recorded.

To address this, the processes and circumstances for purchasing package e-book content remained largely the same but the procedures and recording of information became more rigorous. A spreadsheet was created to maintain information on:

- The numbers of records per package and the years obtained
- The supplier (agency or direct)
- The platform
- The payment type (subscription; one-off purchase; initial purchase with continuing access fee)
- The title sets (evolving or static)
- The administrative access (website administration portal address with passwords; supplier contact details)
- Usage statistics (types of reports available and their source)
- Licence details (e.g. conditions of ongoing access) and in-house information such as the 997 MARC field (described below) and the cataloguer responsible for updating MARC records

Having this information in one updateable area allows the Library to report accurately on its e-book collections, to make informed choices about future purchases (e.g. assessing gaps in the collections) and to manage administration effectively.

Following the launch of the new *Joint Consortia Framework Agreement for the Supply of Print Books, E-Books, Standing Orders and Related Materials* in 2017 (a UK-wide purchasing contract for library book supply), and the inclusion of more suppliers in the agreement, the process for single title e-book purchasing became more complex as it was determined that all suppliers would be used to maximise options for obtaining a text electronically at the best price under the best terms. However, improvements were made to the handling of the metadata for single title e-books. Prior to the review, once an e-book had been purchased the link to the e-book was passed to the Metadata Team who catalogued the book from scratch. As a result of the review, the Acquisitions and Reading Lists Team made arrangements with all e-book suppliers used to obtain MARC records for the e-books purchased via FTP. Now, twice a day, the FTP server is checked for new e-book records, and the records amended as necessary by the Metadata Team, speeding up the process of making e-books available to users.

16.3 Improving the quality of the catalogue records

MARC records for e-books purchased as packages were being obtained from a variety of sources and were of variable quality. Some substandard records had been identified as they were loaded, and were being fixed by performing a series of global updates in the system. These had to be applied one at a time. However, using task lists in MarcEdit meant that records could be uploaded and updated in batches, which was far more efficient. As part of this workstream load profiles in the library management system were also investigated. These were discovered to be extremely powerful as they could apply the required updates to records at the point of loading, rather than having to act on the records before or after loading. As the practice of picking up MARC records from suppliers of single title purchases via the FTP server developed, load profiles were created for each supplier to address the main known issues with the MARC records from the different sources, for example prefixes or suffixes to the URL supplied to enable authentication to take place. The matching profiles also meant that duplication of records could be almost entirely eliminated as if the record already existed a new one would not be loaded.

The removal of URLs in MARC 856 fields (electronic location and access) which were not linking to full text content, such as links to tables of contents and publisher blurbs, was straightforward as indicators are used to denote the type of target, with second indicator '0' (zero) meaning the full resource. A set of records was compiled by looking for second indicators that were not '0', so that the 856 fields that contained links to anything other than the full text content could be deleted.

The separation of records where two or more 'copies' from different suppliers had 856 fields in the same bibliographic record was more complex but relatively quick. The affected records were identified by checking the $z subfield at the end of the 856 field where information about the platform is recorded. A methodology was developed to create duplicate records and then separate the 856 fields between the new records. This meant that users now had access to all copies of a given e-book.

However separating the combined print and e-book records took longer, as a variety of methods had to be deployed to identify affected records. These involved running the various indicators within records for e-books (e.g. the leader or location field) against records for print items. Once identified the records were extracted and when reloaded the load profile created a new e-book record based on the print record. Duplicate records for the same title from the same supplier were identified by searching for duplicate ISBNs, in the first instance, within a shelfmark. Further checks within a given shelfmark were also carried out to pick up those not identified by ISBN. An added complication here was the need to identify these duplicate items on the Library's reading lists so that they could be amended. This was achieved by comparing within Excel, a list of the duplicated records with a list of all titles linked to on reading lists.

Historically Leeds University Library had indicated the e-book supplier in the shelfmark field. However, the shelfmarks had not been consistently applied and a range of variations had crept in (e.g. in spacing, capitalisation and abbreviations). Work began to normalise these, but was superseded by the insertion of a new local MARC field (997) into e-book records. This expands upon the information provided in the shelfmark but gives further detail. The tag was set up to include subfields comprising: 'e-book package' or 'single title purchase' as an initial statement; date of acquisition (in the standardized format of YYYYMMDD for easy analysis in, e.g. Excel); provider name; umbrella collection name and subcollection name (where relevant). An example is given in Fig. 16.1.

This tag can then be used to draw on a range of information from overall e-book package book numbers to specific subcollection details. It enables the monitoring of evolving collections and the assessment of purchases in a given year. In library management systems that do not have a collection level function within the metadata infrastructure it acts as the equivalent, tethering free floating e-books to their collection and corresponding purchase or subscription order information.

The e-book records were further improved by the incorporation of a licence information note, utilising the MARC 506 'Restrictions on access' note field, visible to users on the OPAC. Whilst some e-books (e.g. those bought directly from the publisher) are licence free, the majority available for single title purchase from aggregators are sold with either a 'maximum number of simultaneous sessions' or a 'maximum number of sessions per period' licence type. This can lead to frustration for the user and difficulty for the library as access routes for e-resources is non-uniform. The addition of the note explaining the licence type and its limitations enables both staff and users to understand any loss of access. Furthermore, this supports staff understanding of user demand and 'turnaway' statistics when assessing the potential value of further purchases.

16.4 Auditing the existing content of e-book packages

To ensure that the contents of the Library's e-book packages were up to date and that entitlements were accurately represented on the catalogue, titles lists were obtained from suppliers for comparison with the library catalogue. This large scale but seemingly simple exercise proved more complex to achieve than anticipated, as the obvious point of comparison, the ISBN, is in many cases not reflected accurately in suppliers' title lists. Frequently, for example, the lists feature the ISBN for the print rather than the e-version. In these cases, it was often more effective to use a fresh set of MARC records from the supplier from which to create an inventory list. Two sets of approaches were deployed to turn a batch of MARC records into a

| 997 | | | e-book package\|b20180731\|cCambridge University Press\|dCambridge Histories\|eAsian History |

Figure 16.1 997 example.

list: the first, using a bespoke piece of Python code (see Fig. 16.2) to pull MARC record fields into an Excel spreadsheet; the second, using MarcEdit to similarly export fields from the MARC records into a CSV file which could then be opened in the likes of Excel or OpenRefine.

In many cases, this creation of an entitlement list from a batch of MARC records proved very effective. However, it is not just the case that providers' entitlement lists may contain erroneous ISBNs; frequently this is the case within the MARC records too. A further option was to use the book's URL which also often contains the ISBN. Excel formulas (examples are given in Figs 16.3 and 16.4) were used to capture and extract the ISBN from the URLs in both the providers' title lists and the catalogue, resulting in two comparable lists.

Further exacerbating the problem of inaccurate ISBNs is the issue of multiple ISBNs. Both MARC records and supplier title lists frequently contain more than one ISBN per resource. This heightens the complexity of a title comparison process significantly, requiring more advanced Excel formulas using arrays to cater for matching across multiple columns. An example is given in Fig. 16.5.

When every attempt to match on ISBNs was exhausted, the final fall back was a match on title. A title match is inherently problematic, particularly given differences in the treatment of definite and indefinite articles which throw out a literal match. To combat this, methods of standardisation of titles were deployed. Within Excel, the Macro feature was used to establish a list of amendments that could be made to title lists (e.g. removing 'The') and which could be saved and rolled out repeatedly across any title comparison exercise. A similar technique was used in OpenRefine, taking advantage of the Cluster and Edit feature.

```
from pymarc import MARCReader
import unicodecsv as csv
import os

#gather all files in directory
files = os.listdir(".")

#initalise empty arrays (title, isbn, url)
records = [[],[],[]]

for file in files:
    if file.endswith(".mrc"):
        with open(file, 'rb') as fh:
            reader = MARCReader(fh)
            for record in reader:
                #title
                records[0].append(str(record['245'])[10:])

                #isbn
                records[1].append(str(record['020']))

                #url
                records[2].append(str(record['856'])[10:])

with open("urls.csv", "wb") as file:
    #initialise file with headers
    fieldnames = ["Title","ISBN","URL"]
    writer = csv.DictWriter(file, fieldnames=fieldnames)
    writer.writeheader()

    #write all entries to correct locations
    for i in range(len(records[0])):
        writer.writerow({"Title": records[0][i], "ISBN": records[1][i], "URL": records[2][i]})
```

Figure 16.2 Python code.

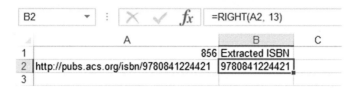

Figure 16.3 Excel formula example 1.

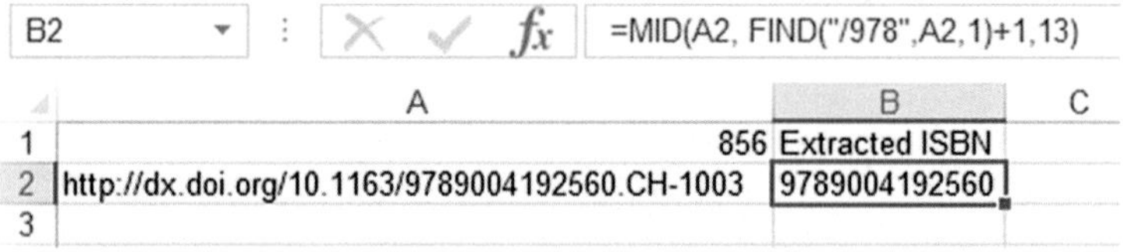

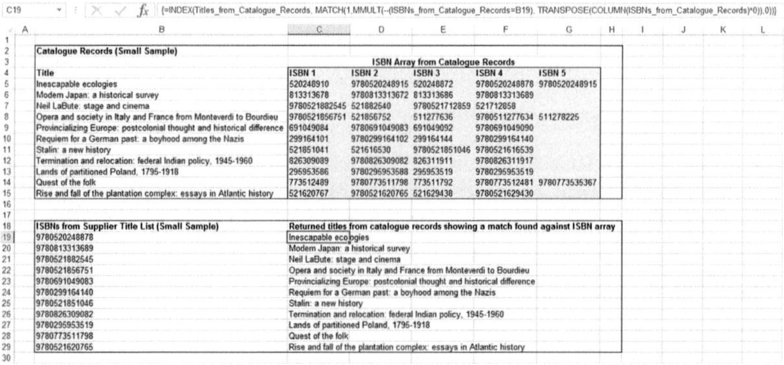

Figure 16.4 Excel formula example 2.

Catalogue Records (Small Sample)					
	ISBN Array from Catalogue Records				
Title	ISBN 1	ISBN 2	ISBN 3	ISBN 4	ISBN 5
Inescapable ecologies	520248910	9780520248915	520248872	9780520248878	9780520248915
Modern Japan: a historical survey	813313678	9780813313672	813313686	9780813313689	
Neil LaBute: stage and cinema	9780521882545	521882540	9780521712859	521712858	
Opera and society in Italy and France from Monteverdi to Bourdieu	9780521856751	521856752	511277636	9780511277634	511278225
Provincializing Europe: postcolonial thought and historical difference	691049084	9780691049083	691049092	9780691049090	
Requiem for a German past: a boyhood among the Nazis	299164101	9780299164102	299164144	9780299164140	
Stalin: a new history	521851041	521616530	9780521851046	9780521616539	
Termination and relocation: federal Indian policy, 1945-1960	826309089	9780826309082	826311911	9780826311917	
Lands of partitioned Poland, 1795-1918	295953586	9780295953588	295953519	9780295953519	
Quest of the folk	773512489	9780773511798	773511792	9780773512481	9780773535367
Rise and fall of the plantation complex: essays in Atlantic history	521620767	9780521620765	521629438	9780521629430	

ISBNs from Supplier Title List (Small Sample)	Returned titles from catalogue records showing a match found against ISBN array
9780520248878	Inescapable ecologies
9780813313689	Modern Japan: a historical survey
9780521882545	Neil LaBute: stage and cinema
9780521856751	Opera and society in Italy and France from Monteverdi to Bourdieu
9780691049083	Provincializing Europe: postcolonial thought and historical difference
9780299164140	Requiem for a German past: a boyhood among the Nazis
9780521851046	Stalin: a new history
9780826309082	Termination and relocation: federal Indian policy, 1945-1960
9780295953519	Lands of partitioned Poland, 1795-1918
9780773511798	Quest of the folk
9780521620765	Rise and fall of the plantation complex: essays in Atlantic history

Figure 16.5 Excel formula example 3.

16.5 Developing approaches to usage statistics to facilitate collection management

Monitoring usage to manage stock is a concept familiar to librarians, but the external hosting of e-books gives rise to a further set of statistics: 'turnaways', or the number of times unpurchased books on the publisher's platform have been denied to users. Whilst it is very useful to be alerted to potential books of interest to users, collection statistics can be manipulated or misrepresented by suppliers. This has prompted the Library to standardise its statistical analysis: collating and recording statistics for all publishers and collections for the same time frames (academic years) and applying a consistent interrogation. In particular, assessments of both strength and breadth are made when considering the current or potential value of an e-book collection: strength being the frequency with which titles are used/turned away; breadth being

Subject	No of Titles	Percentage of titles from unpurchased collection denied access	Average number of times access denied per denied book	Average number of times access denied per no of titles in full collection
Engineering	58	53.45	6.81	3.64
History	45	51.11	4.74	2.42
Linguistics	23	47.83	8.27	3.96
Law	33	42.42	6.93	2.94
History	77	36.36	4.14	1.51
Psychology	181	35.80	4.38	1.57
Drama	531	33.98	2.39	0.81
Earth and Environmental Science	453	31.79	3.19	1.02
Physics and Astronomy	480	19.17	4.52	0.87
Engineering and Computing	45	6.51	1.55	0.10
Various STM	25	0.43	0.00	0.00

Figure 16.6 Usage statistics.

the coverage (or potential coverage) of usage across the full collection. It is common for e-book collections to garner a high strength score for a small number of titles, whilst the remaining majority attract little or no interest from users. In these cases, where, as is often the case, it is not possible to purchase the high use titles individually, the value of this relatively small number of books has to be assessed against the price of the full collection. Similarly, a collection may score well for breadth with a high percentage of titles attracting interest from users but with few, if any, titles attracting a high frequency of interest. In these cases, it is worthwhile considering the collection as an entity in its own right, rather than as a package of individual entities, and therefore deciding if the range of information supplied across the collection makes it of value.

The analysis in Fig. 16.6 shows how this method was applied to decision making on an investment purchase of new e-book packages (the names of suppliers have been removed). These packages were 'finalists' in a number of collections examined and so represent some relatively high potential interest rates from users.

Comparing the Engineering and Linguistics collections, Engineering has a higher cross-section of books for which access has been attempted, suggesting potentially wide coverage of use (breadth). However, the Linguistics collection has had more attempts made on those specific books within it for which there are interested users, suggesting potentially high usage of particular titles (strength). Linguistics also scores higher for average denials across the collection as a whole demonstrating that, whilst Engineering may have a greater range of books of interest, Linguistics has a stronger potential usage to title ratio overall, making it arguably the collection which will most likely attract the highest usage.

16.6 Conclusion

The project described here was successful in resolving the issues initially identified. Indeed, the improvement to the catalogue records for e-books, in particular the separation of the records for print and e-resources, and the inclusion of the local 997 MARC field (enabling records to be easily grouped by supplier and/or package) made the Library's subsequent migration to a new library management system (Alma) in the summer of 2019 far more straightforward than it otherwise would have been. Library staff engaged in the project expanded their knowledge of MARC, MarcEdit, Excel, OpenRefine and Python, as well as the functionality of both the old and new library management systems. However, working with suppliers to establish the correct content of the various packages held by Leeds University Library was surprisingly time consuming. Further work planned at Leeds University Library on e-books is likely to focus on adequacy of provision across the different disciplines. Although the Library has had a consistently high score in the NSS survey (93% for question 19 in 2017, 2018 and 2019), students through their union, Leeds University Union, are asking for increased access to e-books via their module reading lists.

The key benefit of this project is that Leeds University Library can continue to develop its collection of e-books in the context of a robust collection management framework which will ensure that the e-books provided remain accessible and relevant to users. As this case study shows, the management of e-book collections poses particular issues for library processes, processes that have for decades been based around the characteristics of print collections. For both print and e-book collection management the quality of the metadata is critical to effective management and discoverability. However, as e-books are remotely hosted, not available as physical entities to be checked by collections staff, and often purchased in bulk as collections that evolve over time, there is a pressing need for consistency in metadata quality to support interoperability between library systems and supplier platforms. Furthermore, the adaptations to catalogue records made at Leeds indicate the challenges inherent in making the MARC format fit for purpose in the digital age.

References

Chad, K. (2018). The student consumer and the rise of e-textbook platforms. *HELibTech Briefing Paper*, 4, 49. doi: 10.13140/RG.2.2.17262.51525

Fry, A. (2018). Factors affecting the use of print and electronic books: A use study and discussion. *College & Research Libraries*, *79*(1), 68−85. Available from https://doi.org/10.5860/crl.79.1.68.

Newman, T., Beetham, H., & Knight, S. (2018). *Digital experience insights survey 2018: Findings from students in UK further and higher education*. London: Jisc. Available from http://repository.jisc.ac.uk/6967/1/Digital_experience_insights_survey_2018.pdf.

Universities, Jisc and the journey to open

Neil Jacobs[1,2] and William J. Nixon[3]
[1]UK Research and Innovation, Swindon, United Kingdom, [2]Formerly Jisc, Bristol, United Kingdom, [3]University of Glasgow Library, Glasgow, Scotland, United Kingdom

17.1 Introduction

Open access, research and scholarship are now mainstream activities which have increasingly become embedded in the research environment, culture and activity of UK universities. Their impact can be seen in the Research England requirements for open access compliance for REF 2021, initiatives like the UK Scholarly Communications Licence (UK-SCL) and the advent of the Plan S open access initiative.

Over the last 20 years, new tools, processes and services have ensured that 'open' has become increasingly integral, and familiar to our academies, and Jisc has played a key role in enabling that integration and familiarity.

In the early 2000s, Jisc was an innovation engine which jumpstarted the rollout of institutional repositories and related services across the UK higher education community. Building on international initiatives like the Budapest Open Access Initiative (BOAI) and the Open Archives Initiative Protocol for Metadata Harvesting (OAI-PMH) Jisc leveraged this work in the United Kingdom through a series of increasingly focused funding programmes. These programmes provided an environment which encouraged risk, innovation and experimentation to foster a national (and international) culture of open and a national network of institutional repositories and related services. Many of those initial services and repositories are still running today, providing essential institutional and national repository infrastructure.

This chapter will explore the cultural changes which Jisc has enabled and demonstrate their wider impact through its tools and services. These include familiar (and mature) names including EPrints, OpenDOAR, the Repositories Support Project (RSP), SHERPA and RoMEO. It will reflect on the success of this cultural change, policies and practice and how, collectively, they have enabled the United Kingdom to pioneer open. It will also place these changes in the context of the wider environment which Jisc and universities have found themselves working in over the last 20 years. These changes have included the Finch report, the rise of Current Research Information Systems (CRIS), Jisc's own review (and transition) and the emergence of international open initiatives like Plan S.

Technology, Change and the Academic Library. DOI: https://doi.org/10.1016/B978-0-12-822807-4.00017-8

17.2 University libraries: the cultural evolution

'At their core, libraries have always been about sharing information with their communities, advancing knowledge and facilitating connection. The means by which researchers and scholars collect, access and disseminate data, information and research results will continue to transform rapidly' (MIT Task Force on the Future of Libraries) (MIT Libraries, 2016).

In the 21st century, libraries, their role and their culture are evolving and nowhere are this more apparent than in their support for open in digital scholarship. This paradigm shift, which is still ongoing, has provided a focus for libraries to explore, support and expose their own institutional content and assets in support of their own broader research and teaching agenda.

Both print and print collections still have their places in libraries but the last 20 years has seen an accelerating digital shift in which the majority of library collection budgets are spent on digital content (and access) not print material. This shift from print to digital has seen a reconfiguration of libraries, from collection based models to service driven ones which now actively support academic workflows. Dempsey and Malpas (2018) explicitly provide examples of these workflows which include support for open access and research data. This shift to providing support for open access, research data management and new workflows to support these new needs provides new opportunities and the need for new skills in academic libraries in coding, data management, infrastructure as well as the traditional skills of information management, synthesis and advocacy.

Successful libraries have repositioned themselves as trusted partners in the support of open scholarship and they have pivoted to focus and invest in new staff and roles to support open access repositories and publishing. These staff can manage the content, liaise with publishers, advocate for open and support academic colleagues. Jisc and funding for services like the RSP have been critical in the development, transition and training of staff to support these new services. Its early support for UKCoRR, the UK's independent Council of Research Repositories, reflected the recognition of these new roles and needs.

Looking ahead, the 2017 SCONUL report on mapping the future of academic libraries (Pinfield, Cox, & Rutter, 2017) identified open access as the number one trend which would have an impact in the coming 10 years. Open access is embedded in the work of libraries today, but the broader cultural change which bodies like SPARC envision as 'setting the default to open'[1] is a door we are knocking ever louder on.

For libraries, new relationships with researchers and research offices across a spectrum of open and related activity has emerged including:

- Preparedness for broader OA landscape changes, for example Plan S
- Enabling the research environment to support open
- Delivering the Research Excellence Framework

These shifts have not occurred overnight and, as we reflect on the last 20 years, we can be proud of the role libraries and librarians have played in advocating open and working with our academic colleagues, authors and editors to shift the debate from 'Why open?' to 'How?' and increasingly 'Are we there yet?'.

This evolution is also set against the challenge of decreasing budgets, resources and priorities as institutions and funders decide how best to optimise their funding to deliver and support research strategies.

While the United Kingdom can demonstrate its clear commitment to open access in the proportion of published research which is now available, that has not been without cost through article processing charges and changes in subscription models. These costs, borne by a mix of institutions and funders, are no longer sustainable and have been the catalyst for funders like the Wellcome Trust to update their open access policy to support the transition to a fully open access world, and require all publications to be freely available at the time of publication.

The example of the Wellcome Trust shows that the policy and cultural landscape has continued to evolve and, at the time of writing, the proposals of Plan S and the adoption of open access policies by funding bodies have just closed for consultation. Libraries can provide expert support and guidance around these proposals and, has been demonstrated over the last 20 years, are able to refresh and update their services to enable this broader cultural, and systemic change. In each of these challenges, Jisc (and by extension Jisc Collections) has worked with UK libraries as a partner, a critical friend and as a catalyst to help them realign their roles, refocus their resources and reassess their strategic priorities, for example toward new 'read and publish' agreements with publishers.

17.3   New relationships and new models

The last 20 years has seen an ongoing evolution of the markets and the economics around relationships with publishers, an explosion of hybrid models and processing charges and the advent of university open access presses (e.g. White Rose, Huddersfield and UCL). Into that mix libraries have, however patchily, used open source software (e.g. EPrints, DSpace, Fedora) to support open access repositories and publishing initiatives (e.g. PKP's Open Journal Systems). As the software and the needs of open access and open scholarship have matured, these platforms have worked to explore sustainable and mixed business models which ensure they continue to be developed and are part of a broader institutional infrastructure. On top of these platforms, service as software models have evolved to provide some of that support and to provide security and longevity.

Jisc and the HE community have a key role to support not only the open content, but also to support the underlying open global infrastructure which enables this, and is critical to the wider community's vision of open. The Jisc-funded CORE, IRUS-UK and OpenDOAR provide critical elements of this open global infrastructure providing discovery, COUNTER compliant usage statistics and directory services.

While the majority of institutional repositories are built on open source, and in the last 20 years new forks, flavours and software have emerged including

Islandora, Samvera and Zenodo, alternative and more proprietary platforms and services have also emerged as Current Research Information Systems. Many of these CRIS systems are now owned by commercial companies, for instance Pure from Elsevier and Converis from Clarivate. These provide a challenging counterpoint to the open culture of open source for research outputs and has seen the rise of hybrid repository/CRIS systems, if not a wholesale migration from an open source platform.

17.4   Jisc: then and now

JISC (Joint Information Systems Committee, in later years retitled Jisc) emerged from the Computer Board for Universities and Research Councils that was formed in 1966, focusing on the academic network via the formation of a joint network team in 1976 and the launch of Janet in 1984. JISC itself was formed in 1993 at the time of the publication of the Follett report into digital libraries (Higher Education Funding Councils, 1993), soon followed by the first major national innovation programme, the Electronic Libraries programme (eLib). A subsequent programme, Focus on Access to Institutional Resources (FAIR), led in 2003 to the birth of SHERPA services supporting open access and repositories. Further investment followed in both institutional and national capacity for open access and research data management, in the form of, for example, the RSP (2006−13) and the launch of the EThOS service for doctoral theses in 2009. With the growth of open access policies from the mid-2000s and especially with the Finch report in the United Kingdom in 2012, JISC strengthened its attention to negotiations with publishers for deals that offset open access publishing fees against subscription costs.

Today, Jisc is a membership organisation and sector agency, focused on providing services and infrastructure to members to benefit UK research. It has been described as a 'key actor' (Rumsey, 2017) in supporting open access tools and services and it does three things: delivers shared services, for example RoMEO, Publications Router and CORE for open access; does sector deals, for example with publishers large and small for open access publishing; and offers advice and support, for example guides and workshops where professionals can share good practice.

17.5   The journey from coordination to cooperation

In the following sections, we outline how Jisc contributed to institutional change across nearly 20 years of open access developments, highlighting its role against four themes.

17.5.1   Shifts in content and workflows

The last 20 years has seen an accelerating shift in libraries providing support for research outputs and content created by their own academies. This has included digitised content, including electronic theses, research data and the rise in support for open access while continuing to support traditional library activities. Examples of these new workflows include curation and sharing of research artefacts, lab notebooks, research data and data management services.

17.5.2 New library strategies

Reports like the MIT Task Force on the Future of Libraries have recognised the shift for library users from merely consumers to creators working in a broader global landscape, as well as the impact of open and the digital shift in shaping library strategies.

17.5.3 Infrastructure

Open access activities that focus around policy compliance, cost management, discovery, usage and impact, and metadata and interoperability are critical in enabling and supporting institutions to fully realise and manage their commitment to open.

17.5.4 Sustainability (and community building)

Jisc has provided and supported community building through funding for the launch of UKCoRR and the work and training delivered by the RSP.

17.6 Coordination: 2000–2005

As with virtually anything concerning open access, its origins are contested. However, for the purposes of this chapter we can see one origin as being the Santa Fe convention, agreed in 1999 and released in 2000, that then became the OAI-PMH, which is the way most repositories share information even today. At that point, UK libraries were wrapping up the last phases of the first large scale JISC development programme, eLib. That was widely seen as a success both in exploring new technologies and services, and in ushering in a new tide of collaboration between academic libraries. It was a fertile environment, but not one in which Stevan Harnad's 'subversive proposal' for open access or OAI-PMH (Harnad, 1995) had yet achieved much traction. For that, further coordination was needed.

In the United Kingdom, the spark for the rapid engagement, discussion and debate around open access and, in particular, the advent of institutional repositories can be traced back to JISC's activities at this time, which brought some coordination to a nascent and fragmented landscape. At the time there were pockets of world-leading practice, for example at Southampton University developing the EPrints software, but little sense that this might lead to a national infrastructure or widespread cultural change within universities.

JISC readily grasped the possibilities and the opportunities which both open access and repositories could provide through the FAIR programme. This built on repositories such as EPrints and DSpace that used OAI-PMH, and on the clarion call of the BOAI to encourage universities and others to experiment with the uses to which repositories might be put. Research papers, theses and cultural heritage materials were the early focus of the FAIR programme, together with learning resources via its sister X4L (Exchange for Learning) programme.

17.6.1   All's FAIR

The 14 projects in the FAIR programme spawned a range of outputs, including advocacy and guidance resources, software and early shared services. These covered topics such as:

• Setting up a repository
• Addressing the cultural change of this new technology
• Addressing the IPR implications of sharing resources
• Managing e-prints and electronic theses
• Virtual sharing of museum collections
• Presenting shared resources in institutional environments
• Preserving institutionally generated resources

FAIR prompted growth in the number of institutional repositories (Awre & Baldwin, 2005). In 2003 there were only 9 such repositories that used the most common platform, EPrints, whereas by 2006 there were a total of 69 repositories. This sheer momentum was generated by JISC providing coordinating mechanisms such as the SHERPA project at Nottingham, which worked with 18 partner institutions to share lessons and good practice in setting up and running repositories. However, as Alison Allden, then chair of the relevant JISC Committee, noted in her foreword to the FAIR synthesis report:

> 'The main challenges are not technical. Instead they relate to clarity of purpose, quality control, metadata and semantics, legal issues (intellectual property, institutional liability), to ethical issues (consent) and cultural issues, research cultures and variations between disciplines in terms of methodologies and practices, and so on'.

These issues are closely related to culture and practice within universities, and anticipate the four key themes that still resonate today. The new workflows in this case were those that enabled research-related content to be both well managed and effectively shared using the new infrastructure of repositories. Management and sharing of content challenged some institutional policies (such as IPR) and library strategies, and was an early taste of the issues that the 'inside out' library would need to address. One such was described at the time as being about 'advocacy'; persuading people that it was worth the time and effort to use the repositories. In later years this was unpacked a little, to be more clearly about skills and roles (who is best placed to manage and share an institution's research outputs?), and sustainability (how does this become business-as-usual?). During the FAIR programme, however, we believed that the benefits of open access repositories would quickly become self-evident.

It is worth noting that JISC's early efforts to work with publishers toward open access also date from this period. For example, in 2003 JISC secured a deal with BioMed Central on behalf of UK institutions to waive author fees for over 90 biomedical journals. The challenges of hybrid journals were also already apparent. In 2005 the open access fee charged by the *Proceedings of the National Academy of Sciences* was $1000 (today it is $2200 or $1500 for a non-compliant licence). While JISC forums provided some places for institutions to consider the implications of gold OA, there was perhaps insufficient coordination within the sector at this stage.

The move toward open access is, of course, international and JISC joined UK institutions such as UCL and Glasgow in coordinating activities such as CERN's 'OAI' workshop, while other coordination activities, such as that by Cambridge around the DSpace repository platform, were pursued independently of JISC. Clifford Lynch's paper on repositories as essential infrastructure (Lynch, 2003) which focused on DSpace provided an opportunity for JISC-funded institutions to engage with MIT/Cambridge's repository programme and to share experience and lessons. That international engagement has remained a strong strand of the professional culture around open access.

17.7   Consolidation: 2005–2010

After the initial push of FAIR, pilot agreements with publishers, and international initiatives, 2005 was a year of reflection and planning. JISC published a synthesis report from FAIR, and designed a new programme to build on its foundations, helping institutions explore research data repositories, new technologies and repository services. As with all JISC programmes at this time, there were support activities that encouraged participating institutions to share lessons with each other, across the United Kingdom, and more widely.

From 2006 to 2007, the pace of consolidation became even faster, as a major capital investment supported a larger programme that gave support to institutions across the sector to start or enhance their own repositories, for a national service – the RSP – to be established at Nottingham, and for groundbreaking research into the costs and benefits of open access to be commissioned. The programme vision was bold, including that:

- Every UK institution would have repository capability to support research and learning
- Repositories would be embedded into workflows
- Repository services would be interoperating to avoid duplication of effort and to increase access to content
- Institutions would be better equipped and skilled to manage their information assets

Even during the life of the programme, success was marked. For example, in terms of quantity between 2007 and 2008, reports of the electronic sharing and management of research papers rose from 37% to 48%, and of theses from 19% to 30%, and, in terms of variety, repositories were established for the creative arts and music, where open access was, and remains, a challenging concept. Perhaps the best example of consolidation of services, with institutions working together to support a national solution, was the birth of the EThOS e-theses service at the British Library, following and via several JISC development projects. The changes in institutional doctoral workflows that accompanied this change were often significant, in terms of culture, practice and, often, institutional policy. Such changes were increasingly common, as the implications of the 'inside-out' library became apparent and institutions started, for example, adopting their own open access policies as complements to those of research funders.

To support institutions, and the UK more generally, in making those changes, JISC commissioned a landmark piece of research from John Houghton (Houghton et al., 2009), outlining the potential net benefits of open access. It was not uncontroversial, and its place in the evolution of open access policy might perhaps be the subject of a different chapter but, in terms of institutional culture, it emboldened open access advocates and the few institutional leaders, such as Paul Ayris at UCL and Martin Hall at Salford, who were members of the UK Open Access Implementation Group.

It became increasingly clear that consolidation was needed at the professional level too. With some seed project support from JISC, UK institutions formed the UK Council of Research Repositories (UKCoRR), as a safe and effective means by which those implementing the 'inside-out' library could share good practice and learn lessons from each other. With extensive support from the RSP, these professional skills and roles became recognised within institutions, and UKCoRR was perhaps one of the key building blocks that led to the current crop of open science and scholarly communication teams, revived university presses, etc. It also began to cement a much firmer relationship on campus between the library and the research office, as both institutions and the professionals themselves saw increasing synergies between their roles.

Institutions and their engagement with repositories matured and consolidated. Repositories moved away from the role of an institutional silo to one which was more connected and interoperable with other institutional systems. This integration included links into grant and identity management systems and these links enabled not just an integration step change but opportunities for libraries to work in partnership with other teams across the university including IT, web services and human resources. The repository was ideally positioned to provide and blend data from these systems to support new uses including populating staff profiles and readiness for Research Excellence Framework (REF) 2014.

17.8   Collaboration: 2010–2015

By 2010, the UK had a world-leading network of institutional repositories, whose business case was increasingly established but still contested, especially by journal publishers. That formed one context for a radical shift in the UK open access policy landscape. Other drivers were the Finch Report 2012 that recommended open access mainly via hybrid journals, and the subsequent revised policies from the Research Councils (favouring 'gold' open access) and the post-2014 Research Excellence Framework (favouring deposit into repositories). JISC was not part of the Finch group and, by this time, was undergoing a protracted organisational change, during which its attention moved away from national programmes comprising projects based at institutions, and focused much more on establishing national services. The two main strands of service were negotiation and infrastructure. Following Finch, JISC (now a membership organisation, 'Jisc') pioneered 'offset' agreements with journal publishers, which constrained the additional costs of gold open access supplementing journal subscriptions. In doing so, the scope of the conversations between Jisc and institutions broadened, as did the conversations within institutions faced with complex and varied journal deals, their own open access positions, contrasting funder policies and the rapidly evolving broader open research movement among researchers.

Jisc's infrastructure development nationally included an attempt, via the EDINA data centre, to impose collaboration among a range of services that supported open access, including the SHERPA services based at Nottingham, discovery services based at Manchester, and deposit services based at Edinburgh. While not wholly successful, this project did both spawn the Publications Router, and provide important lessons for service interoperability and sustainability. Jisc also contributed to the development of standards, such as COUNTER, whose 2013 release introduced gold open access usage reports, enabling institutions, publishers and Jisc to collaborate in having agreed evidence on the use of open access articles in journals.

At the institutional level, the main theme during this time was the rapid adoption, certainly among universities with wide research interests, of CRIS. These commercial products often took on some of the functionality offered by repositories, and collaboration between customers was limited to participation in user groups. At the same time, library systems and e-resource management systems were rapidly evolving, allowing institutional culture to surface open access content across multiple platforms with new drivers and new vendors.

In this changing context, collaboration involving Jisc, seeking to understand the needs of its new members, and within and between institutions themselves, became essential. In an exception to its move away from sector-wide programmes, Jisc funded a set of projects under the name 'OA Good Practice', that produced a wide range of resources, including a handbook, for institutions adopting open access. Importantly, the programme included a very diverse range of institutions, to ensure that open access did not leave some behind.

17.9   Cooperation: 2015–2020

From 2015, Jisc has been unequivocally a member-driven organisation, and cooperation has been key, with its members, and with the organisations that fund both them and Jisc. At a national level, Jisc worked closely with Universities UK on the Open Access Coordination Group set up under Professor Adam Tickell, to enable stakeholders to work together to implement the Finch recommendations. While that consensus came under increasing strain over this period, the group did achieve some notable successes, producing a common view of progress through two monitoring reports, and a set of practical recommendations on monographs, repositories, efficiencies and standards.

The value of this cooperation is perhaps exemplified by the adoption by UK institutions of ORCiD, a vital component in open access workflows but one that depends on cooperation between researchers, institutions, the enabling consortium, as well as publishers and funders. In this case, the Jisc-led consortium is not only a way for a group of institutions to buy into ORCiD as a solution, but vitally it includes support for ORCiD take-up locally, because the infrastructure depends now on each actor playing their part. It is not simply a matter of either installing local software such as repositories, or purchasing solutions such as access to journal platforms. Open access workflows depend on this cooperative adoption of standards and agreed solutions. Another example of Jisc enabling institutions and their academics to pursue this approach is around the revival of small academic and university presses. Jisc cooperated with institutions who were leading this revival, producing a landmark report in 2017 (Adema & Stone, 2017) and, more recently, a purchasing service that enables new and small presses efficiently to procure the tools they need to operate, where those tools are vetted to ensure they do support the cooperative approach to infrastructure described above, for example supporting ORCiD, etc.

17.10   Conclusion

In *Insights into the economy of open scholarship* (Franck, 2019), Martin Paul Eve posits the questions:

> 'What's the role of the library in the 21st century if it is not facilitating open scholarship? Part of the role of the library has to be to enable new and innovative approaches.'

Libraries have a very important role to play, in partnership with organisations like Jisc, in supporting, innovating and encouraging the journey to open scholarship. Jisc has been critical in enabling and supporting the growth of open access and institutional repositories within the United Kingdom over the last 20 years. Jisc's work laid strong foundations which saw its role in the United Kingdom frequently cited as being the catalyst and coordinator for this growth. The journey for HEIs has moved through various stages with Jisc, reflecting both shifts within the organisation and its role, as well as new and mature relationships to the current one of cooperation.

Endnote

1. SPARC: https://sparcopen.org.

References

Adema, J., & Stone, G. (2017). *Changing publishing ecologies: A landscape study of new university presses and academic-led publishing.* Retrieved from <http://repository.jisc. ac.uk/6666/1/Changing-publishing-ecologies-report.pdf>

Awre, C., & Baldwin, C. (2005). Focus on access to institutional resources: A synthesis of the JISC FAIR programme. New Review of Information Networking, 11(2), 137–158. Available from https://doi.org/10.1080/13614570600573276.

Dempsey, L., & Malpas, C. (2018). Academic library futures in a diversified university system. In N. W. Gleason (Ed.), *Higher education in the era of the fourth industrial revolution* (pp. 65–89). Singapore: Palgrave Macmillan. Available from https://www.oclc.org/research/publications/2018/academic-library-futures.html.

Franck, G. (2019). *Insights into the economy of open scholarship: A look into the Open Library of Humanities with Martin Paul Eve, Co-founder.* Bristol: Knowledge Exchange. Available from http://repository.jisc.ac.uk/7296/1/Insights_into_the_Economy_of_Open_Scholarship_-_A_look_into_the_Open_Library_of_Humanities_March_2019.pdf.

Harnad, S. (1995). A subversive proposal. In A. Okerson, & J. O'Donnell (Eds.), *Scholarly journals at the crossroads: A subversive proposal for electronic publishing.* Washington, DC: Association of Research Libraries. Available from https://eprints.soton.ac.uk/253351/.

Higher Education Funding Councils (1993). *Joint Funding Councils' Libraries Review Group [Follett report].* Bristol: Higher Education Funding Councils Retrieved from <https://www.ukoln.ac.uk/services/papers/follett/report/index.html>.

Houghton, J., Rasmussen, B., Sheehan, P., Oppenheim, C., Morris, A., Creaser, C., Greenwood, H., Summers, M., & Gourlay, A. (2009). *Economic implications of alternative scholarly publishing models: Exploring the costs and benefits.* Loughborough: Loughborough University. Available from https://core.ac.uk/download/pdf/10833825.pdf.

Lynch, C. A. (2003). Institutional repositories: Essential infrastructure for scholarship in the digital age. *Portal: Libraries and the Academy, 3*(2), 327–336. Available from https://doi.org/10.1353/pla.2003.0039.

MIT Libraries. (2016). The future of libraries. Retrieved from <https://future-of-libraries.mit.edu>

Pinfield, S., Cox, A., & Rutter, S. (2017). *Mapping the future of academic libraries: A report for SCONUL.* London: SCONUL. Available from https://www.sconul.ac.uk/sites/default/files/documents/Mapping%20the%20Future%20of%20Academic%20Libraries%20Final%20proof_0.pdf.

Rumsey, S. (2017). OA in the UK: State of the nation. *International Journal of Legal Information, 45*(1), 56–61. Available from https://doi.org/10.1017/jli.2017.15.

Section IV

Reflections

Reflections on technology, change and academic libraries

18

Jeremy Atkinson
Jeremy Atkinson Consultancy, Cardiff, Wales, United Kingdom

18.1 Introduction

The previous chapters and case studies provide very useful insights into the nature and effectiveness of technology and change activities and projects in academic libraries. Embedded within these case studies are some themes, observations and important lessons learned that have been identified by the contributors. I thought it would be useful if I tried to bring some of these themes, observations and lessons learned together with related points from the literature within a concluding chapter. I have amalgamated these key points under a number of headings and subheadings, sometimes using or adapting the wording of the contributors, sometimes using my own wording. The headings used are:

- Benefits
- Constraints
- Key issues (with a number of subheadings)

Many of these points could be included under different headings or subheadings, but I have allocated the points to those headings which seem to be the most appropriate.

I hope the information under the headings below is of value to those planning or implementing technology and change activities and projects. Not all the points will be relevant to all potential activities, but, hopefully, the information can act as a checklist with at least some points providing useful food for thought and helping to make the work more effective.

18.2 Benefits

- A technology and change project can help raise the visibility, profile, status and reputation of the library in the university and beyond.
- A project can provide an opportunity to lift library staff's gaze out of day-to-day work and engage with a vision of developing services. In collaborative projects, staff are exposed to a wider pool of ideas, knowledge, expertise and ambitions from other departments or institutions.
- Library staff involved in a successful project can gain confidence and develop a change of mindset and different approaches to work and staff development.

Technology, Change and the Academic Library. DOI: https://doi.org/10.1016/B978-0-12-822807-4.00018-X

- There may be opportunities to utilise the skills and expertise developed in other projects and with other clients.
- In collaborative projects, academic staff, researchers and students who are involved may develop a deeper understanding about the library's work and see the benefits of further collaboration.

18.3   Constraints

- There is the challenge of which technologies to adopt in a rapidly changing landscape, as well as the cost implications.
- If the library does not participate in particular initiatives, there is a danger it may be side-lined in technological developments.
- Time is the greatest difficulty and risk in technology and change projects. The time commitment can easily be underestimated in terms of planning, building, consulting with stakeholders and testing. Members of the project team are often not solely employed on the project. The project work has to fit in around business-as-usual and service development activities and balanced against other priorities.
- Short timescales can also be a problem for other stakeholders involved in the project, including academic staff, who have high workloads. System rejection by end users can be a major risk to implementation.
- Constraints can be imposed by institutional procedures and processes.
- There is a danger of overcomplicating the design at a time of rapid technological change. The service, system or content may have a short shelf life and it could take a lot of work to review and restructure.
- There can be a steep learning curve for library staff and other stakeholders involved in a changeover of a system or service.
- There may be no system or service like it in any other university, reducing the help and advice available.
- There may a risk of a low level of participation by academic staff and students related to a lack of understanding or interest. There may also be concerns about the quality or status of the new service or content.
- There can be risks associated with how the library is perceived if a new system results in it adopting a compliance or monitoring role in addition to a service-orientated role.
- There is a need to identify and quantify the risks associated with failure of the project.

18.4   Key issues

18.4.1   Strategic planning, and relationship to strategies, policies and procedures

- The project should link in appropriate ways to existing university strategies, programmes and policies.
- There may be a need to produce a strategic vision for the project which links explicitly to university and library strategies.

- A linkage to a major programme or project at a high level in the university can help with ownership and prioritisation.
- Important areas for strategic linkages could include: supporting university teaching, learning and research; improving the student experience; making systems more user friendly; enhancing access to quality content; delivering collaborative approaches that work across institutional silos; ensuring more effective use of physical space; delivering value for money, affordability and efficiency gains.
- The project may impact on or bring about revision to institutional policies. Example could include policies relating to social media, research data management and learning spaces.

18.4.2 Leadership and management

- Innovative leadership is often important in technology and change projects. Key aspects include the ability to remove barriers, generate short term wins, produce a sense of urgency and acceleration, and gain strong commitment from all those involved.
- Strong leadership is required to ensure the project is appropriately resourced in terms of space, equipment and software, staff, access to IT support and administrative support.
- Effective change management is a key part of good leadership. The staff need to see that organisational leaders consider the change important. Any change agent used should remain behind the scenes; the local leadership must be seen as the face of change.
- An open and collaborative management style enables the project staff to feel highly valued members of the team, consulted and able to make contributions.
- Universities can benefit from leadership skills developed by staff involved in the project.

18.4.3 Project management, change management, governance and communication

- Transparent governance arrangements for the project will need to be put in place. A project group with representatives of appropriate stakeholders will need to be set up, the size and nature of the group depending on the project, but potentially including different library teams, academic staff, researchers, students, other departments, other universities and external experts. A team approach will ensure a diversity and breadth of input. For larger and more complex projects, a two tier governance structure may be needed, with groups such as a working group and a steering group, with good communication between the two. A project manager and project administrator may also be required.
- Projects with good change management processes, addressing the people side of change, are more likely to meet their objectives. Consideration should be given to using a change agent, with the role being carried out by a person from inside or outside the library. The communication process is important in change management; there is a need to engage with library staff to understand how they regard the change and to ensure the communication addresses their key areas of concern.
- Effective project management should be put in place. A project plan should be developed with clear aims and objectives and rationale for the work, work packages and timelines and funding requirements. A testing stage may be needed to gain feedback, before the final development phase. Prince2 or a similar project management methodology may need to be employed. The plan will need to be signed off by the relevant senior manager.

- There may be value in having a segmented development with each stage carried out as a separate, self-contained smaller project, with a review carried out at each stage to consider what has been achieved and the next stage of development.
- In developing project plans, it is important not to let the technology dictate. Technology should be viewed as the enabling agent, not the driver. There is a need to fully understand the underlying purpose of the development, including the perspective of users and their needs.
- Processes should be put in place to review and incorporate ideas from similar projects elsewhere, to ensure quality, and, in appropriate cases, to make the transition from project to service.
- Regular meetings of the project group should be held in order to maintain momentum, monitor the project plan and review progress.
- Managers of the project should seek to value contributions from all members of the project group, ensure mutual trust and respect and arrange for success to be celebrated by the whole group.

18.4.4 Finance and staffing

- There is a need to ensure that there is sufficient staff capacity to undertake the project, in particular the changes planned in systems, services and staffing. Any expert staffing and support requirements need to be defined. Changes in project staffing can slow the project down.
- The changes to staffing levels, roles and responsibilities, and organisational structures to operate the new or revised service or system need to be defined.
- The project costs and ongoing costs of the resulting business-as-usual service or system need to be defined and procured, either from the university or externally. The university may require savings as a result of investment in the technology.
- There can be a danger that ongoing system costs take up too high a percentage of revenue budgets. It may be necessary to walk away from all or part of a project proposal that is not value for money.

18.4.5 Advocacy, consultation and engagement

- For many projects, success will be dependent on gaining strong support from other staff in the university, in some cases senior university staff.
- Taking an evidence-based approach involving consultation with an appropriate range of stakeholders can ensure that the project is focused on the needs and priorities of users. Interviews or focus groups with potential users of the new service or system, such as academic staff or students, or seeking feedback on prototypes can help to obtain faculty buy-in. Consulting with staff or students in their own physical or virtual spaces can be useful. Advocacy to persuade users to take up the new service should focus on the benefits to them. If academic staff or students are involved in the project work, they can usefully act as 'champions' promoting the new service or system to their colleagues.
- There may be a need to engage directly with appropriate library staff early in the project in order to surface and address issues that they have. Methods such as events, focus groups and suggestions schemes can be useful to obtain feedback and gain buy-in.
- Engagement with suppliers and other external providers about the project can sometimes be difficult and often time-consuming.

- Contact with other academic libraries that have developed the same or similar services and systems can be useful to obtain advice and share information.

18.4.6   Institutional culture and cultural change

- The culture in many academic libraries is deep seated and can tend to preserve the status quo, making it difficult to implement new innovations that require flexibility and creativity. The strength of ownership to existing services and practices and the length of time before new initiatives become embedded in the culture of the library can be underestimated.
- Where academic libraries have a track record of being pioneering and innovative and refreshing and updating their services, change can become normalised for library staff, with an understanding of the change cycle helping to navigate the process successfully.
- There is a need to create an environment which encourages risk, innovation and experimentation. Librarians increasingly need to demonstrate agility and the ability to change rapidly in addition to providing stable services.
- Attitudes to risk need to be balanced against the appetite for change. Consideration should be given to the extent of innovation that is sensible in order to retain ownership amongst all stakeholders.
- Following a change, initial uptake can often be slow with staff or users feeling disconnected and not seeing the relevance or value of the new service or system. However, a change in culture can occur when library staff or users have to use the new service in their day-to-day work.
- Cultural adjustment and training may be required for new roles and a redefinition of support requirements.

18.4.7   Values

- There can be a conventional view, held by some librarians and users, that adoption of digital technologies goes against the purpose and tradition of libraries.
- Technologies can come embedded with their own set of values and assumptions, with the consequence that the professional values of libraries may be in conflict with the values embedded in the technology.
- Developments can support the value of openness in the distribution of research.
- It may be necessary to retain some of the values inherent in the original services and systems prior to technological development.
- There may be cultural values and sensitivities associated with the materials and artefacts intended for digitisation.
- The project may need to relate to university values, for example, social justice or the importance of the individual.

18.4.8   Changes in roles and responsibilities

- Technology developments provide opportunities for academic librarians to move into new roles beyond traditional activities. Examples include the management of research outputs, research data management, digital humanities and digital literacy. This can result in librarians moving from a peripheral role to a more central role in teaching and research support.

- Librarians can often become involved in a wider range of activities in the project lifecycle or research lifecycle, such as exploring potential sources of funding. In time this can result in new professional skills and roles becoming recognised within institutions.
- Consideration should be given to roles and responsibilities as the project evolves into a service. Those managing the project may not be the most appropriate people to manage the new service.

18.4.9   Partnerships and collaboration

- Technology and change projects require a greater emphasis on collaboration of library staff with academic and support staff across the university, particularly areas such as IT services, technology developers, research offices and commercial services. Collaborative approaches bring together a wider range of expertise and knowledge and different ways of thinking. Academic libraries become more of a partner than a service provider. It is important that new library systems and services interact and align with existing systems and processes that other departments manage.
- New partnerships between different library teams may also be required.
- In some projects, close partnerships may be needed with external providers and vendors. The library may need to take an active role in activities managed by the external provider, for example, user groups or early adopter programmes.
- In some cases, it may be useful to involve experts and mentors with relevant experience who are external to the library.
- There may be opportunities for a number of academic libraries to work collaboratively in areas such as the procurement of e-resources, out-of-hours virtual enquiry services and open access presses. Shared services or approaches may help to deliver cost efficiencies, improve service levels and deal with complex activities which would be difficult for any library to undertake on its own.
- National organisations, such as Jisc in the United Kingdom, can help academic libraries realign their roles, refocus resources and reassess their strategic priorities in technology-based projects. They can link with libraries as a partner, a critical friend or as a catalyst to enable libraries to work together and share lessons learned and good practice.
- In technological developments, the library can have an increasing dependency on external systems providers and on individuals and teams external to the library but acting on the library's behalf.

18.4.10   Impact on staff, services and users, on workflows and processes and on university teaching, learning and research

- Technology and change projects can help to make academic libraries more user- and service-based rather than collection-based. The library service portfolio can be extended, including engaging beyond traditional user groups. They can be beneficial to service development, with projects benefitting provision in a wide range of areas including support for teaching learning and research, user discovery, acquisition processes, metadata management, collection management, document supply, support and training for users, study facilities, and evaluation.

- Projects can help to support the creation, capture, preservation and discovery of content. Access to a broader range of resources related to user needs can be enabled, including access, via digitisation, to material that previously had limited availability.
- Projects can help to support new approaches to learning and knowledge creation, enable pedagogical innovation and provide support for teaching, through digital initiatives help to support and develop research and scholarship, and provide development opportunities for university staff and students.
- Projects can have an impact on the nature and extent of library staff workloads and can help to streamline workflows, automate processes, and rationalise and speed up services. There can also be impacts on requirements for numbers of library staff and staff responsibilities, organisational structures and service models.
- In appropriate cases, resources need to be allocated to enable the transition from project phase to a business-as-usual service.

18.4.11   Skills, attitudes and behaviours of library staff

- The presence of skilled and expert staff is an important factor in the success of a project. For library staff involved in technology and change projects, there may be constraints to overcome in terms of staff skills, knowledge, confidence, competency, capability and capacity. They may need to expand their skills and competencies beyond traditional areas and to adapt to new practices through targeted staff development and training. As with training for library users, a decision will need to be made on whether the training is compulsory or optional.
- Existing skills of academic librarians should be utilised. These could be in areas such as: information management; relationship and partnership management; skills in communication, problem solving, critical thinking and evaluation; research skills; strategic and operational planning; service development and delivery.
- There are a number of areas where library staff skills may need to be enhanced, including: technical and higher level IT skills; project and change management; leadership, negotiation and persuasion skills; knowledge of new technologies and systems; use of collaborative tools.
- A number of behaviours and attitudes are required for effective project working, including: openness and being outward facing; trust; pooling of skills and attributes; creativity; flexibility; enthusiasm; determination.
- Some of the skills developed by librarians in technology and change projects will be transferable to future initiatives, including: increased knowledge of current technological developments, systems and software; prototyping; usability testing; accessibility testing.

18.4.12   Skills, attitudes and behaviours of users

- The project should aim to be in line with changing user behaviour and expectations, including changing information searching behaviour. This is particularly true of younger students who, as digital natives, can have very different needs and preferences in relation to areas such as use of mobile devices, social media and learning spaces.
- There is a need to analyse and aim to meet the needs of different stakeholder groups. Stakeholder assessment provides a careful consideration of everyone who has a stake in

the change. User experience techniques can be utilised to understand and improve the experience of users, and user driven approaches, such as patron driven acquisition and personalised support, can help to provide a stronger user focus.

- The project may need to appreciate and understand the differing levels of technology acceptance among different stakeholder groups.
- Training and support may need to be delivered to different user groups to enhance skills, knowledge and competencies in new services and systems and in the different aspects of digital and information literacy. Online training can be used to deliver to a large number of people at scale, but its effectiveness compared with face-to-face training needs to be considered.

18.4.13   Ethical and legal issues, including privacy, confidentiality and security

- The needs of disabled students and accessibility standards and requirements should be addressed when implementing technological developments.
- Implications such as information security, IPR, copyright and data protection need to be considered fully.
- Access issues should be carefully balanced against issues of user privacy.
- Traditionally in academic libraries, user data has been siloed to the library and treated as private and confidential and not identifiable to individual users. The benefits of libraries' involvement in initiatives such as learning analytics should be balanced against ethical issues such as privacy, confidentiality and intellectual freedom.

18.4.14   Technical infrastructure and support

- Good integration and interoperability of new or revised systems with relevant existing library and university systems will be required as part of a broader institutional infrastructure. In many cases, a single user interface will be preferable.
- Effective interoperability with external platforms, including supplier platforms, is also required.
- In appropriate cases, effective digital preservation and enhanced metadata provision to aid discoverability need to be put in place as more electronic material is provided.
- Ongoing technical support for new systems will need to be provided and be fit for purpose. In some cases, library staff or university IT staff will need to enhance their technical knowledge and expertise relating to the new systems.

18.4.15   Promotion and marketing

- Marketing and promotion strategies related to the new developments will be required. Promotion methods could include email, messaging, social media, websites, leaflets and, in appropriate cases, meetings, events and exhibitions.
- The danger of 'over promotion' should be recognised and the methods adopted should focus on the tools different audiences use or the places they visit.
- Marketing and promotion will need to relate to a diverse range of university stakeholders, including library staff, and, in some cases, external stakeholders. There may be subcategories

in the stakeholder groups and different messages or promotion in different forms may be needed for the different subcategories.

- Promotion needs to aim to increase knowledge and understanding of the work of the project and encourage use of the service or system. The promotion may need to convey the transformational nature of the technological change and embed revised perceptions of the library's role. Consideration should also be given to the need for ongoing promotion.

18.4.16   Evaluation, monitoring and review

- Although it is not an exact science, at the beginning of the project it can be useful to define what success for the change project will look like and the measures of success.
- Interim evaluation is important. A new or revised system or service need not be complete before asking for stakeholder feedback. It is useful to obtain detailed comments and to gauge interest on a prototype before implementing an initiative permanently.
- At the end of the project methods such as analytics and metrics, focus groups and surveys should be used to obtain feedback and assess uptake and impact of the new service or system. This will enable evidence-based decisions to be made on future developments.
- Further periodic reviews may be necessary to ensure the service or system remains up-to-date and any technology changes are addressed.

ABBREVIATIONS AND ACRONYMS

The following list explains general abbreviations and acronyms used in the book. It does not include all the abbreviations and acronyms related to a particular institution or organisation.

ACRL	Association of College and Research Libraries (USA)
ADKAR (in change management)	awareness desire knowledge ability reinforcement
APC	article processing charge
API	application programming interface
APUC	Advanced Procurement for Universities and Colleges (Scotland)
ARC	automated reserve collection
ARDC	Australian Research Data Commons
ASRS	automated storage and retrieval system
BA	Bachelor of Arts
BOAI	Budapest Open Access Initiative
BYOD	bring your own device
CAUL	Council of Australian University Librarians
CERN	European Council for Nuclear Research (Conseil Européen pour la Recherche Nucléaire)
CIO	chief information officer
CORE	Connecting Repositories
COUNTER	Counting Online Usage of Networked Electronic Resources
CPD	continuing professional development
CRIS	current research information system
CSC	cascading style sheets
CSIRO	Commonwealth Scientific and Industrial Research Organisation (Australia)
CSV	comma-separated values
DDA	demand-driven acquisition
DOI	digital object identifier
DRM	digital rights management
EDI	electronic data interchange
EDINA	Edinburgh Data and Information Access (UK)
EThOS	Electronic Theses Online Service (UK)
EU	European Union
FAIR (in research data management)	findable, accessible, interoperable, reusable
FAIR (Jisc programme)	Focus on Access to Institutional Resources (UK)
FAQs	frequently asked questions

Fedora	Flexible Extensible Digital Object Repository Architecture
FRBR	Functional Requirements for Bibliographic Records
FTE	full-time equivalent
FTP	File Transfer Protocol
GDPR	General Data Protection Regulation (EU)
GLAM	galleries, libraries, archives and museums
GPS	Global Positioning System
HDR	higher degree research
HEI	higher education institution
HPECM	Hewlett Packard Enterprise Content Manager
HTML	Hypertext Markup Language
HUP	Helsinki University Press (Finland)
IATUL	International Association of Technological University Libraries (name changed to International Association of University Libraries in 2014)
IIP	infrastructure investment plan
IPR	intellectual property rights
IRUS-UK	International Repository Usage Statistics UK
ISBN	International Standard Book Number
IT	information technology
Janet	Joint Academic Network (UK)
JAWS	Job Access With Speech
JESLA	Journal of the European Second Language Association
Jisc	Joint Information Systems Committee (UK)
JPEG	Joint Photographic Experts Group
JSTOR	short for Journal Storage
LMS	learning management system/library management system
LSE	London School of Economics (UK)
LTI	Learning Tools Interoperability
MAP	Modern Academic Publishing (Germany)
MARC	Machine Readable Cataloguing
MBA	Master of Business Administration
MIT	Massachusetts Institute of Technology (USA)
MOOC	massive open online course
MySQL	My Structured Query Language
NBK	National Bibliographic Knowledgebase (UK)
NBN	Newcastle Broadcasting New South Wales (Australia)
NERS	New Enhancements Request System
NFSA	National Film and Sound Archive (Australia)
NSS	National Student Survey (UK)
OA	open access
OAI-PMH	Open Archives Initiative Protocol for Metadata Harvesting
OER	open educational resources
OJS	Open Journal Systems
OPAC	Online Public Access Catalogue
OpenDOAR	Directory of Open Access Repositories
ORCiD	Open Researcher and Contributor ID
PDA	patron-driven acquisition
PhD	Doctor of Philosophy

PHP	PHP Hypertext Processor (originally derived from Personal Home Page tools)
PKP	Public Knowledge Project
PMC	PubMed Central
PNG	Portable Network Graphics
PoD	print on demand
Q&A	question and answer
QR	quick response
RDA	Resource Description and Access
READ	Reference Effort Assessment Data
REF	Research Excellence Framework (UK)
RFID	radio-frequency identification
RLUK	Research Libraries UK
RoMEO	Rights Metadata for Open Archiving (UK)
RSP	Repositories Support Project (UK)
SCONUL	Society of College, National and University Libraries (UK)
SCURL	Scottish Confederation of University and Research Libraries
SHEDL	Scottish Higher Education Digital Library
SHERPA	Securing a Hybrid Environment for Research Preservation and Access (UK)
SMS	short message service
SPARC	Scholarly Publishing and Academic Resources Coalition
TEQSA	Tertiary Education Quality and Standards Agency (Australia)
UCL	University College London (UK)
UDA	user-driven acquisition
UI	user interface
UJPIR	Undergraduate Journal of Politics and International Relations
UKCoRR	United Kingdom Council of Research Repositories
UK-SCL	UK Scholarly Communications Licence
URL	Uniform Resource Locator
UX	user experience
VHS	Video Home System
VLE	virtual learning environment
VR	virtual reality
WCAG	Web Content Accessibility Guidelines
WHEEL	Wales Higher Education Electronic Library
WHELF	Wales Higher Education Libraries Forum
WIL	work integrated learning
WREO	White Rose eTheses Online (UK)
WRL	White Rose Libraries (UK)
X4L	Exchange for Learning (UK)

Further reading

The references provided at the end of each chapter or case study provide some signposts for those wishing to explore specific themes and aspects further. There is a considerable amount of literature relating to technology, change, and academic libraries, and good access to this literature is provided by abstracting and indexing journals and contents list providers. However, I thought it would be helpful if I put together a very selective list of further reading, concentrating on some of the more readable and accessible articles and books I have used in putting this book together, which are additional to those listed in my overview and literature review in Chapter 2.

Section 1: Introduction
Critical reflection

Fook, J., & Gardner, F. (2007). *Practising critical reflection: A resource handbook.* Maidenhead: Open University Press.

Fook, J., & Gardner, F. (Eds.), (2013). *Critical reflection in context: Applications in health and social care.* London: Routledge.

Jasper, M. (2013). *Beginning reflective practice* (2nd ed.). Andover: Cengage Learning EMEA.

Reale, M. (2017). *Becoming a reflective librarian and teacher: Strategies for mindful academic practice.* Chicago, IL: ALA Editions.

Rolfe, G., Jasper, M., & Freshwater, D. (2010). *Critical reflection in practice: Generating knowledge for care* (2nd ed.). London: Palgrave Macmillan.

Thompson, S., & Thompson, N. (2008). *The critically reflective practitioner.* London: Palgrave Macmillan.

White, S., Fook, J., & Gardner, F. (Eds.), (2006). *Critical reflection in health and social care.* Maidenhead: Open University Press.

Section 2: Technology, change management, and academic libraries
Technology in academic libraries

Baker, D., & Evans, W. (Eds.), (2015). *Digital information strategies: From applications and content to libraries and people.* Oxford: Chandos Publishing.

Baker, D., & Evans, W. (Eds.), (2016). *Innovation in libraries and information services.* Bingley: Emerald Group Publishing.

Dempsey, L., & Varnum, K. J. (2014). *The network reshapes the library: Lorcan Dempsey on libraries, services and networks.* London: Facet Publishing.

Hall, M., Harrow, M., & Estelle, L. (Eds.), (2015). *Digital futures: Expert briefings on digital technologies for education and research.* Oxford: Chandos Publishing.

Henning, N. (2017). *Keeping up with emerging technologies: Best practices for information professionals.* Santa Barbara, CA: Libraries Unlimited.

Ippoliti, C. (2018). *The savvy academic librarian's guide to technology innovation: Moving beyond the wow factor.* Lanham, MD: Rowman & Littlefield.

Varnum, K. J. (Ed.), (2014). *The top technologies every librarian needs to know: A LITA guide.* London: Facet Publishing.

Yang, S. Q., & Li, L. (2015). *Emerging technologies for librarians.* Oxford: Chandos Publishing.

Change management in academic libraries

Atkinson, J. (2003). Managing change and embedding innovation in academic libraries and information services. *New Review of Academic Librarianship, 9*(1), 25−41. Available from https://doi.org/10.1080/13614530410001692013.

Duren, P. (2013). *Leadership in academic and public libraries: A time of change.* Oxford: Chandos Publishing.

Jantz, R. C. (2015). The determinants of organizational innovation: An interpretation and implications for research libraries. *College & Research Libraries, 76*(4), 512−536. Retrieved from: https://crl.acrl.org/index.php/crl/article/view/16440.

Limwichitr, S., Broady-Preston, J., & Ellis, D. (2015). A discussion of problems in implementing organisational cultural change: Developing a learning organisation in university libraries. *Library Review, 64*(6/7), 480−488. Available from https://doi.org/10.1108/LR-10-2014-0116.

O'Connor, S. (Ed.), (2015). *Library management in disruptive times: Skills and knowledge for an uncertain future.* London: Facet Publishing.

Simons, M. (2017). *Academic library metamorphosis and regeneration.* Lanham, MD: Rowman & Littlefield.

Technology and change management in academic libraries

Eden, B. L. (Ed.), (2015a). *Cutting-edge research in developing the library of the future: New paths for building future services.* Lanham, MD: Rowman & Littlefield.

Eden, B. L. (Ed.), (2015b). Partnerships and new roles in the 21st-century academic library: Collaborating, embedding, and cross-training for the future. Lanham, MD: Rowman & Littlefield.

Eden, B. L. (Ed.), (2015c). *Rethinking technical services: New frameworks, new skill sets, new tools, new roles.* Lanham, MD: Rowman & Littlefield.

Mackenzie, A., & Martin, L. (Eds.), (2013). *Mastering digital librarianship: Strategy, networking and discovery in academic libraries.* London: Facet Publishing.

Michalak, S. C. (2012). This changes everything: Transforming the academic library. *Journal of Library Administration, 52*(5), 411−423. Available from https://doi.org/10.1080/01930826.2012.700801.

Stachokas, G. (2018). *Reengineering the library: Issues in electronic resources management.* Chicago, IL: ALA Editions.

Trends

ACRL Research Planning and Review Committee. (2018). 2018 top trends in academic libraries: A review of the trends and issues affecting academic libraries in higher education. *College & Research Libraries News, 79*(6). 286-293, 300. Retrieved from: https://crln.acrl.org/index.php/crlnews/article/view/17001/18739.

Delaney, G., & Bates, J. (2015). Envisioning the academic library: A reflection on roles, relevancy and relationships. *New Review of Academic Librarianship*, *21*(1), 30−51. Available from https://doi.org/10.1080/13614533.2014.911194.

IFLA. (2019). *IFLA trend report 2019 update: Insights from the IFLA trend report*. The Hague, Netherlands: IFLA. Retrieved from: https://trends.ifla.org/files/trends/assets/documents/ifla_trend_report_2019.pdf

Meier, J. (2016). The future of academic libraries: Conversations with today's leaders about tomorrow. *Portal: Libraries and the Academy*, *16*(2), 263−288. Available from https://doi.org/10.1353/pla.2016.0015.

Section 3: Specific technologies
Library systems and library services platforms

Jordan, J. (2010). Climbing out of the box and into the cloud: Building web-scale for libraries. *Journal of Library Administration*, *51*(1), 3−17. Available from https://doi.org/10.1080/01930826.2011.531637.

Stone, G. (2010). Searching life, the universe and everything? The implementation of Summon at the University of Huddersfield. *LIBER Quarterly*, *20*(1), 25−51. Available from https://doi.org/10.18352/lq.7974.

Zimerman, M. (2012). Digital natives, searching behaviour and the library. *New Library World*, *113*(3/4), 174−201. Available from https://doi.org/10.1108/03074801211218552.

Research support

Brown, S., Alvey, E., Danilova, E., Morgan, H., & Thomas, A. (2018). Evolution of research support services at an academic library: Specialist knowledge linked by core infrastructure. *New Review of Academic Librarianship*, *24*(3−4), 337−348. Available from https://doi.org/10.1080/13614533.2018.1473259.

Corrall, S. (2014). Designing libraries for research collaboration in the network world: An exploratory study. *LIBER Quarterly*, *24*(1), 17−48. Available from https://doi.org/10.18352/lq.9525.

Cox, J. (2017). New directions for academic libraries in research staffing: A case study at National University of Ireland Galway. *New Review of Academic Librarianship*, *23*(2−3), 110−124. Available from https://doi.org/10.1080/13614533.2017.1316748.

McRostie, D. (2016). The only constant is change: Evolving the library support model for research at the University of Melbourne. *Library Management*, *37*(6/7), 363−372. Available from https://doi.org/10.1108/LM-04-2016-0027.

Thomas, J. (2011). Future-proofing: The academic library's role in e-research support. *Library Management*, *32*(1/2), 37−47. Available from https://doi.org/10.1108/01435121111102566.

Open access, scholarly communication, and repositories

Chan, G. R., & Cheung, A. S.-C. (2017). The transition toward open access: The University of Hong Kong experience. *Library Management*, *38*(8/9), 488−496. Available from https://doi.org/10.1108/LM-02-2017-0013.

Holley, R. P. (2018). Open access: Current overview and future prospects. *Library Trends*, *67*(2), 214−240. Available from https://doi.org/10.1353/lib.2018.0034.

Novak, J., & Day, A. (2018). The IR has two faces: Positioning institutional repositories for success. *New Review of Academic Librarianship*, *24*(2), 157−174. Available from https://doi.org/10.1080/13614533.2018.1425887.

Otto, J. J., & Mullen, L. B. (2019). The Rutgers open access policy goes into effect: Faculty reaction and implementation lessons learned. *Library Management*, *40*(1/2), 59−73. Available from https://doi.org/10.1108/LM-10-2017-0105.

Shorley, D., & Jubb, M. (Eds.), (2013). *The future of scholarly communication*. London: Facet Publishing.

Bibliometrics

Cox, A., Gadd, E., Petersohn, S., & Sbaffi, L. (2019). Competencies for bibliometrics. *Journal of Librarianship and Information Science*, *51*(3), 746−762. Available from https://doi.org/10.1177/0961000617728111.

Drummond, R. (2014). RMIS revisited: The evolution of the research impact measurement service at UNSW library. *Australian Academic & Research Libraries*, *45*(4), 309−322. Available from https://doi.org/10.1080/00048623.2014.945065.

Open access university presses

Adema, J., & Schmidt, B. (2010). From service providers to content producers: New opportunities for libraries in collaborative open access book publishing. *New Review of Academic Librarianship*, *16*(Suppl. 1), 28−43. Available from https://doi.org/10.1080/13614533.2010.509542.

Bonn, M., & Furlough, M. (Eds.), (2015). *Getting the word out: Academic libraries and scholarly publishers*. Chicago, IL: Association of College and Research Libraries.

Li, Y., Lippincott, S. K., Hare, S., Wittenberg, J., Preate, S. M., Page, A., & Guiod, S. E. (2018). The library-press partnership: An overview and two case studies. *Library Trends*, *67*(2), 319−334. Available from https://doi.org/10.1353/lib.2018.0039.

Research data management

Brochu, L., & Burns, J. (2019). Librarians and research data management − a literature review: Commentary from a senior professional and a new professional librarian. *New Review of Academic Librarianship*, *25*(1), 49−58. Available from https://doi.org/10.1080/13614533.2018.1501715.

Cox, A., & Verbaan, E. (2018). *Exploring research data management*. London: Facet Publishing.

Tenopir, C., Talja, S., Horstmann, W., Late, E., Hughes, D., Pollock, D., ... Allard, S. (2017). Research data services in European academic research libraries. *LIBER Quarterly*, *27*(1), 23−44. Available from https://doi.org/10.18352/lq.10180.

Yu, F., Deuble, R., & Morgan, H. (2017). Designing research data management services based on the research lifecycle: A consultative leadership approach. *Journal of the Australian Library and Information Association*, *66*(3), 287−298. Available from https://doi.org/10.1080/24750158.2017.1364835.

Web services

Gonzales, A. C., & Westbrook, T. (2010). Reaching out with libguides: Establishing a working set of best practices. *Journal of Library Administration*, *50*(6), 638−656. Available from https://doi.org/10.1080/01930826.2010.488941.

Kim, Y.-M. (2010). Gender role and the use of university library website resources: A social cognitive theory perspective. *Journal of Information Science*, *36*(5), 603−617. Available from https://doi.org/10.1177/0165551510377709.

Nicol, E. C., & O'English, M. (2012). Rising tides: Faculty expectations of library websites. *Portal: Libraries and the Academy*, *12*(4), 371−386. Available from https://doi.org/10.1353/pla.2012.0038.

Digital resources, including e-books

Carroll, A. J., Corlett-Rivera, K., Hackman, T., & Zou, J. (2016). E-book perceptions and use in STEM and non-STEM disciplines: A comparative follow-up study. *Portal: Libraries and the Academy*, *16*(1), 131−162. Available from https://doi.org/10.1353/pla.2016.0002.

Corlett-Rivera, K., & Hackman, T. (2014). E-book use and attitudes in the humanities, social sciences, and education. *Portal: Libraries and the Academy*, *14*(2), 255−286. Available from https://doi.org/10.1353/pla.2014.0008.

Daigle, B. J. (2012). The digital transformation of special collections. *Journal of Library Administration*, *52*(3−4), 244−264. Available from https://doi.org/10.1080/01930826.2012.684504.

Hogenboom, K., & Hayslett, M. (2017). Pioneers in the wild west: Managing data collections. *Portal: Libraries in the Academy*, *17*(2), 295−319. Available from https://doi.org/10.1353/pla.2017.0018.

McLure, M., Level, A. V., Cranston, C. L., Oehlerts, B., & Culbertson, M. (2014). Data curation: A study of researcher practices and needs. *Portal: Libraries and the Academy*, *14*(2), 139−164. Available from https://doi.org/10.1353/pla.2014.0009.

Nicholas, D., Williams, P., Rowlands, I., & Jamali, H. R. (2010). Researchers' e-journal use and information seeking behaviour. *Journal of Information Science*, *36*(4), 494−516. Available from https://doi.org/10.1177/0165551510371883.

Ovadia, S. (2019). Addressing the technical challenges of open educational resources. *Portal: Libraries and the Academy*, *19*(1), 79−93. Available from https://doi.org/10.1353/pla.2019.0005.

Plum, T., & Franklin, B. (2015). What is different about e-books?: A MINES for Libraries analysis of academic and health sciences research libraries' e-book usage. *Portal: Libraries and the Academy*, *15*(1), 93−121. Available from https://doi.org/10.1353/pla.2015.0007.

Library spaces

Blummer, B., & Kenton, J. M. (2017). Learning commons in academic libraries: Discussing themes in the literature from 2001 to the present. *New Review of Academic Librarianship*, *23*(4), 329−352. Available from https://doi.org/10.1080/13614533.2017.1366925.

Burke, J. J., & Kroski, E. (2018). *Makerspaces: A practical guide for librarians* (2nd ed.). Lanham, MD: Rowman & Littlefield.

Cunningham, M., & Walton, G. (2016). Informal learning spaces (ILS) in university libraries and their campuses: A Loughborough University case study. *New Library World*, *117*(1/2), 49−62. Available from https://doi.org/10.1108/NLW-04-2015-0031.

Heitsch, E. K., & Holley, R. P. (2011). The information and learning commons: Some reflections. *New Review of Academic Librarianship*, *17*(1), 64−77. Available from https://doi.org/10.1080/13614533.2011.547416.

Letnikova, G., & Xu, N. (2017). Academic library innovation through 3D printing services. *Library Management*, *38*(4/5), 208−218. Available from https://doi.org/10.1108/LM-12-2016-0094.

Nichols, J., Melo, M., & Dewland, J. (2017). Unifying space and service for makers, entre-preneurs, and digital scholars. *Portal: Libraries and the Academy, 17*(2), 363–374. Available from https://doi.org/10.1353/pla.2017.0022.

Watson, L. (Ed.), (2013). *Better library and learning space: Projects, trends, ideas.* London: Facet Publishing.

Virtual reference services

Barry, E., Kelli Bedoya, J., Groom, C., & Patterson, L. (2010). Virtual reference in UK aca-demic libraries: The virtual enquiry project 2008-2009. *Library Review, 59*(1), 40–55. Available from https://doi.org/10.1108/00242531011014673.

Prieto, A. G. (2017). Humanistic perspectives in virtual reference. *Library Review, 66*(8/9), 695–710. Available from https://doi.org/10.1108/LR-01-2017-0005.

Shaw, K., & Spink, A. (2009). University library virtual reference services: Best practices and continuous improvement. *Australian Academic & Research Libraries, 40*(3), 192–205. Available from https://doi.org/10.1080/00048623.2009.10721404.

Digitisation

Petersohn, B., Drummond, T., Maxwell, M., & Pepper, K. (2013). Resource leveling for a mass digitization project. *Library Management, 34*(6/7), 486–497. Available from https://doi.org/10.1108/LM-05-2012-0029.

Wiederkehr, S. (2018). ETH Zurich's university collections and archives in the digital age: Innovative indexing, digitisation and publication of unique materials. *LIBER Quarterly, 28*(1), 1–11. Available from https://doi.org/10.18352/lq.10229.

Social media technologies in learning, research, communication and marketing

Bradley, P. (2015). *Social media for creative libraries.* London: Facet Publishing.

Harmon, C., & Messina, M. (Eds.), (2013). *Using social media in libraries: Best practices.* Lanham, MD: Rowman & Littlefield / Scarecrow Press.

Saw, G., Abbott, W., Donaghey, J., & McDonald, C. (2013). Social media for international students: It's not all about Facebook. *Library Management, 34*(3), 156–174. Available from https://doi.org/10.1108/01435121311310860.

Thomsett-Scott, B. C. (2014). *Marketing with social media: A LITA guide.* Chicago, IL: Neal-Schuman/American Library Association.

Learning analytics

Burke, S., MacIntyre, R., & Stone, G. (2018). Library data labs: Using an agile approach to develop library analytics in UK higher education. *Information and Learning Sciences, 119*(1/2), 5–15. Available from https://doi.org/10.1108/ILS-05-2017-0035.

Farney, T. (2018). *Using digital analytics for smart assessment.* Chicago, IL: ALA Editions.

Robertshaw, M. B., & Asher, A. (2019). Unethical numbers?: A meta-analysis of library learning analytics studies. *Library Trends, 68*(1), 76–101. Available from https://doi.org/10.1353/lib.2019.0031.

Showers, B. (Ed.), (2015). *Library analytics and metrics: Using data to drive decisions and services.* London: Facet Publishing.

MOOCs

Ackerman, S., Mooney, M., Morrill, S., Morrill, J., Thompson, M., & Balenovich, L. K. (2016). Libraries, massive, open online courses and the importance of place: Partnering with libraries to explore change in the Great Lakes. *New Library World*, *117*(11/12), 688−701. Available from https://doi.org/10.1108/NLW-08-2016-0054.

Dreisiebner, S. (2019). Content and instructional design of MOOCs on information literacy: A comprehensive analysis of 11 xMOOCs. *Information and Learning Sciences*, *120*(3/4), 173−189. Available from https://doi.org/10.1108/ILS-08-2018-0079.

Online learning

Allan, B. (2016). *Emerging strategies for supporting student learning: A practical guide for librarians and educators*. London: Facet Publishing.

Han, Y., & Yates, S. (2016). eLearning integration in the library: A case study. *Library Management*, *37*(8/9), 441−453. Available from https://doi.org/10.1108/LM-04-2016-0025.

Rae, S., Hunn, M., & Lobo, A. (2019). Sustainable continuous improvement in online academic and information literacy support. *Journal of the Australian Library and Information Association*, *68*(1), 68−77. Available from https://doi.org/10.1080/24750158.2018.1561600.

Digital scholarship and digital humanities

Fay, E., & Nyhan, J. (2015). Webbs on the web: Libraries, digital humanities and collaboration. *Library Review*, *64*(1/2), 118−134. Available from https://doi.org/10.1108/LR-08-2014-0089.

Hartsell-Gundy, A., Braunstein, L., & Golomb, L. (Eds.), (2015). *Digital humanities in the library: Challenges and opportunities for subject specialists*. Chicago, IL: Association of Research Libraries.

Mackenzie, A., & Martin, L. (Eds.), (2016). *Developing digital scholarship: Emerging practices in academic libraries*. London: Facet Publishing.

Mitchem, P. P., & Rice, D. M. (2017). Creating digital scholarship services at Appalachian State University. *Portal: Libraries and the Academy*, *17*(4), 827−841. Available from https://doi.org/10.1353/pla.2017.0048.

Warwick, C., Terras, M., & Nyhan, J. (2012). *Digital humanities in practice*. London: Facet Publishing.

Disability technology and accessibility of services and resources

Howe, A. (2011). Best practice in disability provision in higher education libraries in England specializing in art, media, and design. *New Review of Academic Librarianship*, *17*(2), 155−184. Available from https://doi.org/10.1080/13614533.2011.610213.

Rosen, S. (2018). What does a library accessibility specialist do?: How a new role advances accessibility through education and advocacy. *College & Research Libraries News*, *79*(1), 23−24. Retrieved from: https://crln.acrl.org/index.php/crlnews/article/view/16861/18482.

Tripathi, M., & Shukla, A. (2014). Use of assistive technologies in academic libraries: A survey. *Assistive Technology*, *26*(2), 105−118. Available from https://doi.org/10.1080/10400435.2013.853329.

Digital literacy

Carlson, J., & Johnston, L. R. (Eds.), (2015). *Data information literacy: Librarians, data and the education of a new generation of researchers*. West Lafayette: Purdue University Press.

Ince, S., Hoadley, C., & Kirschner, P. A. (2019). The role of libraries in teaching doctoral students to become information-literate researchers. *Information and Learning Sciences*, *120*(3/4), 158−172. Available from https://doi.org/10.1108/ILS-07-2018-0058.

Reedy, K., & Parker, J. (Eds.), (2018). *Digital literacy unpacked*. London: Facet Publishing.

Focus on the user

Allison, D. E. (2013). *The patron-driven library: A practical guide for managing collections and services in the digital age*. Oxford: Chandos Publishing.

Appleton, L. (2016). User experience (UX) in libraries: Let's get physical (and digital). *Insights*, *29*(3), 224−227. Available from https://doi.org/10.1629/uksg.317.

Priestner, A., & Borg, M. (Eds.), (2016). *User experience in libraries: Applying ethnography and human-centred design*. London: Routledge.

Mobile technologies and devices

Al-Daihani, S. M., Almutairi, M. R., Alonaizi, R., & Mubarak, S. (2018). Perceptions toward academic library app implementation. *Information and Learning Sciences*, *119*(5/6), 330−341. Available from https://doi.org/10.1108/ILS-02-2018-0007.

Canuel, R., & Crichton, C. (Eds.), (2017). *Mobile technology and academic libraries: Innovative services for research and learning*. Chicago, IL: ALA Editions.

Goodwin, S., Shurtz, S., Gonzalez, A., & Clark, D. (2012). Assessing an e-reader lending program: From pilot to mainstream service. *Library Review*, *61*(1), 8−17. Available from https://doi.org/10.1108/00242531211207389.

Peters, T. A., & Bell, L. (Eds.), (2013). *The handheld library: Mobile technology and the librarian*. Santa Barbara, CA: Libraries Unlimited.

Saravani, S.-J., & Haddow, G. (2017). A theory of mobile library service delivery. *Journal of Librarianship and Information Science*, *49*(2), 131−143. Available from https://doi.org/10.1177/0961000615595854.

Robotics, including automated storage and retrieval

Burton, F., & Kattau, M. (2013). Out of sight but not lost to view: Macquarie University Library's stored print collection. *Australian Academic & Research Libraries*, *44*(2), 102−113. Available from https://doi.org/10.1080/00048623.2013.795473.

Calvert, P. (2017). Robots, the quiet workers, are you ready to take over? *Public Library Quarterly*, *36*(2), 167−172. Available from https://doi.org/10.1080/01616846.2017.1275787.

Iglesias, E. (2013). *Robots in academic libraries: Advances in library automation*. Hersey, PA: IGI Global.

Artificial intelligence

Arlitsch, K., & Newell, B. (2017). Thriving in the age of accelerations: A brief look at the societal effects of artificial intelligence and the opportunities for libraries. *Journal of Library Administration*, *57*(7), 789−798. Available from https://doi.org/10.1080/01930826.2017.1362912.

Massis, B. (2018). Artificial intelligence arrives in the library. *Information and Learning Sciences*, *119*(7/8), 456−459. Available from https://doi.org/10.1108/ILS-02-2018-0011.

Internet of things

Liang, X. (2018). Internet of things and its applications in libraries: A literature review. *Library Hi Tech*. Available from https://doi.org/10.1108/LHT-01-2018-0014.

Lo, L., Coleman, J., & Theiss, D. (2013). Putting QR codes to the test. *New Library World*, *114*(11/12), 459−477. Available from https://doi.org/10.1108/NLW-05-2013-0044.

Makori, E. O. (2017). Promoting innovation and application of internet of things in academic and research information organizations. *Library Review*, *66*(8/9), 655−678. Available from https://doi.org/10.1108/LR-01-2017-0002.

Palmer, M. (2009). *Making the most of RFID in libraries*. London: Facet Publishing.

Index

Printed in the United States
By Bookmasters